The Quest for Paradise

The Quest for Paradise

A History of the World's Gardens

RONALD KING

With an Introduction by Anthony Huxley

WHITTET/WINDWARD

Contents

First published 1979
Introduction © 1979 by Anthony Huxley
Text © 1979 by Ronald King

Whittet Books Ltd, The Oil Mills, Weybridge, Surrey

Designed by Nicholas Maddren, Campion Design, Baldock, Hertfordshire

British Library Cataloguing in Publication Data

King, Ronald, b.1914
  The quest for paradise.
  1. Gardens – History
  I. Title
  712′.6′09   SB451
  ISBN 0-905483-10-3

Printed in Great Britain by
Sackville Press Billericay Ltd

Introduction

One of the redeeming features about the human race is its continuing desire to make gardens and grow plants for pleasure rather than mere utility. As Ronald King says early on in this book, 'a study of pleasure gardens is a study of the way in which man has tried to capture some of the universal beauty that he perceives' — the beauty and wonder of the natural world around him. One of man's less pleasing aspects is his facility for destroying this natural world. But the instinct for its appreciation still shows up in his gardens. Something in him seems to require contact with the green world of plants; we have only to consider the amazing quantities of indoor plants sold today to see what a need for this contact there is among those deprived of the possibility of gardening in the normal sense.

As Ronald King points out, the word 'paradise' was originally used, by Xenophon, to describe the nature-imitating parks of the Persian kings and nobility. That the word now means the abode of the blessed after this mortal life reaffirms how powerfully mankind needs gardens, how much the concept of their desirability is embedded in our subconscious mind. This need, and its realization, are not confined to any single religion but have raised themselves independently in many cultures, separated in both time and distance. It is true, of course, that pleasure gardening can only blossom among the more affluent and in times of relative economic and social stability. Those Persian paradises were the prerogative of a few among a population most of whom were barely able to earn their daily bread. Many workers in this country may not think themselves very well off, but the fact that so many of them have gardens undoubtedly points to a society that is relatively comfortable overall.

Paradise does not always equate with idealized nature, at any rate as interpreted by gardeners. To some it is wild, to others it needs formalizing, sometimes to the most acute pitch of symmetry. Some prefer a garden to be filled with naturally growing plants, some to train or clip their plants to quite unnatural forms, yet others to reduce planting to a symbolic minimum or even — as in the Orient — to replace plants with carefully chosen rocks, and streams with raked sand. Here we have the influence of a contemplative religion under which the garden is transformed into a place for meditation, where the active growth of plants, and the seasonal changes they undergo, are distractions.

One of the oldest traditions in garden design is that of dividing an area into four parts, as described in the Biblical account of the Garden of Eden: 'And a river went out of Eden to water the garden, and from thence it was parted, and became into four heads . . .' Beginning in Persia, this concept can be traced to many parts of the world — the Tudor garden in Britain often followed it — and even now, in more formal layouts, a rectangular design transected by water or paths is frequently seen.

Once you have a garden, it becomes a new abode for plants brought there from any part of the world with a reasonably similar climate. This desire to collect new and unfamiliar plants and as it were domesticate them is as old as the ancient civilizations of Assyria and Egypt. In modern times the collection of plants abroad has been enormously supplemented by deliberate plant breeding, which satisfies an urge for novelty which I believe has always been very strong in most gardeners, although Ronald King deplores its most modern manifestations. I can see little essential difference in the desire to establish exotic species at home and to grow new man-made hybrids. They both stem from a desire to extend the possibilities of the garden, and if one happens to prefer a pure species to a highly bred hybrid, or vice versa, this is in the end a matter of taste.

Equally it is a matter of taste what else besides plants one puts into a garden — water-works, for instance, grottoes, temples, aviaries, statuary — and how these additional items are set out in relation to the created landscape. But the kind of garden, even the kinds of plant preferred, are subject to changes of fashion, from which gardening is certainly not immune. Changes of direction are also brought about by new technical developments and techniques, by economic and social pressures. Such pressures, acting on space and time available, have for instance reduced the original Persian *paradeisoi* to the present-day German *paradiesgartenlein*, a formal kind of small patio garden adapted to outdoor leisure.

These developments, transitions, influences, in cultures ancient and modern, form the subject of Ronald King's book. It is not by any means a series of generalizations, however, for a great many individual gardens are recorded and described — much of this material having never before been combined in this way. Equally the large number of illustrations include many unfamiliar gardens and fresh views of better known ones.

In his final chapter the author paints a depressing picture of man separating himself from nature and in so doing making himself mentally unhealthy. As he quotes from Christina Rossetti,

Who can tell what memories
Of lost beloved Paradise
Saddened Eve with sleepless eyes?

For Eve, read mankind; for sleepless eyes, read restlessness, aggressiveness, discontent. I wonder if it is quite as bad as this? What a future garden historian will be able to write of the coming decades is difficult to imagine; but meanwhile the overall interest in gardening seems stronger than ever, and since most of the gardeners I know are relatively happy people, perhaps we have not lost Paradise entirely. This book will certainly provide an admirable background to the continuing quest.

Anthony Huxley

Acknowledgements

The author and publishers are grateful to Professor J. P. M. Brenan, Director of the Royal Botanic Gardens, Kew and to Mr V. T. H. Parry, Chief Librarian and Archivist of the Royal Botanic Gardens, for permission to use the resources and facilities of the Library of the Gardens. The publisher would also like to thank Mr Ben Weinreb for his help.

The picture on p.178 is Reproduced by Gracious Permission of Her Majesty the Queen.

The pictures in the book are reproduced by kind permission of the following: (the number of pictures on a page is indicated by a bracketed number)

J. Allan Cash, 134, 136 top right, 137, 139, 148, 214, 258, 267 bottom; PBP International Picture Library, 150, 213 top, 264, 266 top, 272; The Basilisk Press, from the *Red Books of Humphry Repton*, 196, 197; Belgian National Tourist Office, 263; Birmingham Museums and Art Gallery, 182 top; Bodleian Library, 80, 83(2), 84 bottom, 116; British Library Board, 16, 19, 40, 42(2), 43, 46, 47, 48, 49, 74, 81, 84 top, 85, 118, 119; British Tourist Authority, 9, 162, 176, 179 bottom, 191 top, 193, 201 top right; Cooper-Bridgeman Library, 182 bottom; C. Cottrell-Dormer, 183 bottom, 189 bottom; Kenneth Collier, 227 top; *Country Life,* 223, 224 bottom, 225; Editora Abril, 271 bottom; Mary Evans Picture Library, 23 bottom, 155, 200 top; Finnish Tourist Board U.K., 278(2); French Government Tourist Office, 2, 136 top left, 138, 157 top, 160 top, 194 top; Peter Hayden, 115 right, 145(2), 172(3), 173, 178 bottom, 179 top, 204 top, 206, 219, 274, 275 top; Arthur Hellyer, 239, 245 bottom, 246 top, 247(2), 248, 251 bottom; Angelo Hornack, 156, top, 160 bottom; Anthony Huxley, 124 top, 125(2), 128 bottom; India Office Library, 128 top; Iranian Tourist Office, 65; Italian State Tourist Office, 101, 104 top right, 111(2); Japan Information Centre, London, 62 top, 63 top; S. Jellicoe, 126 top left, 129; Patricia Johnson, 18 bottom; Michael Lancaster, 124 bottom, 130 bottom; William MacQuitty, jacket, 10, 54(2), 60, 64, 68, 69 top, 76, 94, 120, 123, 126 top right, 130 top, 131, 132, 133(2), 158 bottom left, 168, 260 right, 269 right, 270; His Grace the Duke of Marlborough, 184; Metropolitan Museum of Art, New York, 18 top; Paul Miles, 146(3), 147(2), 164 bottom, 175(2), 207(2), 220(2), 224 top, 228 top, 235, 236 left, 240(2), 242, 243, 245 top, 250(2), 251 top, 253 bottom, 254, 259 bottom left, 262 top, 266 bottom; Tony Mott, 5, 32, 33, 36, 37(2), 38, 77, 78, 79, 86, 87, 88, 89, 90(2), 91, 92, 93(2), 95(2), 96, 97(2), 98, 99, 102, 103(2), 104 top left, 104 bottom, 105(2), 106(2), 107 top, 109(2), 112 top, 113(2), 140(2), 151, 161 bottom, 163, 164 top, 165(2), 166(2), 167 bottom, 177, 181(2), 182 top, 187, 189 top, 191 bottom, 194 bottom, 215, 265 top right, 269 left; Norwegian National Tourist Office, 265 top left; Royal Horticultural Society, 202 top, 203, 208, 209 top; Lord Salisbury, 149 bottom right; Scala, 39, 186 (Private Collection); Geoffrey Shakerley, 210, 211; Stanley Schuler, from *America's Great Private Gardens,* 241, 255(2), 257; Edwin Smith, 100, 107 bottom, 108(2), 110, 114, 149 top, 174 top, 183 top, 232, 233, 234 bottom, 236 right; Harry Smith Horticultural Photographic Collection, 71 bottom, 112 bottom, 154, 157 bottom, 158 top, 174 bottom, 190, 198, 218, 222, 226(2), 227 bottom, 228 bottom, 229, 230, 231(2), 234 top, 237, 238, 244(2), 252, 253 top, 256, 260 left, 262 bottom, 265 bottom left, 267 top, 268, 271 top, 275 bottom; Spanish National Tourist Office, 70, 71 top, 73 top; Syndication International, 277 top; Sun Slide Co., 50, 51, 53, 57, 58; James Turner, 69 bottom, 72, 73 bottom, 143, 152, 158 bottom right, 159, 161 top, 188 top, 216, 246 bottom; Urasenke Foundation, 1, 52, 59(2), 61 top, 63 bottom; Victoria and Albert Museum, 13 top, 41, 66, 82, 122; Elizabeth Whiting and Associates, 259 top, 159 bottom right, 176(2), 277 bottom; John Whittet, 6; Wiggins Teape, 279

1
Eastward in Eden

There was a time when meadow, grove and stream,
The earth, and every common sight, To me did seem
Apparelled in celestial light,
The glory and the freshness of a dream.

Wordsworth

For many centuries and in many countries the name 'Paradise' was applied to pleasure gardens and even now when a beautiful garden is described it is often said to be a 'paradise'. The reasons why this term is particularly apt have become obscured in modern times but they remain valid and much of what is found distasteful in today's world may be traced to a disregard of their implications.

Pleasure gardens are outdoor places designed by man which induce in the beholder a sense of well-being. Like drugs, they can be addictive but, unlike drugs, they have no unpleasant after-effects unless the addict undertakes to create a pleasure garden of his own, when he must resign himself to unremitting backaching toil, first in creating the garden and then in preventing nature from reclaiming her territory. Nature has a fifth column, as anyone will agree who has tried to repel the creeping underground stems of that demure virgin of the late spring, the lily-of-the-valley, which will take over the garden on a light sandy soil, or fought with the forget-me-not, whose flowers remind one that there is a blue sky behind the clouds, or with stout honesty, both of which scatter seeds prolifically.

He who sets out to write a history of pleasure gardens must of necessity search his own brain for information about their origin, for he soon discovers that no one else can tell him how they began. He must look into himself for the answer and, if he is shrouded in the smog of Western industrial society, he will need to peer hard into the dimness for inspiration. He must examine the springs of his being and the nature of the universe and rid himself of that notion of the past, if he still has it, that the history of his species is a matter wholly of the random play of economic forces generally hidden from the actors in the contemporary scene.

Even in the unlikely cliffs and caverns of industrial centres artists have found beauty and put it into words or music, or spread it upon canvas. They have rid themselves of the misconceptions of their milieu and looked afresh upon the 'dark Satanic mills' with the eye of a child, that sees everything as pleasing, and is taught by its elders where beauty to them is not. Those of such vision may suspect or believe that, if they could see with absolute clarity, they would find that the child's first impression was right, and that everything is beautiful. The philosopher and aesthete will ask 'What is beauty?', and construct their own models for an answer, but a sense that universal beauty exists has always informed the actions and beliefs of men. A study of pleasure gardens is a study of one way that man has tried to bring some part of that beauty closer to him.

In the organization of nature, from the tiny particles that absorb the study of the physicist, through atoms and molecules, cells and tissue, to man and society, there is an inexorable trend of combination into a unity of ever-increasing complexity which points to an end where, while all parts remain individual, all, in the sublime paradox, have become one. To the small child, who cannot yet formulate such a concept, but only live it, the unity and integration of the part of the universe that it perceives is self-evident. Our ancestors who, so long ago, crossed that divide between the animal existence unconscious of self and that of man capable of reflecting upon his own actions, must have looked out upon the world very much as a small child does, seeing itself as part of nature and accepted by it.

Kipling's character Mowgli and Edgar Rice Burrough's character Tarzan are probably nearer in spirit to the truth of the relationship of early man to his environment than those accounts which set him under constant harassment of the beasts of the wild. Even now, though his natural body is almost defenceless and he would appear to be an easy prey, few animals will attack man unless provoked. The most primitive men who have survived into modern times, the Bushmen of

LEFT *This wall painting, showing at the bottom what are probably intended to be fruiting date and doum palms and fig-trees, is from a tomb at Senedjem.*

A mediaeval Garden of Eden from Leven Jhesu Christi *by Ludolphus de Saxonia (Antwerp, 1503), showing both the Tree of Life and the Tree of Knowledge of Good and Evil. Note the four rivers issuing from drainpipe-like orifices.*

the Kalahari, the food-gathering Indians of the Amazon forest, the aborigines of Australia, the Tasaday of Mindanao and others, are less aggressive than more advanced tribes. They attack only when they feel threatened. This suggests that primitive man, when the species first evolved, would be even less aggressive. The violent and aggressive nature of modern man makes this hard to believe, but, at the beginning, when man was wholly unsophisticated and childlike and his relationship with the living scenes of natural beauty around him uncomplicated and straightforward, there was surely a time when he was almost entirely free from that aggression. Rousseau's 'noble savage' had no real existence, but the core of his notion may be valid.

The small intelligent Semitic tribe of Hebrews, hardly big enough for a long time to be called a nation, that lived around Jerusalem, and the world later called the Jews, seems to have preserved a race-memory of that time of innocence. An articulate race, its earliest poet wrote a sublime account of his people's beliefs in which his percipient genius captured the memory for ever. His work is enshrined in the Bible in the Book of Genesis and he set his characters, the progenitors of humanity, in the context of untouched nature, precisely as they

really had been when they first emerged, in the course of evolution, from the ruck of animal kind; he called their place of origin the 'Garden of Eden'. Here is his account from the King James version of the Bible:

> And the Lord God planted a garden eastward in Eden and there he put the man whom he had formed.
> And out of the ground made the Lord God to grow every tree that is pleasant to the sight
> and good for food . . .
> And a river went out of Eden to water the garden, and from thence it was parted, and became into foure heades.
> And the name of the first is Phison; that is it which compasseth the whole land of Havilah . . .
> And the name of the second river is Gihon [Hebrew: Cush]:
> the same it is that compasseth the whole land of Ethiopia.
> And the name of the third river is Hiddekel [Tigris]: that is it which goeth towards the east of Assyria.
> And the fourth river is Euphrates.

The word 'Eden' means 'pleasantness' or 'delight', so that some translations of the Bible do not use the phrase 'Garden of Eden' but render it as 'paradise of pleasure' or 'garden of delight'. It seems likely from the occurrence of the names of two rivers which can be identified as the modern Tigris and Euphrates that the poet had a specific place in mind. The Babylonian word *edinnu* referred to the plain of Shinar between the Euphrates and the Tigris and may locate it in that district, which is certainly east of Palestine, but the two other rivers named, Phison and Cush, cannot be found in the present landscape of that area, nor can Havilah or Ethiopia (not the modern country which bears this name) be placed, so that it seems unlikely that, even if a particular place were intended, the exact site of the Garden will ever be fixed with certainty.

Sir Leonard Woolley, in his book *The Sumerians,* has some interesting comments to make. He says that the silt brought down by the Euphrates and the Tigris, and the river Karun of Persia, created 'a vast delta of clay and sand and mud, diversified by marshes and reed-beds, through which wound rivers so flush with their banks that they were for ever changing their courses: it was a delta periodically flooded, and in the summer scorched by a pitiless sun, but its soil, light and stoneless, was as rich as could be found anywhere on earth, and scarcely needed man's labour to produce man's food.' He goes on to say that the description in Genesis of the creation of the earth as man's home agrees admirably with the process of formation of the Mesopotamian delta: 'Let the waters under the heavens be gathered together under one place, and let the dry land appear: and it was so . . . And the earth brought forth grass, and herb yielding seed after his kind: and God saw that it was good.' Abraham, father of the Hebrew people, came from the Euphrates-Tigris delta; he was a native of Ur of the Chaldees in Sumeria. The poet's description may therefore be based on fact, stemming from Abraham's account of his origins handed down by word of mouth, and relating the way in which the earliest settlements in the delta were established.

ABOVE *The Garden of Eden was a favourite subject of early painters. This Flemish version by Jan Brueghel (1568-1625) shows very well a northern version of the idyllic parkland in which man first wandered.*

RIGHT *An impression of the Garden of Eden by a nineteenth-century French artist, V. Foulquier, from* Histoire des Jardins *by Arthur Mangin (Tours, 1883).*

We know from this Genesis account that, in the nation which events proved to have a special role in history, man was thought to have lived first in pleasant surroundings in harmony with his fellow-creatures, that the surroundings were a 'paradise', i.e. a park-like garden with ornamental trees which also provided food, and that streams ran through it. We are entitled to deduce also, because the poet placed man in these surroundings in a state of complete happiness, that the early Jews regarded a garden environment as the natural home of man, and his first requirement for a happy existence. Further, their idea of a garden environment was not the roughness of the mountain glen, nor the darkness of the thick forest, nor the flat meadows of the treeless plain, but the warm and verdant 'in-between' land where sun and shade are equal and the pleasant waters flow. Who can doubt that here in this ancient poem from the Middle East, man is looking back far down the corridors of time to that carefree era when he was first himself? To the time when, after he had ventured down from the trees, he

Nymphaea lotus, *the white water-lily characteristic of ancient Egypt:* Illustrations of the Lotus of the Ancients and Tamara of India, *by R. Duppa (London, 1816).*

moved about, first on the borders of the forest where the shrubs and climbers grow freely, and then among the more scattered trees further out, particularly along the edges of rivers and lakes, for he must have water, gathering his daily food of fruits and roots and learning to kill animals for food also. Short-lived and prone to sudden death because he knew nothing of medical science, surgery or sanitation, and could not combat the attacks of infection or alleviate the results of accidental injury, he still in his short life enjoyed his surroundings. As his knowledge increased he peopled these surroundings with fantastic mythologies and brought down upon himself self-created evils. Those who choose, may interpret the rest of the poet's story in Genesis as a symbolized racial memory of that change also.

The story of that loss of innocence has been the subject of one of the greatest poems in the English language. In *Paradise Lost* John Milton, who doubtless took the Genesis story literally and wrote for those who believed it to be a record of fact, used his majestic genius to describe the Garden of Eden. He set it upon the top of a rocky height, where:

> . . . overhead up grew
> Insuperable heighth of loftiest shade,
> Cedar, and Pine, and Fir, and branching Palm:
> A sylvan scene, and as the ranks ascend
> Shade above shade, a woody Theatre
> of stateliest view. Yet higher than their tops
> The verdurous wall of Paradise up sprung . . .

But the description of the Garden itself portrays a kindlier scene: it was

> A happy rural seat of various view:
> Groves of rich trees . . .
> Betwixt them Lawns, or level Downs . . .
> Or palmy hillock, or the flowery Lap
> Of some irriguous valley spread her store
> Flowers of all hue, and without Thorn the Rose:
> Another side, umbrageous Grots and Caves
> Of cool recess, o'er which the mantling Vine
> Lays forth her purple Grape, and gently creeps
> Luxuriant; meanwhile murmuring waters fall
> Down the slope hills . . .

The Garden of Eden has been the recurring subject of painters and illustrators throughout the ages. One of the most pleasing attempts to depict it was that of the Italian artist Salvator Rosa, painted in Rome in the middle of the seventeenth century, almost at the same time as Milton was composing *Paradise Lost*. The picture shows the Garden very much as Milton described it. It is a curious fact that earlier pictures painted by this artist in a different style from the series of Biblical pictures painted in Rome, and regarded in this largely post-Christian age as artistically superior to that series, had a very great influence on the development of garden design in Europe. It would probably be stretching the facts to suggest that the basic cast of mind which produced such pictures as that of the Garden of Eden would have influenced the earlier style and connected the Biblical Garden with those developments. Nevertheless, the garden concept of the ancient Hebrew poet as set out in Genesis, which C. G. Jung would perhaps classify as archetypal, dredged up from the earliest days of the human species, has had a continuous attraction for the minds of men. It runs, as we shall see, like a coloured thread through much of western garden history, not only that of Christian countries, but of Islam also.

The very earliest man, concerned with the simple facts of maintaining his existence, seems to have made no move for a very long time to adapt the environment to his convenience: the first traces of agriculture that have been discovered date to no more than ten thousand years ago. This is so recent as to be almost yesterday, chronologically speaking. His first attempts to induce things to grow where he was likely to want them were directed wholly towards food plants. As the men were concerned with hunting and fishing while the women were more tied to the camp because of the need to care for the smaller children, it is likely that the first efforts to grow crops were made by the women. Certainly, in primitive societies, it is the women who till the ground. In the poet's story, it is the woman who is moved by intellectual curiosity, not the man, since we are told that it was she who desired the apple because 'it would make one wise'. Again the poet may be recording the long-preserved symbolic memory of what actually happened, i.e. that it was the women whose curiosity was aroused by the growth of food seeds dropped while eating or the regrowth of a dropped root accidentally trampled in and who realized that a food crop could be raised near the camp, obviating the need to go searching for it. From this discovery sprang the first permanent settlements and then civilization with all its attendant ills, blame for which was attached to the women for having begun the process.

Although man's first interest was in food plants, he must have been conscious from time to time of the attractive scent of some of the plants surrounding him and the bright colours of their flowers, fruit and sometimes their leaves, and sooner or later moved with an impulse to use them in some way. Nevertheless, the cave paintings of prehistoric man are almost wholly concerned with the depiction of animals and his three-dimensional art with fertility, which would seem to indicate that the impulse did not appear in the earlier stages of his development. The restriction of the paintings to animals may, however, mean no more than that those which survived were the productions of hunters rather than pastoralists, who would have to move with their flocks and herds and probably rarely, if ever, dwelt in caves. The artistic efforts of the latter, if any, are likely to have been in more exposed places and thus long since effaced by the weather.

RIGHT Nelumbium speciosum, *the Sacred Lotus of the East and possibly the lotus of ancient Egypt:* Illustrations of the Lotus of the Ancients and Tamara of India, *by R. Duppa (London, 1816). Unlike the water-lilies, this plant holds its leaves and flowers above the water instead of floating on it.*

BELOW *A drawing of the doum palm* (Hyphaene thebaica) *by the famous botanical artist Pierre-Joseph Redouté for the* Flora of Egypt *(1807-9). The doum palm is the only member of the palm family having a stem that branches.*

Religion and mythology played a large part in the life of our ancestors: the priest and the sacred places of worship and disposal of the dead appear in the earliest civilizations as the focus of activity apart from the struggle for existence and it may be that the practice of cultivating plants for their ornamental or scented qualities arose from their use in religious practices. Whether it occurred first in the Middle East, the civilization of the Indus valley, China, America or elsewhere it is impossible to tell, but the most reasonable assumption is that it happened in various places at different times independently. Where it happened the action is likely to have been the same as that which occurred with food plants: a notion was born in someone's head that flowers could be grown where they were likely to be wanted instead of gathered at random, and the train of events was initiated. Like the invention of the wheel, which someone suddenly saw as a disc with an axle instead of a rolling log, from which it doubtless evolved, the last jump was a leap of the mind, rather than a physical change.

One of the countries of which we possess any record of early gardens is China where early traditions, mainly mythical, seem to take us back to 2,000 B.C. In view of the age of Chinese civilization, however, the first gardens in that country may have been made very much earlier, perhaps as early as the fourth or even fifth millenium B.C. West of China, while civilization in that country was still comparatively young, in the third millenium B.C., another great civilization arose on the silt of the Indus valley to the north-west of the Indian sub-continent. The chief city of the new group of communities was Mohenjo-daro, but the structure of the habitations of this city and others in this civilization do not seem to have made any provision for gardens to the houses although they may have used plants in pots and tubs for courtyard and internal decoration. The inhabitants were certainly interested in plants, as the tree had a religious significance for them, the tree spirit

appearing on seals. A design for the leaf of the pipal (*Ficus religiosa*), a member of the fig family noted for its great size and long life, was also used on these.

The Indus valley civilization had early contact with the civilizations to the west of it in the countries of the Middle East, about which we know a great deal because they discovered the art of writing very early, in the fourth millenium B.C., and great quantities of clay tablets have not only survived but have been deciphered by scholars. These civilizations arose in the area now called Iraq, formerly Mesopotamia and in ancient times Babylonia, the 'Fertile Crescent' of the Tigris and Euphrates, the country of Abraham, the description of which in early times by Sir Leonard Woolley has already been quoted. This rich new land invited settlers, who came from several sources, the inhabitants of the land of Sumer in the south first becoming prominent. Among the very earliest relics to survive are several that show an interest in and use of flowers. The royal cemetery of Ur, dating from the middle of the fourth millennium B.C., contains the grave of Qvueen Shub-Ad, whose elaborate head-dress was crowned with wreathes of gold leaves and flowers. On the temple of Al 'Ubaid was found ornamentation of clay flower rosettes with inlaid petals of red, black and white. A vase from Uruk which has survived is decorated with an offering scene to a goddess in bas-relief, and includes in its ornament representations of plants, so that, even as early as this, plants and their flowers had achieved some significance in the culture.

States and dynasties rose and fell as the centuries

An ancient Egyptian wall painting of workers gathering figs from Ficus sycomorus, *helped by monkeys which seem more interested in sniffing the fruit than picking it; perhaps they were driven away if they dared to eat it, but could not resist the temptation of smelling the delectable mouthful.*

passed until, for the first time, in the second half of the third millennium B.C., an empire arose on Babylonian soil. The state of Akkad to the north succeeded Sumer as the dominent entity and under King Sargon numerous conquests extended its sway over a wide area. Merchants from Mesopotamia had formed a trading colony in Cappadocia in Asia Minor, probably at Ganes, but had been harshly treated by the local ruler. They appealed to Sargon who, undeterred by the long distance his troops had to cover, crossed the Taurus and defeated the offending monarch. There would be nothing to distinguish this foray from other adventures except the distance were it not that an account of it has survived which records the interesting fact that Sargon brought back foreign trees, vines, figs and roses to grow in his own land. He would not have done this unless a well-established practice of ornamental gardening already existed in his home country. An interesting Akkadian story relates that Sargon himself was abandoned as a child but rescued by an irrigation worker and brought up as a gardener. An inscription was recorded on his behalf saying: 'My service as a gardener was pleasing to Ishtar and I became king.'

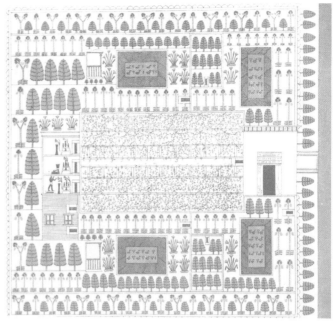

This picture shows how a nineteenth-century French artist, D. Lancelot, saw an Egyptian villa: from Histoire des Jardins *by Arthur Mangin (Tours, 1883).*

BELOW LEFT *A proposed restoration of Queen Hatsheput's terrace garden at Deir-al-Bahari, the first terraced garden of which a record exists, the ruins of which may still be seen. The picture is taken from* Deir-el-Bahari *by Auguste Mariette-Bey (Leipzig, 1877).*

ABOVE *A drawing made from his tomb at Thebes of the garden of a high official of Amenhotep II reproduced from Rossellini's* Monumenti dell' Egitto é della Nubia. *This is the Theban garden described in the text.*

Other later rulers of the Mesopotamian countries were also actively interested in plants and gardens. Tiglath-Pileser, king of the Assyrians about 1100 B.C., was interested in trees. The record he left says, 'Cedars and box, & allakanu wood have I carried off from the countries I conquered, trees that none of my forefathers have possessed, these trees have I taken, and planted them in mine own country, in the parks of Assyria have I planted them.' This would suggest that his interest was in park-like gardens rather than the smaller ornamental gardens, but nothing has in fact been discovered that would give an idea of what gardens in the Fertile Crescent lands were like in these early days.

West across the Arabian desert from the land of the

Tigris and the Euphrates another great river gave rise to a civilization. The Nile coming down from Africa into the Mediterranean passes between the Arabian and the Western Deserts, laying a green road to the sea. Isolated by these barren lands from other contacts, the civilization was in-turned upon itself and developed remarkable characteristics unmatched elsewhere. Early settlements resembled those of other civilizations but the whole of the country was united just before the end of the fourth millennium B.C. and from that time history begins. A method of writing by hieroglyphics was soon discovered. Written records were left in the temples and tombs and many scenes depicted on walls and furniture so that much has been learnt about Egyptian history and customs.

The alluvial soil of the Nile was so fertile that the country had many periods of great prosperity. Being comparatively isolated, it was less troubled with wars against foreign enemies for the early part of its history than other countries of the time, although it had its quota of internal dissension. Many substantial houses were built for nobles and many temples erected. The nearness of the hot deserts rendered the shade of trees particularly attractive and every temple had its sacred grove, each specializing in the cult of a particular variety

TOP *A wall painting from the tomb of Ken-Amun at Thebes showing monkeys in branched palms which are probably intended to represent doum palms. The flowers below show what could be the 'pepper pot' seed pods of* Nelumbium speciosum, *the sacred lotus.*

ABOVE *A line drawing of a scene carved in low relief on a panel which is part of a chest found in the tomb of Tutankhamun, who reigned from 1361-1352* B.C. *This is the chest referred to in the text which shows in the background a number of plants and flowers.*

of tree. The coolness of water was also greatly appreciated and the gardens of private houses were well furnished with ponds. A typical Theban house of the 18th Dynasty, about the middle of the second millennium B.C., illustrated in a tomb painting, showed the massive main gate of the garden of the house opening on to a tree-lined canal, the garden being divided by low stone walls into symmetrical compartments. All the lines were straight and the detail of the design severely rectangular. There was a large vine-covered trellis in the centre of the garden supported on four rows of slender pillars and there were no less than four small ponds, stocked with waterfowl and water-lilies, including the sacred lotus,

emblem of lower Egypt, the papyrus reed being the emblem of upper Egypt. A number of avenues of trees, including a member of the fig family, *Ficus sycomorus*, the date palm and the doum palm (also known as the gingerbread tree, from the resemblance of the rind of its fruit to gingerbread) provided shady walks and there were two summerhouses.

The interest of the Egyptians did not at first extend abroad, but in later times, when conquests had been made in Asia, Pharaoh Thutmose III, who reigned about the middle of the second millennium B.C., brought back foreign plants which he had depicted in his festival hall at Karnak. Ornamental gardening within the limits imposed by the climate and the nature of the buildings had by this time reached a high level of skill. Queen Hatsheput, who reigned during the minority of Thutmose III, built a most beautiful terrace garden, the first of this style of which a record has survived, at Deir-al-Bahari. Arriving from the river the visitor passed through a long avenue of sphinxes backed by trees to approach the garden, which comprised three terraces adorned with pillared cloisters, with stairways and gentle slopes for ascent to the shrine hewn out of the rock at the top. There were ponds for coolness and the garden was well furnished with trees, for which large holes had to be cut out of the rock. The queen was interested in plants from other countries and some of the trees in her garden were imported from Punt (Somalia). The expedition she sent there brought back 32 large incense trees (probably *Boswellia,* the olibanum tree from which frankincense was derived) which were taken up very carefully with a ball of soil to keep the roots from drying out in almost exactly the manner in which, until the advent of the mechanical shovel, such large trees used to be taken up in modern times. The care and skill paid off, for the trees flourished when planted.

The temples of Egypt benefited greatly during the reign of another of the greatest Egyptian monarchs, Rameses III, who reigned about three hundred years later than Queen Hatsheput. It is recorded of him that during his reign he gave 514 gardens or garden sites to temples. He is also stated to have originated the practice in Egypt of planting small trees and shrubs in large decorated earthenware vases.

The plants and trees most familiar to the Egyptians, the sacred lotus, the papyrus, the sycomore fig, and the date and doum palms appear frequently in Egyptian pictures and ornaments, and others are also shown. By a stroke of great good fortune the tomb of Tutankhamen, who ruled from 1361 to 1352 B.C., survived until modern times almost untouched, so that all his grave goods were found where they were buried. They contain some excellent examples of the use of flowers by the Egyptians. The most striking, perhaps, are found in the ornamental panels of a fine chest with a desk-shaped lid. Also significant is the panel which shows the young Tutankhamen and his wife Ankhesenanum at the beginning of his reign in a garden, where the queen is offering the king flowers. Another panel shows a hunting scene, in which the artist has filled in the background with festoons, garlands and bouquets in which the flowers and petals of the blue lily, buds of the white lotus, leaves and fruit of the mandrake, convolvulus, cornflowers and possibly a vine can be recognized. When Tutankhamen's coffin was opened, a small wreath of flowers lay on the first shell; on the second was a great necklace of olive and willow leaves and lotus flowers; and a necklace of flowers on a backing of papyrus lay on the third. Only in a nation in which a love for flowers and gardens had become part of the national make up would a king have been buried in such a way.

Egyptians loved their gardens so much that they created small gardens around grates and some of their inscriptions seem to imply that the deceased would continue to enjoy his garden after his death. Their love of gardens comes out also in their writings, such as the following passage taken from a 19th Dynasty source, written about 1900 B.C. and called by the translator the 'Tale of the Garden of Flowers':

She led me, hand in hand, and we went into
her garden to converse together.
There she made me taste of excellent honey:
The rushes of the garden were verdant,
and all its bushes flourishing.
There were currant trees and cherries redder
than the ruby;
The ripe peaches of the garden resembled bronze
and the groves had the lustre of the stone 'nashem'.
The 'menni' unshelled like cocoa-nuts they brought
to us,
Its shade was fresh and airy, and soft for the
repose of love.
'Come to me' she called to me,
'and enjoy thyself a day in the room of

Detail from a papyrus of Nakht of the time of the New Kingdom (1567-1085 B.C.) showing the master and his wife with their house and garden, which is well stocked with fruit-trees and water-fowl.

a young girl who belongs to me,
the garden is today in its glory;
there is a terrace and a parlour.'

The various fruits are the guesses of the translator as to what is meant. 'Nashem' he identifies as 'green felspar, or Amazon stone'. These vaguenesses do not, however, conceal the spirit of the piece.

Marie Luise Gothein, in her *History of Garden Art*, written in the first years of this century, said this about the Egyptians:

'The Egyptian shows his whole relation to Nature in his love for the garden — not an extravagant Nature, but one who deserves the care and pains of man, because of her great beauty, her protecting shade, her wonderful flowers and her costly fruits. To Nature the dweller in the Nile valley linked all that was dear to him: his happiest fetes, poetry and love — all were bound up with the garden and its products, especially flowers. Few Oriental nations can think of a festival without flowers, but nowhere are they so completely a part of human life as portrayed by the Egyptians on the monuments they have left.'

Here in this most ancient of civilizations the urge impelling men to seek after beauty by making gardens was given full rein with superb results. The gardener was an honoured man in Egypt, so much so that he is sometimes named in pictures. Marie Luise Gothein's further comment is well justified: in considering the first Egyptian garden described above she says, 'We recognise with astonishment that we have a formal garden in an advanced state of development on the very threshold of our history.' Not only was western Europe still in the Stone Age when the vine flourished in Egyptian gardens and the nodding sycamore and palm were reflected in their lotus-filled pools, but the great age of Greece and Rome had not yet begun.

2
The Four Rivers

On either hand
The lawns and meadow-ledges midway down
Hang rich in flowers, and far below them roars
The long brook falling thro' the clov'n ravine
In cataract after cataract to the sea.

Tennyson

East of the Fertile Crescent, across the Zagros Mountains, stretching mile after thristy mile towards the East to Afghanistan and Baluchistan, lies the upland country of Persia, modern Iran. A romantic land, praised in literature, Persia gave birth to gardens the influence of which has been of great importance in the history of man's search after beauty. Yet it is not a country in which garden-making is easy. The mountains take most of the rainfall, leaving a meagre amount only for the Iranian plains. The cold of the bitter winters of these uplands gives way at last to a March and April when, as by a wizard's wand, the country is transformed to a brightly patterned carpet of colour as all the wild-flowers bloom. But the time of spring passes quickly; too soon the blossoms fade in the heat of the summer sun.

The civilizations of Mesopotamia, drawing their sustenance from the fertile soil of the great rivers, rose and fell, but the scattered communities of upland Persia, confined in action by their struggle to obtain a living in much less favourable conditions, made slower progress. Not until the invention of a simple but clever piece of water engineering called the *qanat*, an underground conduit from hill country to the flatter lands designed to raise the level of the water in the latter, did progress quicken because better irrigation could support larger communities. There were few settlements of any size in early Persia, nor was it possible to unite the country until the first millennium B.C.

The ancient Persians must have felt, during their summer, the same need as the Egyptians to keep back the encroaching heat. Like the Egyptians they turned to the shade of trees and the coolness of the pool to make their living places more bearable and so, where economic circumstances permitted, the classic Persian garden must have been born. The central feature was the water tank, slightly sloped so that the water gradually overflowed and could be carried to irrigate the garden. Around it and along the water channels

LEFT Iris florentina, *found by John Sibthorp among the wild-flowers of Greece, drawn by Ferdinand Bauer: Volume I of the* Flora Graeca *(1806).*

ABOVE *Sennacherib had a terraced garden around his palace such as that depicted in this Assyrian relief of a 'hanging' (terraced) garden at Kuyundjik: from* A History of Garden Art *(1913) by Marie Luise Gothein.*

grew shrubs and flowers, particularly roses, of which the Persians were very fond. Shade was provided by regular rows of trees and the garden was enclosed by walls to keep out the desiccation of the dry lands beyond.

The water in the Persian garden traditionally divided it into four parts, exactly as described by the Hebrew poet in his account of the Garden of Eden. The Old Testament was compiled after the Jewish exile in Babylon and it is possible that the poet was describing something that he had seen in captivity, which the Babylonians had adopted from Persia. On the other hand, it may be recording a tradition very much older from which the Persians had derived the practice. However it began, this fourfold division of the garden

21

Drawing of an Assyrian relief of a temple and artificial hill at Khorsabad: from A History of Garden Art *(1913) by Marie Luise Gothein.*

by water came to be adopted as standard, and may be traced up to almost modern times in gardens far away from Iran.

Apart from ornamental gardens around their dwelling places, the Persians also planted groves of trees around places of burial. The grove planted at the tomb of Cyrus, the great Persian king of the sixth century B.C., at Pasagardae was still there when Alexander the Great visited it nearly two centuries afterwards. The Persians had great veneration for trees and training in the right way to plant them was part of normal education. In later times large hunting parks came into being in Persia as an inheritance from Assyria to the north-west rather than as an indigenous production, such parks having been created in that country while settlements in Persia were still small and isolated. By the time of Cyrus, however, they had attained great importance in Persia itself. In these parks, the royal family and the great nobles could enjoy themselves in time of peace and, in time of war, use them as a mustering place for their armies.

Xenophon, the Greek historian who lived around 400 B.C., was acquainted with Persian customs because of his military service with Persian troops, and reports a dialogue of Socrates on the subject. Socrates is made to say that the King of Persia considered agriculture to be among the most necessary and honourable occupations and that 'in whatever province he resides, and wheresoever he travels, he takes care that there may be gardens, such as are called *paradeisoi*, stocked with everything good and valuable that the soil will produce; and that in these gardens he himself spends the greatest part of his time, whenever the season of the year does not prevent him.' Cyrus the Younger, who lived just before the end of the fifth century B.C., was so proud of his park at Sardis that he showed it to the Greek Lysander. Socrates is reported by Xenophon as saying,

'When Lysander expressed his admiration of it, observing how fine the trees were, how regularly they were planted, how straight the rows of them were, and how elegantly all the rows formed angles with one another, while many sweet odours attended on Lysander and Cyrus as they walked about', he also added, ' "I look with astonishment on all these trees on account of their beauty, but am still more astonished at the art of him who measured out the ground, and arranged them all for you." His astonishment was all the greater when the delighted Cyrus replied, "It was I, let me say, Lysander, that measured the ground and arranged all the trees myself; and there are some of them that I planted with my own hand. " '

The term *paradeisoi*, used by Xenophon as if it were a word not of his own language, but nevertheless quite familiar, gave rise to our word 'paradise', which has come to mean in English-speaking countries primarily the abode of the blessed. The use of it by Xenophon is the first occasion when it appears in literature. Sir William Temple defined its original meaning in his essay 'On the Gardens of Epicurus' in the seventeenth century. His description may serve as a definition of these larger gardens which, at their most extensive, were virtually a stretch of countryside:

'A Paradise seems to have been a large space of ground, adorned and beautified with all sorts of trees, both of fruits and of forests, either found before it was enclosed, or planted after; either cultivated, like gardens, for shades and for walks, with fountains or streams, and all sorts of plants usual in the climate, and pleasant to the eye, the smell or the taste; or else employed like our parks for enclosure and harbour of all sorts of wild beasts, as well as for the pleasure of riding and walking: and so they were of more or less extent, and of differing entertainment, according to the several humours of the princes that ordered and inclosed them.'

The Assyrian parks from which the Persian counterparts were probably developed were magnificent in conception and execution, there being no problem with regard to labour because the conquests of the Assyrians enabled them to enslave whole nations. One of their kings, Tiglath-Pileser, has already been mentioned as an importer of foreign trees. Another, bearing the great name of Sargon, reigned at the end of the eighth century B.C., and created in the vicinity of Nineveh a park 'like the Amanus mountains, wherein all flowers from the Hittite land and herbs from the hill are planted together'. The reference to the Hittite country of the Amanus, which was on the extreme north-east coast of the Mediterranean, extending to the Cilician Taurus, appears elsewhere in Assyrian inscriptions. It was a beautiful, well watered and fertile mountain country.

The son of Sargon, Sennacherib, the dread Assyrian king of the Bible who, in the words of Lord Byron, came down on the Jews 'like a wolf on the fold', only to be soundly defeated, was also a maker of gardens. One of those made by him was hewn out of the rock around a

JARDINS DE BABYLONE

CHAPITRE V

PARADIS DES PERSES — JARDINS SUSPENDUS DE BABYLONE
— LES JARDINS CHEZ LES JUIFS

L'HISTOIRE authentique des Perses ne commence qu'à Cyrus, environ cinq cent cinquante ans avant Jésus-Christ. Tous les rois ses prédécesseurs, mentionnés dans les traditions persanes, sont des personnages fabuleux, dont chacun, s'il fallait en croire ces traditions, aurait vécu et régné pendant plusieurs siècles. Xénophon, qui écrivait quatre cents ans avant l'ère chrétienne, parle du goût des rois de Perse pour les jardins, qu'ils appelaient, dit-il, *paradis*, et dans lesquels on cultivait à la fois des plantes d'ornement et des végétaux à fruits comestibles. « Dans toutes ses résidences et dans toutes les parties de ses domaines qu'il visite, dit l'historien grec, le roi veille à

RIGHT *The Hanging Gardens of Babylon as they appeared to a nineteenth-century artist, D. Lancelot: from* Histoire des Jardins *by Arthur Mangin (Tours, 1883).*

BELOW *In this eighteenth-century artist's impression of the Hanging Gardens of Babylon there is little to suggest 'hanging', i.e. terraces; the gardens are more reminiscent of a seventeenth-century French garden. Published* c. 1760 *by John Bowles at the Black Horse in Cornhill.*

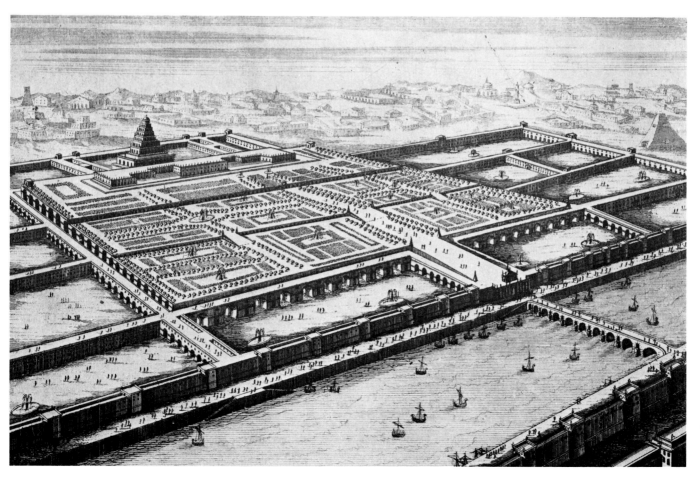

temple he had built to the god Assur. There was a canal in front of the building feeding smaller water-courses between the plants and trees. The round holes for the latter, about five feet deep, were, like those made for Queen Hatsheput to plant trees at Deir-al-Bahari, cut out of the rock, and have been traced over an area of about five acres. Sennacherib says:

'I made gardens in the upper and lower town, with the earth's produce from the mountains and the countries round about, all the spices from the land of the Hittites, myrrh (which grows better in my garden than in its native land), vines from the hills, fruits from every country; spices and Sirdu-trees have I planted for my subjects. Moreover, I have cut down and levelled mountain and field from the land about the town of Kisri into the country near Nineveh, so that the plants may thrive there, and I have made a canal; one and a half hour's journey from the Chusur river have I brought water to flow in my canal and between my plantations for their good watering. I have set a pond in the garden to keep water there, and in it I have planted reeds . . . By the grace of the gods the garden prospered, vines and fruit, Sirdu-wood and spices. They grew tall and flourished greatly, trees and reeds also . . . palms, cypresses, and the fruits of the trees . . . The reeds in the pond I cut down, and used them for divers purposes in my lordly palace.'

Sennacherib lived in magnificent style, erecting his palace on splendid terraces, and having his conquests

LEFT *The garden of Alcinous from Homer's Odyssey as seen through the eyes of the French artist D. Lancelot in* Histoire des Jardins *(Tours, 1883).*

ABOVE *A painting of Mount Olympus, where the gods of the Greeks had their home: Volume III of John Sibthorp's* Flora Graeca *(1819).*

RIGHT Vitis vinifera, *the common grape vine, which might have trailed over the grotto of Calypso as described in Homer's Odyssey, depicted by Ferdinand Bauer in the same work.*

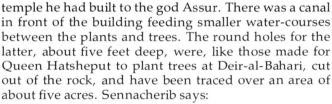

and other activities recorded in reliefs in his rooms, many of which have survived. The gardens on these terraces probably surpassed the terrace gardens of Queen Hatsheput, but it is doubtful whether they equalled those that were built to the south in Babylon in the early part of the first millennium B.C., which were known as the 'Hanging Gardens of Babylon' and listed among the Seven Wonders of the ancient World. It is possible, indeed, that the terrace gardens of Assyria were the inspiration of those at Babylon, as one of the accounts of them says that an Assyrian king devised them. There is also an account by Berosus which ascribes the making of the gardens at Babylon to King Nebuchadnezzar, who is alleged to have had them constructed for his wife, who was a native of Media, adjacent to Assyria on the east.

The most complete account of the Hanging Gardens is that of Diodorus Siculus, who wrote about 50 B.C.:

of the twentieth century he discovered a vaulted building in the Southern Citadel area of Babylon which fits the account of Diodorus Siculus quite well. It was the only building in which stone was used and stone was specifically mentioned in the account. He also found a special well which fits the way the water was said to be raised. There were three adjoining shafts, a square one in the middle with a rectangular shaft on each side. Leather buckets would have been lowered down one of the side shafts, filled with water at the bottom, and returned up the other. At the top the contents would have been tipped into a trough and then sent down the side shaft to be filled again and the process repeated. The central shaft doubtless afforded access to the buckets at the bottom if required because of some hitch. There would probably have been a similar system carrying the water from this first stage up to the top, but no trace of this was found. From their wide reputation, there seems little doubt that the Hanging Gardens of Babylon were a magnificent set of terrace gardens, worthy of the great capital city they adorned.

The Bible establishes that the Hebrews also possessed the love of gardens that distinguished their neighbours. From early times their great men were buried in garden surroundings and from stories such as that of Susannah some idea can be gained of the gardens to which they were accustomed. Her adventure took place in a garden in Babylon during the exile in which oaks and mastic trees (*Pistacia lentiscus*) grew around a pool. Their love of gardens is also evident from the Song of Solomon, probably the most sensuous and beautiful mystical poem written in any language. Here, under the guise of the burgeoning garden of spring, to be understood on many levels, the lover greets the loved one, the Jewish nation welcomes its Messiah, the young Christian church expects the imminent coming of the Kingdom, the convert to Christianity perceives the beauties of his faith, the nun addresses her bridegroom Christ and all may feel the call of goodness when grace enters their hearts:

'The Hanging Garden of Babylon was not built by Semiramis who founded the city, but by a later prince called Cyrus, for the sake of a courtezan, who, being a Persian, as they say, by birth, and creating meadows on mountain tops [this is an interesting comment, bearing in mind that it was made by someone almost contemporary, on ancient Persian gardens], desired the king, by an artificial plantation, to imitate the land in Persia. This garden was 100 feet long by 100 wide and built up in tiers so that it resembled a theatre. Vaults had been constructed under the ascending terraces which carried the entire weight of the planted garden; the uppermost vault, which was 75 feet high, was the highest part of the garden which, at this point, was on the same level as the city walls. The roofs of the vault which supported the garden were constructed of stone beams some sixteen feet long, and over these were laid first a layer of reeds set in thick tar, then two courses of baked brick bonded by cement and finally a covering of lead to prevent the moisture in the soil penetrating the roof. On top of this roof enough topsoil was heaped to allow the biggest trees to take root. The earth was levelled off and thickly planted with every kind of tree. And since the galleries projected one beyond the other where they were sunlit, they contained many royal lodges. The highest gallery contained conduits for the water which was raised by pumps in great abundance from the river, though no one outside could see it being done.'

When the German archaeologist Robert Koldewey was excavating the ruins of Babylon in the first decade

Arise, my love, my fair one, and come away;
For lo, the winter is past, the rain is over and gone.
The flowers appear on the earth and the time of
     singing has come,
The voice of the turtle dove is heard in our land.
The fig tree puts forth its figs, and the vines are in
     blossom . . .
A garden locked is my sister, my bride, a garden
     locked, a fountain sealed.
Your shoots are an orchard of pomegranates with all
     choicest fruits,
Henna with nard, nard and saffron, calamus and
     cinnamon, with all trees of frankincense,
Myrrh and aloes, with all chief spices:
A garden fountain, a well of living water, and flowing
     streams from Lebanon.
Awake, O north wind, and come, O south wind:
Blow upon my garden, let its fragrance be wafted
     abroad.

BELOW LEFT *A poppy* (Papaver pilosum) *mentioned by Dame Ethel Smyth in* A Three-Legged Tour of Greece *as one of the wild-flowers she saw, as depicted by Ferdinand Bauer in Volume V of John Sibthorp's* Flora Graeca.

BELOW RIGHT *Theophrastus, the ancient Greek, pupil of Plato and Aristotle, whose work on plants earned him the title of 'Father of Botany'. He had a garden of his own which he left for the use of his friends when he died.*

Solomon built the great Temple in Jerusalem which is associated with his name. Although there is no mention of gardens attached to it, flowers and palm trees figured prominently in the decorations. The Jewish historian Josephus describes the splendour of the palace which Solomon also built for himself. In a part constructed from fine stone there were represented 'trees, and all sorts of plants, with the shadows that arose from their branches, and leaves that hung down from them. These trees and plants covered the stone beneath them completely, and their leaves were made so finely and delicately that you would think they were in motion.' Solomon was particularly fond of a place about six miles from Jerusalem to which he used to ride every morning. Josephus records that this place was called Etham. 'Very pleasant it is in fine gardens,' he says, 'and abounding in rivulets of water; thither did he use to go out in the morning, sitting high in his chariot.'

The Assyrian empire went down in the sixth century B.C. and the Medes and Persians, now united into a formidable power under Cyrus, conquered Babylonia and obtained possession of the countries between Persia and the Mediterranean, including the Greek colonies in Asia Minor. Darius, who followed Cyrus, consolidated the Persian power and made the frontiers of the Persian empire secure. Away to the West a new civilization had arisen, that of Greece and its islands, the first civilization on European soil. Over that civilization the vast Persian power hung like an enormous and threatening cloud on the eastern horizon.

Papaver pilosum.

THEOPHRASTVS

The earliest civilization of Greece at Mycenae had links with that of Crete to the south, which preceded it. The Minoan civilization of the island of Crete, named after King Minos, whose great palace at Knossos has been excavated, was almost as old as the civilization of Egypt to the south-east and in its art reached standards of taste and excellence fully the equal of that of Egypt. In the painting on their vases, the ornamentation of other vessels, and the decoration of the palace rooms the Cretans portrayed flowers and trees in a most pleasing way. The design of the palace at Knossos, built on a hill, includes open pillared halls and terraces which look down into a valley. Although no trace of it remains, it seems very likely that the surroundings, including the valley, would have been gardens. If this surmise is correct, and the standard of these was equal to that of the art of which remains are extant, they would have been memorable. All this, however, was lost when the civilization of Crete was destroyed about 1450 B.C. by volcanic action.

The poetry of the great Grecian poet Homer echoes perpetually down the years, capturing in words at the very beginning of European civilization some of the eternal beauty. His works were probably composed around the beginning of the first millennium B.C. and the scenes described may be related to that period of history. The gardens praised by him in the Odyssey are useful rather than ornamental. Of the garden of Alcinous he wrote (Pope's verse translation):

Close to the gates a spacious garden lies
From storms defended and inclement skies:
Four acres was the allotted space of ground,
Pen'd with a green enclosure all around.
Tall thriving trees confess the fruitful mould;
The redd'ning apple ripens here to gold;
Here the blue fig with luscious juice o'erflows,
With deeper red the full pomegranate glows:
The branch here bends beneath the weighty pear,
And verdant olives flourish round the year.
The balmy spirit of the western gale,
Eternal breathes on fruits untaught to fail:
Each dropping pear a following pear supplies,
On apples apples, figs on figs arise;
The same mild season gives the blooms to blow,
The buds to harden, and the fruits to grow,
Here order'd vines in equal ranks appear,
With all the united labours of the year.
Some to unload the fertile branches run,
Some dry the blackening clusters in the sun.
Others to tread the liquid harvest join,
The groaning presses foam with floods of wine.
Here are the vines in early flower descry'd,
Here grapes discolour'd on the sunny side
And here in Autumn's richest purple dy'd.
Beds of all various herbs for ever green,
In beauteous order terminate the scene.

A painting of Delphi, where the temple of Apollo was situated, whose oracle was the most renowned in ancient times: Volume X of John Sibthorp's Flora Graeca *(1840).*

Two plenteous fountains the whole prospect
  crown'd;
This through the gardens leads its streams around,
Visits each plant and waters all the ground:
While that in pipes beneath the palace flows,
And thence its current on the town bestows;
To various use their various streams they bring,
The people one and one supplies the king.

There seems little doubt that in this passage Homer is picturing the kind of garden that rich men of his country possessed and with which he was familiar. It is also clear that, if any flowers were grown in the garden their place was so minor that they were not thought worthy of mention.

Various reasons have been advanced to explain why the Greeks did not in the earlier years of their culture make ornamental gardens. It has been said, for example, that the narrow valleys opening to the sea, with the mountains behind, in which most of their settlements were situated, did not encourage such gardens; or that they were confined in outlook because of the high development of city life. It has also been said that it just never occurred to the Greeks to bring flowers in from the wild; but, if this is true, why did it not occur to them to do so, when this seems to have happened to other communities in a similar stage of development? The answer to this question stares out both from the Greek countryside and from Grecian literature and, indeed, from the whole of the Greek artistic achievement.

Greece was, and still is, a natural flower-garden. Dame Ethel Smyth, in *A Three-Legged Tour of Greece*, has drawn a picture of the country that brings it to life. 'No-one who has not visited that vast rock-garden', she says, 'knows what wild flowers can be . . . For a mile or two the dominating fact in the carpet would be scarlet and pink anemones; then suddenly a hillside of blue or yellow flowers; then a divine whiff, stronger and sweeter than any scent known in our northern climes . . . of huge violets . . .' There was, she continues, 'a terra-cotta six-leaved poppy which grows together with the usual blood-red kind, and combines with white, yellow and blue anemones and orchids to produce an effect so ludicrously like a Turkey carpet that it made you think of Wilde's paradox about Nature imitating art . . .' As one came in from the sea in ancient times the blue of the water contrasted with the gold and pink of the coastline. Behind this a stretch of plain stood out a beautiful golden-green in the brilliant light: and nowhere does the light seem so bright as in Greece. This was broken in places by dark masses of olive and laurel groves, which led up into the wooded mountain slopes and the wilder country beyond, where snow-clad peaks and precipices give birth to rushing streams and quieter springs. So Greece was of old and still, in spite of the alterations of three thousand years, retains its ancient magic.

In these surroundings it is not surprising that, more than any other people, perhaps because they were so articulate and able to explain themselves, the ancient Greeks give the impression of retaining the primal sense of one-ness with nature that characterized our first ancestors. Their gods were all around them, always with them and part of the same scene, with the same faults and the same virtues, appearing when they chose in natural forms, and often transforming human beings into those forms. Arcadia was where the Greeks lived, with the gods as awesome but familiar companions. To have moved plants nearer to their houses solely because they were beautiful would have been a senseless act in their eyes because the plants there already were just as beautiful. When, therefore, Homer sang of gardens, it was of the fruits of the earth, because these were necessarily grown near to where they would be used, and when Hesiod wrote of plants, it was agriculture, not ornamental gardening, which concerned him. To both, the recognition of the beauty of natural things was so fundamental to their life that it did not need to be stated explicitly. It informed not only all that they said and did as individuals, but the whole society in which they lived.

Acceptance of this situation is not to say that the Greeks did not use plants ornamentally when they felt it necessary to do so, but when they did it was in the nature of an offering rather than for other reasons. Sacred groves were planted around altars and individual trees near a spring were often enclosed in ornamental fashion as sacred. Homer himself describes an ornamental scene, but it is a natural one, not man-made. Calypso, the nymph that held Odysseus captive, inhabited a grotto, which the poet describes as a 'great cave':

Where from a brazier by her, burning well,
A fire of cloven cedar-wood and pine
Far through the island sent a goodly smell.
And in it she with voice melodious sang,
While through the warp the golden shuttle rang
As to and fro before the loom she went.
But round the cave a verdurous forest sprang
Of poplars, and sweet-scented cypresses,
And alders . . .
. . . round the hollow cavern trailing went
A garden-vine with heavy clusters bent;
And rising all arow, four springs abroad
This way and that their shining waters sent.
And on both sides fair-flowering meads were set,
Soft clad with parsley and with violet.

(Pope)

This is the prototype of all grottoes, which became in later years and in other civilizations a feature of ornamental gardens. An interesting point is the reference once again to the four sources of water. The description is too near that of the four rivers of the Garden of Eden and the fourfold division by water of the Persian garden to be coincidence and points to a common origin for all three.

RIGHT Asphodelus ramosus, *one of the plants known as the asphodel, the principal plant associated by the ancient Greeks with the dead and the underworld: portrayed by Ferdinand Bauer in Volume IV of John Sibthorp's* Flora Graeca *(1823).*

Asphodelus ramosus.

Greek philosphers in discussion in a garden as seen by a twentieth-century artist: Landscape Art Past and Present by Harriet Hammond McCormick (New York, 1923).

In the fifth century B.C. the Persian storm broke over Greece. After a revolt of the Greek colonies in Asia Minor, to which Greece sent ships, the Persians invaded Greece but in 490 B.C. were defeated at Marathon, victory gaining a respite of some ten years for the Greeks. Then, under Xerxes, the Persians came again, in much larger force this time. Defeating the Greeks after the heroic stand of Leonidas and his Spartans at the pass of Thermopylae, they ravaged Athens but were eventually confronted again at the naval battle of Salamis and the land battle of Plataea, in both of which they were defeated. Although the threat was thus decisively repelled, things were never the same in Greece. The old estates broke up into smaller properties and the vigorous city-states fought among themselves. The Peloponnesian wars between Athens and Sparta dragged on interminably and the countryside became deserted as, for safety's sake, the population moved to the towns. Town life flourished and in this forcing-ground political and intellectual life developed to an unprecedented vigour, the great minds of Socrates, Plato and Aristotle setting the basic patterns for European thought. The places where the intellectuals and athletes congregated, the 'academy' and the 'gymnasium' respectively, began to be planted with trees and to assume a park-like aspect. Flowers begin to be mentioned: Herodotus speaks of a many-petalled sweetly-scented rose that grew in Macedonia and Demosthenes mentions rose-gardens. Theophrastus, a pupil of Aristotle, possessed a garden of his own which, in his will, he left jointly to his friends to enjoy. He was the first to study plants methodically: the works he compiled on this subject have survived, although most of the rest that he wrote has perished, and have earned him the title of 'Father of Botany'. The philosopher Epicurus is credited with the creation of the first garden within town walls, retreating with his students inside its enclosure to savour the niceties of the Epicurean approach to life.

Greek private houses of this period were small and the internal courtyard paved, so that the growing of plants within the latter, if any took place, would have been limited to those in pots and tubs. There was, indeed, a pot-plant cult. Quick-growing plants which came up, matured and died very quickly, symbolized the life of Adonis, and were very popular. The growing of plants in tubs was facilitated by the development of the peristyle, a colonnade around the court open to the sky. The peristyle had a very long future in front of it, up into modern times.

In the fourth century B.C. the Greeks were revenged upon the Persians. Alexander the Great of Macedonia swept across the map with his armies, conquering all in his path until in 330 B.C. he battered his way into Persia and the great empire passed for ever from the descendants of Cyrus. The victory revealed to the astonished Greeks the splendour of Persian gardens and parks. Alexander recognized the merit of what he saw and took steps to see that these beautiful places should be preserved. Among other things he punished the Magi who were supposed to maintain the tomb of Cyrus but had neglected it.

The Greeks were astonished not only by the Persian gardens but also by the gardens of Egypt which Alexander had conquered and which they had also seen. Here they found an ancient garden culture that laid emphasis on flowers and used them extensively in its festivities. Moreover, the Egyptians had flowers all the year round. From this time on, in the wider Hellenistic world that came into being as a result of Alexander's conquests, flowers and gardens played a very prominent part in social as well as religious life. The change was particularly marked in the large towns which, because of the greater distance of most of the inhabitants from the countryside, now developed town gardens. Towns particularly renowned for their gardens were Alexandria in Egypt, founded by Alexander, where a quarter of the town was given over to them, and Antioch in Syria, the gardens of which are greatly praised by writers. The Greeks of Asia Minor had been subject to influences not felt in the homeland of Greece and had always been in advance of the latter. In Antioch there was a one-sided colonnaded main street on the other side of which there were gardens stretching to the mountain; a second similar street ran down to the Orontes. The greatest attraction was, however, a beautiful park called Daphne, originally a sacred grove, which was described by some as the finest spot on earth.

With increasing prosperity and luxury, the garden activities of the rich of the Hellenistic world degenerated into extravagances. Accounts are extant of a feast of Ptolemy Philadelphus at Alexandria the main feature of which was a 'Great Tent' erected for the guests, supported by garden courts and ceremonial chariots decked with plants and flowers. The principal

ABOVE RIGHT *The Oleander* (Nerium oleander) *is such a common plant of Mediterranean regions that it is often neglected, but grown in a favourable situation it is a most beautiful shrub: from Volume III of John Sibthorp's* Flora Graeca *(1819).*

BELOW Clematis viticella, *a climber that hangs its long stems bearing lovely purple flowers among the shrubs of Greece: Volume VI* Flora Graeca.

chariot, which carried the goddess Semele, included a creeper-clad grotto with two streams surmounted by a colossal statue of Bacchus. Artificial grottoes were often a feature of the gardens of the wealthy. Pliny mentions one in Lycia which, although inside a plane tree, was capacious enough to hold eighteen people. Large groups of statuary were also made for such gardens. One which is still extant is a large and vigorous group struggling with a bull, which probably appeared superb in its original setting but is a little overpowering under a roof. Hieron II of Sicily, helped by the famous Archimedes, built a gigantic pleasure raft to house a lavish garden, including the usual walks and pools, in which he could conduct state business, apeing the monarchs of the older empires further east, who loved to dispense justice in beautiful surroundings in the open air.

About 750 B.C. a small settlement was established on the River Tiber in Italy. As the centuries passed it grew into a town spreading over seven hills and fought with its neighbours until, by about the middle of the third century B.C., it had become supreme in Italy and, as the considerable power of Rome, was ready to enter on the world's stage. Romans of the Republic were an austere race, much attached to the countryside and leading lives not far removed from the primitive, but as outside influences came into the country the simple life, championed by Cato and Censor, who would not even have plaster on his walls, gave way to more luxurious ideas. Hellenistic styles became Roman styles and Roman farms became elaborate estates. The Hellenistic gardens became, in the new world which arose, the gardens of the Roman villa.

3
Peristyle and Portico

I sometimes think that never blows so red
The Rose as where some buried Caesar bled;
That every Hyacinth the Garden wears
Dropt in its Lap from some once lovely Head.

Omar Khayyam

The military preoccupations of the great men of the Roman Republic, concerned with those conquests that were eventually to turn their Republic into an Empire, found one avenue of expression in their early villa buildings, which had more than a touch of the fortress about them. Scipio Africanus was the first to adopt the Greek style but the comparative simplicity of the military building which he still continued was soon lost. Before the Republic gave way to the Empire in 27 B.C. the opportunity for luxury afforded by the wealth acquired from campaigning had broken down the old austere ideals. It became the fashion for gentlemen to have a number of country estates as well as a town house in Rome, the latter being required because their rank and standing carried with it duties in and to Rome.

The grounds of the original villas changed from being areas solely for food-production to estates supporting leisure retreats modelled on the tree-lined gymnasia and academies of Greece. They were almost always provided with a grotto or nymphaeum, often very beautiful. An idea of the nature of one of these may be obtained from a fresco at Pompeii, where a falling stream feeds first a decorative fountain and then a basin under a gloomy rocky pile surmounted by a pillared rose pergola. There are accounts of such grottoes on a larger scale, open above to the sky. These gardens, consciously modelled by Cicero and others on those of Greece, so as to preserve the continuity with the philosophers of whom they felt they were the heirs, were comparatively modest compared with later developments. Even in Cicero's time, however, the earlier half of the first century B.C., large hunting parks were being established like those of the ancient Assyrians (whose civilization was already no more than a half-buried heap of forgotten ruins) and there came a time when they began to crowd the farmland so that the general view gained ground, and was expressed by Pliny, that 'large estates have ruined Italy'.

The peace, prosperity and prestige brought to Rome by its conquests enabled the Romans of the first days of

LEFT *A close-up view of one of the arches and statues of the Canopus Canal of Hadrian's Villa at Tivoli showing the triclinium (dining room) in the distance.*

ABOVE *The Casa dei Vettii at Pompeii, which was buried in the eruption of Vesuvius in A.D. 79. This picture shows the peristyle, a feature derived from the Greeks which was adopted in Roman houses.*

the Empire to turn to quieter pursuits. They very soon surrounded the city with gardens and established within its walls many public and private places of this kind. One such public place of which the plan has survived was the Portico of Livia created by Augustus which was wholly Greek in style. A colonnade (or 'portico') completely surrounded a sunken lawn, to which access was obtained by steps. In the centre of this was a great tank, the remainder being laid out with plantations of trees, flower-beds and pergolas, which provided a pleasant shady retreat in which to walk and talk. Such places were always embellished with statuary and fine works of art breathing the Greek spirit. The gardens of the tomb destined for Augustus were used as a park in his lifetime.

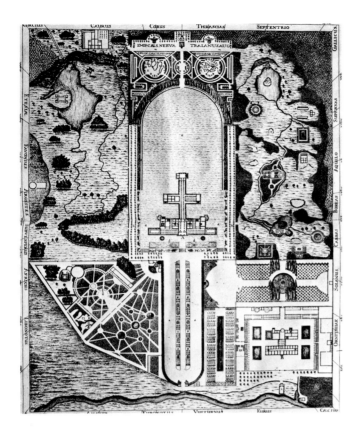

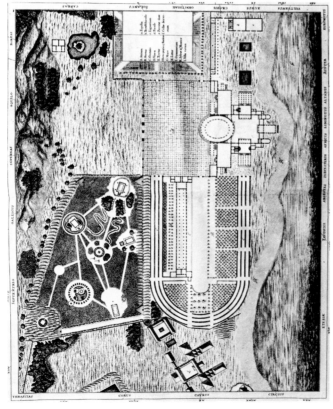

A plan of the younger Pliny's smaller seaside villa at Laurentium, not far from Rome, reconstructed from the description in his letters for The Villas of the Ancients Illustrated *by Robert Castell (London, 1728). The plan was drawn by T. Wilson and engraved by P. Fourdrinier.*

LEFT *A plan of the younger Pliny's villa in Tuscany, known as the Tusculan, reconstructed from the description in his letters for* The Villas of the Ancients Illustrated *by Robert Castell (London, 1728). The plan was drawn by T. Wilson and engraved by P. Fourdrinier.*

RIGHT *A drawing of a restoration by Schinkel of the seaside villa of Pliny the Younger at Laurentium from* L'Art des Jardins *by J. Rothschild (Paris).*

The private gardens made during these times were so extensive and varied that the whole area within and around Rome, except the Plebeian Quarter south of the Capitol, must have appeared to be a garden city extending over several square miles. Many of these villas are mentioned, and sometimes described, in contemporary or near-contemporary works. Some of them were: Caesar's garden on the Via Portuensis; the gardens of Antony nearby; the gardens in the Campus Martius in which a huge pool named Naumachia was made by Augustus in which to stage a mock sea-fight; the gardens of Caligula's mother Agrippina on the site now occupied by the Vatican, which ran down to the Tiber; the hill to the north of the town which was called the Collis Hortulorum because of the gardens upon it; the gardens of Sallust the historian in the valley near the Porta Salaria, bought with funds extracted from the conquered Numidians, which became, after A.D. 20, a favourite place of several emperors; and the gardens of the Esquiline estates near the high Servian wall, with its fine views of the Sabine and Alban mountains, where Maecenas was one of the first to settle, and the poets lived — Virgil, Propertius and Martial.

According to Sallust, the Romans tried to make the town like the country and the country like the town. Pliny the Elder, who lived about the middle of the first century A.D., had something to say on the first point. In his *Natural History* he explains that the Romans regarded almost any piece of land that they inherited as a 'garden', even though they were more properly farms or estates. It was no disgrace that their land grew vegetables or fruits; indeed, some noble families took their names from these, some of the Valerii, for example, taking their name Lactucini from the lettuce, with which they had a particular connection, and Pliny's own family giving its name to a cherry. He adds the interesting information (using Philemon Holland's translation from the seventeenth century, which has a quaint flavour of its own):

'And as for the other quarters set out with beds of floures and sweet smelling hearbs, what reckoning was made of them in old time may appeare by this, That a man could not heretofore come by a commoner's house within the citie, but he should see the windows beautified with greene quishins [cushions], wrought and tapissed with flowers of all colours; resembling daily to their view the Gardens indeed which were in out-villages, as being in the very heart of the citie, they might think themselves in the countrey . . .'

Pliny the Younger, nephew of the Elder Pliny, describes his villas so delightfully and lingers with such obvious pleasure on each detail that he not only gives a very good and clear description of what they were like but conveys unconsciously an excellent picture of the very great love the Romans bore for their estates and their interest in everything pertaining to them. His principal villa was in Tuscany, and of this he says (the translation is that of William Melmoth):

'My villa is so advantageously situated, that it commands a full view of all the country around; yet you approach it by so insensible a rise that you find yourself upon an eminence, without perceiving you ascended. Behind, but at a great distance, stand the Apennine Mountains. In the calmest days we are refreshed by the winds that blow from thence, but so spent, as it were, by the long tract of land they travel over, that they are entirely divested of all their strength and violence before they reach us. The exposure of the principal front of the house is full south, and seems to invite the afternoon sun in summer (but somewhat earlier in winter) into a spacious and well-proportioned portico, consisting of several members, particularly a porch built in the ancient manner.'

'In the front of the portico', he continues, 'is a sort of terrace, embellished with various figures and bounded with a box hedge, from whence you descend by an easy slope, adorned with the representation of divers animals in box, answering alternately to each other, into a lawn overspread with the soft, I had almost said the liquid, *Acanthus*.' This is not the plant now known as *Acanthus*, but some low-growing plant, perhaps moss.

'This is surrounded by a walk enclosed with clipped evergreens, shaped into a variety of forms. Beyond it is the *gestatio* [a place for exercise in vehicles] laid out in the form of a *circus* [a place for public games], ornamented in the middle with box cut in numberless different figures, together with a plantation of shrubs, prevented by the shears from shooting up too high; the whole shut in by a wall covered with box, rising by different ranges to the top. On the outside of the wall lies a meadow that owes as many beauties to nature, as all I have been describing within does to art; at the end of which are several other meadows and fields interspersed with thickets.'

Returning now to the house, Pliny says:

'At the extremity of this portico stands a grand dining-room, which opens upon one end of the terrace [the word used is *xystus*, which is properly a large portico used for athletic exercises]: from the windows there is a very extensive prospect over the meadows and to the country . . . you also have a view of the terrace and such parts of the house as project forward, together with the woods enclosing the adjacent *hippodrome* [a racecourse for horses and chariots]. Opposite almost to the centre of the portico stands a square edifice, which encompasses a small area, shaded by four plane trees, in the midst of which a fountain rises, from whence the water, running over the edges of a marble basin, gently refreshes the surrounding plane trees and the verdure underneath them . . .

'In the front of these agreeable buildings lies the very spacious *hippodrome* entirely open in the middle, by which means the eye, upon your first entrance, takes in its whole extent at one glance. It is encompassed on every side with plane-trees covered with ivy, so that while their heads flourish with their own foliage, their bodies enjoy a borrowed verdure; and thus the ivy, twining round the trunk and branches, spreads from tree to tree, and connects them together. Between each plane-tree and the next are planted box-trees and behind these bay-trees, which blend their shade with that of the planes. This plantation, forming a straight boundary on both sides of the *hippodrome*, bends at the farther end into a semi-circle which, being set round and sheltered with cypress-trees, varies the prospect, and casts a deeper gloom; while the inward circular walks (for there are several), enjoying an open exposure, are perfumed with roses and correct, by a very pleasing contrast, the coolness of the shade with the warmth of the sun.

'Having passed through these winding alleys, you enter a straight walk, which breaks out into a variety of others, divided by box-hedges. In one place you have a little meadow, in another the box is cut into a thousand different forms: sometimes into letters expressing the name of the master; sometimes that of the artificer; whilst here and there little obelisks rise, inter-mixed alternately with fruit-trees: when, on a sudden, in the midst of this elegant regularity, you are surprised with an imitation of the negligent beauties of rural nature: in the centre of which lies a spot surrounded with a knot of dwarf plane-trees.'

So far, Pliny's account has been concerned with a description of his grounds. He now turns to the way in which he lived in the villa, and the parts principally used in what, under the warm Italian sun and the cool breeze from the Apennines, must have been a delightful existence:

'Beyond these is a walk planted with the smooth and twining *Acanthus*, where the trees are also cut into a variety of names and shapes. At the upper end is an alcove of white marble, shaded by vines, supported by four small Carystian pillars. From this bench the water, gushing through several little pipes, as if it were pressed out by the weight of the persons who repose themselves upon it, falls into a stone cistern underneath, from whence it is received into a fine polished marble basin, so artfully contrived that it is always full without ever overflowing. When I sup here, this basin serves as a table, the larger sort of dishes being placed round the margin, while the smaller ones swim about in the form of little vessels and water-fowl. Corresponding to this, is a fountain which is incessantly emptying and filling; for the water, which it throws up to a great height, falling back into it, is by means of two openings, returned as fast as it is received.

'Fronting the alcove, and reflecting as great an ornament to it as it borrows from it, stands a summer-house of exquisite marble, the doors whereof project and open into a green enclosure; as from its upper and lower windows the eye is presented with a variety of different verdures. Next to this is a little private recess, which, though it seems to be distinct, may be part of the same room, and is furnished with a couch; notwithstanding it has windows on every side, yet it enjoys a very agreeable gloominess, by means of a spreading vine which climbs to the top and entirely overshades it. Here you may recline and fancy yourself in a wood, with this difference only, you are not exposed to the weather. In this place a fountain also rises and instantly disappears; in different quarters are disposed marble seats which serve, no less than the summer-house, as so many reliefs after one is wearied with walking. Near each seat is a little fountain; and throughout the whole *hippodrome*, several small rills run murmuring along, whereso ever the hand of art thought proper to conduct them, watering here and there different spots of verdure and in their progress refreshing the whole.'

Pliny apologises for the length of his description, little knowing its value, for it is the only really detailed account we have of a Roman country estate and it is for this reason that it has been quoted at length. One interesting feature is the extensive use of clipped shrubs and trees, which we now call topiary. Cicero calls a gardener *toparius* but his use of the word does not seem to be connected with topiary as such, but with the general care of the garden. Pliny himself ascribes the introduction of this specialization to a slightly later time than that of Cicero, saying that it was the invention of a friend of Augustus, the Roman knight Cnaeus Martius. By Pliny's time the art had become very skilful, fleets of ships and hunting scenes being cut out of box and cypress.

Pliny's other villa, the Laurentum, was near Rome and smaller, having no large park or important pleasure garden attached, but he speaks of it in the same terms as he does his Tuscan villa, describing his life there and how he was able to achieve the peace and quiet he loved among beautiful scenery. The farm buildings were on the land side and the house next to the sea but sheltered from storms. Of such garden as there was he says:

'The dining-room looks out onto the garden and the promenade running round it, planted with box hedges or with rosemary where box will not grow. I find the box grows excellently where it is protected by the buildings. In the open, where it is exposed to the wind and the salt spray of the sea it is apt to wither. Within the promenade young vines are planted . . . Mulberry and fig trees also do very well in this soil and are as attractive to look at as the sea itself. Round at the back towards the vestibule lies the kitchen garden. From this point cloisters run out [in front of which] is a terrace walk fragrant with violets.'

Apart from the houses on the great estates, there were also many smaller properties of the type which have been preserved at Pompeii. Roman houses were typically built round the *atrium*, which was the heart of the house, being a roofed and floored court with a central opening in the roof through which the smoke escaped, the rain which fell through being caught in a pool below it. Plants were grown in boxes around the walls. Many houses adopted the Greek peristyle. One such at Pompeii was the House of the Vettii. In this house the internal space open to the sky is ten metres by eighteen, the area being bordered by eighteen white pillars with coloured capitals. On the edges of eight basins, fan-sided but with rounded corners, there are twelve statues pouring out water. There are two more basins with fountains in the centre of the garden, which is also provided with marble tables, small pillars bearing statues, and shells. Box-bordered flower-beds and clumps of shrubs and climbers fill the remainder of

ABOVE LEFT *Part of the ruins of the Casa di Mario Lecrezio at Pompeii, showing a fountain and pool in the foreground.*

TOP *The restored central tank, garden and peristyle of the House of the Golden Cupids at Pompeii.*

ABOVE *Part of the portico and circular canal of the Marine Theatre at Hadrian's Villa at Tivoli; this part of the garden probably served as a personal private retreat for the emperor as the small garden house within it could be isolated by movable bridges. The house was itself furnished with a portico leading to a small central garden with a fountain and flower-beds, around which were a dining room, a library and a small bathroom with stairs leading to the pool.*

the space. Such garden areas usually had scenes painted on the walls in order to give the impression of space.

In Rome itself congestion got so great as the years went on that even gardens of this kind diminished in number, although there was a vogue for balcony and rooftop gardens. Nero removed a great portion of older Rome between the Palatine Hill and the Esquiline, stretching from above the baths of Trajan to the garden of Maecenas, and created a belt of parkland across the heart of Rome, but the existence of this great reserved portion was a barrier to trade and later emperors destroyed it. As time went on other emperors constructed gardens on the grand scale, Hadrian's villa at the foot of the Tivoli hill, some of the monuments of which still remain to be seen, being particularly impressive. The lack of garden space for lesser citizens within Rome led to a great demand for flowers, large nurseries being set up in the Campagna to supply this need. The Romans had learnt from Egypt the art of producing flowers out of season and in heated greenhouses induced both roses and lilies to blossom in winter. Fine bunches of grapes were produced in heated glasshouses with windows of mica. Even the smaller towns exhibited similar luxury, a nursery being discovered at Pompeii with a large stock of painted pots. Not only did the Romans rival later ages in the gardens and landscapes of their villas, they also made considerable progress in other horticultural practices. Only in the range of plants were they deficient, as they had but a tiny fraction of what is available today, the fruit of long centuries of plant-collecting.

ABOVE *The restored summer* triclinium *(dining room) and* euripus *(channel filled with water) of the Casa de Lorio Tiburtina at Pompeii, showing the fresco at one end designed to lengthen the view and give the impression of opening on to the countryside.*

RIGHT *A wall painting from an underground room in the Villa Livia by the Porta Prima in ancient Rome, designed to create the illusion of being in a garden, with a flower border and fruiting orange trees, with a background of vegetation and the mountains in the distance. Such a room was doubtless used as a retreat from the heat of summer, providing, in effect, an indoor garden much cooler than the real gardens outside.*

What they did at home, the Romans also did abroad. In North Africa, their villas were enlarged to become fortified houses in hunting parks, but in the European countries they built many fine villas after the Roman model. Even in the far-off colony of Britain, where the savage inhabitants still tried to breach the Roman wall and the sun was but a watery remnant of the warm Italian orb to which the Romans were accustomed, they built after the home fashion, setting their villas where there were fine scenes to view and dreamed that, like Pliny, they looked out from their hills across the Tuscan landscape to the sea.

In truth, the Roman was still at heart at one with the ancient Greeks. In spite of their down-to-earth outlook and the discarding of the ancient gods, the Romans still hankered, as they did in the early days of the Republic, for the basic feeling of one-ness with nature that they had found so satisfying on their farms and which was essential to their well-being. During the days of Alexander the Great Greek poets and writers expressed for the first time a nostalgia for their origins, writing of the shepherd life in the pastures on the hills, amid the rocks and trees and flowers, as if it were the Eden of the Hebrew poet, a life of innocence contrasted with the complexity and corruption of city life. Here is Theocritus expressing that fundamental yearning in what came to be called pastoral literature, of which he was one of the first and greatest exponents. In his seventh Idyll, the *Thalysia*, he is describing the resting-place provided by Phrasidamus for his guests at a harvest feast in honour of the harvest-giver:

> . . . presently we lay,
> Where Phrasidamus dwelt, on loosened sheaves
> Of lentisk, and the vines new-gathered leaves.
> Near by, a fountain murmured from its bed,
> A cavern of the Nymphs: elms overhead,
> And poplars rustled; and the summer-keen
> *Cicadae* sung aloft amid the green;
> Afar the tree-frog in the thorn-bush cried;
> Nor larks nor goldfinches their song denied
> Of golden summer all was redolent,
> And of brown autumn; boughs with damsons bent
> We had; and pears were scattered at our feet,
> And by our side a heap of apples sweet.

Others also wrote such poetry, forming a school, but as the Greek world changed into the Hellenistic world, the music faded for a time, only to be heard again in Rome in the second century A.D. John Dryden

translated Virgil's Eclogues, the first of which, 'the Dispossessed', is a dialogue between one deprived of his land with another fortunate enough to retain it:

O fortunate old man! whose farm remains
For you sufficient, and requites your pains;
Though rushes overspread the neighbouring plains,
Though here the marshy grounds approach your
    fields,
And there the soil a stony harvest yields.
Your teeming ewes shall no strange meadows try,
Nor fear a rot from tainted company.
Behold! yon bordering fence of sallow-trees
Is fraught with flowers; the flowers are fraught with
    bees:
The busy bees, with a soft murmuring strain,
Invite to gentle sleep the labouring swain.
While from the neighbouring rock, with rural songs,
The pruner's voice the pleasing dream prolongs,
Stock doves and turtles tell their amorous pain,
And, from the lofty elms, of love complain.

Rome itself decayed and went down into the darkness, but the feeling lived on and writers still tried to express it. It is fitting, perhaps, that almost the very last flicker of the ancient light was one of the most beautiful. The story of Daphnis and Chloe, written in Greek by Longus about the third century A.D., is the love story of all young virgin lovers, immortalized for all time in the setting of nature. Here is Philetas, an old man, beginning the story in which he reveals to the lovers the existence of Eros, the god of love:

'I am that old Philetas, children, who in former times sang many songs to the nymphs . . . I have a garden that I have planted and cared for, cropped and trimmed ever since old age fell upon me and I could no longer lead flocks to the fields. All that anybody may wish for comes to this garden in its appointed time. In the spring roses, lilies, violets, single and double; in summer poppies, pears, and apples of many different kinds; and the autumn season having returned there are grapes and figs and pomegranates and green myrtles. And come thither every morning great flocks of birds, some to feed, some to sing, for it is thickly planted with trees; and there are three fountains; and if the fencing wall were removed you would think the garden was a wood. Today at noon as I entered I saw a young boy . . . Eros. He is young, beautiful and he has wings.'

Long after ancient Rome had tumbled into ruin, the old strain was heard again among the poets and writers of the Renaissance of western Europe, influenced by the Christian tradition of the 'Good Shepherd'. In Elizabethan England it inspired many voices, including that of Shakespeare and in the years that followed there was a new flowering, culminating in the poets Robert Herrick and Andrew Marvell, who brought a new freshness to it. It has continued into modern times, often tempered, however, by a bitter realism earlier unknown, the roots of which lie in the growth of the great cities and the divorce of ever larger and larger sections of mankind from contact with natural things. Recognized in literature as a distinct genre, the deeper significance of the pastoral has been missed. Like the urge to create gardens it is a manifestation, rising inexorably to the surface from time to time, no matter how often it is thrust down, of the universal longing for the ancient environment, later called Paradise, through which the early ancestors of man roved for so long.

4
The Long Springtime

In spring for sheer delight
I set the lanterns swinging through the trees,
Bright as the myriad argosies of night,
That ride the clouded billows of the sky,
Red dragons leap and plunge in gold and silver seas,
And O my garden gleaming cold and white,
Thou hast outshone the far faint moon on high.

Yuan Mei

While the cool water from the far-off mountains was trapped and guided to trickle through the early Persian gardens; while those whose gods drank with them quenched their thirst at Grecian springs; and while the peristyle of Athens gave way as the centuries passed to the atrium and portico of Rome, other men away to the east beyond the borders of Persia and Baluchistan turned their minds to the beauties of the natural scene. The civilization of Mohenjo-daro in the Indus valley succumbed to invaders in 1700 B.C., but beyond the dusty ruins of its cities, in the land of India, new princedoms developed. The sacredness of the pipal *(Ficus religiosa)* and other trees passed on into these societies which now, in their turn, produced fine gardens.

The infant Gautama later to become the Buddha was, according to tradition, born under a tree in Nepal in the sixth century B.C. Sacred trees and gardens played a large part in his life and the lives of those who followed him, since under the trees they found the shade and congenial quiet in which they could meditate. These gardens and parks did not, perhaps, differ greatly from those further west except that the trees hanging over the pools were palms rather than trees used to cooler conditions. It seems likely also that there was a greater variety of flowers in the Indian gardens: a Chinese visitor to India in the fifth century A.D. did, indeed, say of one garden, which had been given to the Buddha himself and was a favourite resort of his, that it contained 'countless flowers of many colours'.

Two centuries after the Buddha's death Buddhism spread to Ceylon (Sri Lanka). Very soon sacred buildings, parks and gardens were created which outshone those of India: ruins of many of these still exist. A magnificently carved stone enclosure was constructed for a tree grown from a branch of one under which the Buddha received enlightenment. A costly replica of this tree over fifty feet high was made in the second century B.C. The roots were of coral set in an emerald floor, the trunk was of silver and the leaves,

LEFT *Chinese scholars, as depicted by the Chinese artist Yu Chi, enjoying the quiet and repose of a garden.*

ABOVE *The Taoist idea of Paradise, as a garden set against the background of the Hills of Longevity. The pines, peach trees and polyporus fungus that grow from the rocks are sacred plants. Storks bearing messages in their beaks fly across the water between the pavilions.*

41

which were decorated with precious stones, were of coral and gold.

Further east still, in China, there were also developments. The earliest religion of China was animist in nature: mountains and rocks, seas and rivers and even the sky were thought each to have its spirit, fellow creatures with man in the world. Some aspects of this view of nature have persisted throughout Chinese history. The special veneration of the Chinese for mountains was noticed by the Jesuit Martinus Martini in *Novus Atlas Sinensis,* published in the seventeenth century at Amsterdam. 'They investigate', he said, 'the psychology of a mountain, its formation, its actual veins, just as astrologers examine the heavens, and chiromancers the hand of man.' A collector of the early nineteenth century commented that rocks were much used about Chinese houses. These, he said, were 'mostly in one piece; but some of them are like pyramids and pieced together; some are like obelisks; and several are broken up into irregular shapes. When they are like rocks, water flows through the crevices, and they are all of different sizes. Frequently they are set on a wooden base, and they are usually close to some building in the foreground of a small garden, where their peculiar shape may serve as a table or stool.'

Against this background Lao Tzu, whose existence as a real person is somewhat shadowy, taught in the sixth century B.C. the Taoist view that man should integrate himself with the rhythms of life. Among other things he spoke of Wu Wei, 'a paradox', says the Shrine of Wisdom Manual No.8, 'in which is contained the secret of the Simple Way which is the middle path between all extremes.'

'This is the Simple Way: to revert to our original simplicity and naturalness . . . the way of the gentle breeze that whispers in the trees; of the bird that lightly soars into the free, clear, blue sky. It is the way of the artless flowers, which bloom without effort, and through Wu Wei catch the warmth and blessing of the sun. It is the way of the waters which course through the veins of Mother Earth, reaching the most inaccessible places and overcoming obstacles without

LEFT *The villa of Wang Chu'an among the mountains, as protrayed by Wang Wei.*

ABOVE *A Japanese artist's painting of a Chinese garden.*

RIGHT *Shen Chou (1427-1509), in this painting of 'Peach Blossom Valley', has combined the Chinese love for peach-blossom with their equal devotion to mountains.*

striving, passing eventually into the wide-spreading ocean. It is the way of fire, ever tending upwards; and of light, ever shedding itself without becoming less. To feel the touch of Wu Wei is to know and realise the inner pulse of Tao, which is reality itself.'

Confucius, contemporary with Lao Tzu, taught the way to achieve spiritual calm. He spent a great deal of his time researching into the past, convinced that he lived in an age when things were less well managed than they had been in times past. There were undoubtedly great emperors and great estates in the millennia before Confucius but little other than myths, such as that of the miraculous gardens of Kuen-len, has survived of them and there are no traces of ancient gardens. Although grand show gardens were made for the emperor Chou about 2,000 B.C. nothing is known about them. It is not until the time of the Ch'in dynasty, 221 to 206 B.C., and the Han dynasty, which ruled China for the four centuries 206 B.C. to A.D. 201, that the story passes into the pages of recorded history.

The energetic but repressive Ch'in emperor Shih Huang Ti had the great park Ah Fang Kung, but it was the emperor Wu-ti of the Han dynasty, who reigned from 140 to 87 B.C., who was the greatest maker of gardens. His capital was at Chang-an in the west of China and his gardens are stated to have extended for fifty square miles, every valley between the mountains having palaces, pavilions and grottoes scattered over it. Many were built for his beloved Fey-yen, about whose beauty writers such as the great lyrical poet Li-tai-pe

were still composing verses 800 years later. The summer palace of Chao-Yang is described by the poet as having been a sumptuous paradise of spring. The Han emperors expressed their adherence to the old reverence to mountains by making large mounds in their gardens. On these simulated mountains they built their palaces, linking the buildings by bridges. When, therefore, Buddhism came to China in the first century A.D. it found a garden culture already in existence against a background of established philosophies. These philosophies slowed down its acceptance and it was not until the fourth century A.D. that it could be said to have made considerable progress. When it finally caught hold it elevated the attainment of calm so prized by Confucius to a mystical plane.

The Buddhist expansion began with the founding by Hui Yüan in A.D. 370 of the Society of the White Lotus. The park-like garden in which the novices received instruction was copied elsewhere, such gardens becoming known as Lu Shan parks, after the mother house. The process by which Chinese modes of thought had been formed drew them irresistibly to the countryside for enjoyment where the calmness of the landscape was in tune with their desire for peace. Small gardens at this time were often created by poets. Hsieh Lung-yin wrote in A.D. 410: 'I have banished all worldly care from my garden; it is a clean and open spot. I chose the place in the lee of the mountains to the north; the windows open towards the hills in the south. I have dammed up the stream and built a pond. I have planted roses in front of the windows, but beyond them appear the hills.' A little more than a hundred years later Lo yang described in Chia Lang Chi a large garden which had been bequeathed by Chang Lun to a monastery:

'With its hills and ponds this garden exceeded in beauty many princely pleasure grounds. Here had been built up a number of hills that were called the Ching Yang mountains; they looked as if they had been formed by nature. Within these heights there were double peaks and curving ridges by the sides of deep streams and valleys. There were plenty of tall leafy trees which afforded protection against the rays of the sun and moon, and hanging creepers which did not prevent the mist from stealing in. The paths ran zig-zag up the hills and down in the valleys: it looked as if they had suddenly been broken off at certain points, although actually they continued in another direction. The stony and curious watercourses flowed in some places in winding bends but in other places were straight.'

Philosophers, like poets, found conditions more congenial in the countryside than elsewhere and often fixed their dwellings far from those of others. The great painter-gardener of the sixth century A.D., Chang Seng-yu, described such a retreat. The 'thatched cottage for the resident philosopher-hermit', he said, 'was set among trees at the foot of a mountain; there was a stream, a lily-pond, some chrysanthemums, a few fruit trees grown for their blossom, an old and preferably gnarled pine, perhaps a clump of bamboo

Four of the palaces which the Emperor K'ang-hsi of the Manchu dynasty built in the early years of the eighteenth century at Jehol in southern Manchuria about 150 miles north-east of Peking. He had 36 paintings made of these which he commissioned Father Ripa, a secular priest attached to the mission at the Chinese court, to reproduce in copper-plate engravings. This he did very successfully as can be seen from the examples shown.

and some fantastic rocks'. The delight of the poets and philosophers in the solitude and beauty of their gardens was expressed by Tao Yuan-ming. On returning to his garden after a period of absence he wrote:

'Now my eyes light upon my door and the ridge of my roof, exultingly I hasten forward . . . The paths are overgrown, but the pine tree and my chrysanthemums are as of yore . . . To ramble in my garden is my daily joy: its stillness is guarded by a constantly closed gate. The evening mist rises lingeringly out of the valleys; tired birds find their way home. The shadows fade and soon they have disappeared: leaning with my hand against the solitary pine I linger.'

Early in the ninth century A.D. Po chü-i, in his poem 'T'ao T'ang Chi' described another garden, that of his own cottage on the lower slopes of the Kuang-lu mountains in Kiang-si:

'Before the hut extended an open court covering about a hundred square feet and in the middle of the court rose a terrace. On the south side lay a square pond, twice the size of the terrace. Around the pond were planted bamboos from the hillside and wild flowers. White lotus flowers and white fish were placed in the water. Further south wound a stony stream and along this grew pines and other conifers: bushes throve at their feet. The paths, which led in and out, were paved with white stones. To the north the hall steps had been hewn in the mountainside, so that one could ascend to the top and to cleared spaces where stones were piled up [simulating mountains]. There were also a spring and a tea plantation, inviting to the pleasure of tea drinking. On the eastern side of the hill the water fell from a height of three feet, and on the opposite side it was led from the height by an open bamboo pipe to above the house whence it flowed down by a terrace.'

The advent of the Sung dynasty in A.D. 960, which

lasted until the Mongol invasion in the early thirteenth century A.D., brought with it a period of comparative stability in which great cultural advances were made. A poem written in the eleventh century about the garden of the great statesman Hsi-ma-kuang provides a very clear and detailed picture of what the garden of a great mandarin was like at that time:

'Twenty acres are all the space I need. In the middle is a large summerhouse [which he used as a library] . . . On the south side there is a pavilion in the middle of the water, by whose side runs a stream that flows down from the hill on the east. The waters make a deep pond, whence they part in five branches like a leopard's claws . . . At the border of the first stream, which falls in cascades, there stands a steep rock with overhanging top like an elephant's trunk. At the summit stands a pleasant open pavilion . . . The second arm is divided after a few feet into two canals, which twist and turn about a gallery, bordered by a double terrace. The eastern arm turns backward towards the north, beside the arch of a pillared hall which stands in an isolated position and is thus made into an island. The shores of this island are covered with sand, shells and pebbles of different colours. One part of it is planted with evergreen trees. There is also . . . a fisherman's hut . . . The two other arms seem alternately approaching and retreating, for they follow the turns of a flowery meadow and keep it fresh. They often overflow their banks and make little pools, which are edged with soft grass; then they escape into the meadow and flow on in narrow canals, which disperse in a labyrinth of rocks which hinder their course, confine them and break them up so that they burst forth in foaming waves to follow again their prescribed course. There are several pavilions on the north of the large summerhouse, scattered about here and there; some of them are on hills, one above the other, standing like a mother among her children, while others are built on the slope; several of them are in little gaps made by the hills, and

only half of them can be seen. The whole region is overshadowed by a forest of bamboos, intersected by sandy footpaths, where the sun never penetrates. Towards the east there is a little level of irregular shape, protected from the cold north wind by a cedar wood.

'All the valleys are full of sweet-smelling plants, medicinal herbs, bushes and flowers. In this lovely place there is always spring. At the edge of the horizon there is a copse of pomegranates, citrons and oranges, always in flower and fruit. In the middle there is a green pavilion to which one mounts by an imperceptible slope along several spiral paths, which become narrower as they get near the top. The paths on this hill are bordered by grass . . . On the west a walk of weeping willows leads to the bank of the river, which comes down from the top of a rock covered with ivy and wild flowers of all kinds and colours. All round there are rocks piled anyhow, with an odd effect like that of an amphitheatre. Right on the ground there is a deep grotto which gets wider the further one goes, and makes a kind of irregularly shaped room with an arched ceiling. The light comes in through a somewhat large opening hung round with wild vine and honeysuckle . . . A small stream comes out on one side and fills the hollow of a great stone, and then drops out in small trickles to the floor, winding about in the cracks and fissures until it falls into a reservoir bath.

'This basin deepens until it reaches an arch, where it makes a small turn and flows into a pond at the bottom of the grotto. This pond leaves only a narrow footpath between the shapeless rocks which are grotesquely heaped together in piles all around . . . The second pond has small islands of sedge on it . . . Access from one to the other is by the big stones that project above the water, or by the small wooden bridges that are scattered about, some of them arched, some in straight lines or zigzags, according to the space available. When the water-lilies are in flower, the pond seems to be wreathed in purple and scarlet, like the edge of the southern sea when the sun rises . . . Those on foot

ABOVE *The Chinese love for the menace of overhanging mountain crags is well illustrated in this seventeenth-century Chinese picture of a pavilion in the mountains.*

RIGHT *The Sacred Lotus of the Buddhists* (Nelumbium speciosum) *fills the foreground of this painting by Chang Shang-ssu while the white heron soars above.*

must make up their minds either to go back the same way they came, or climb up the rocks that close the place in on every side. Nature intended that these rocks should be approached from one end only of the pond. They seem to be fastened together where the waters have forced a passage among the willows that stand in the gap: the stream breaks through on the other side with a roar. Old fir trees conceal the dip and nothing can be seen among their top branches but stones that have become embedded . . . Leading up to the summit of this rocky wall there is a steep narrow stairway which has been chipped out with a hatchet . . . The pavilion which is set up . . . is simple in design, but is

remarkable for its view of a wide plain where the River Kiang follows a serpentine course in the rice-fields.'

The Sung emperor Hui Tsung, who reigned from A.D. 1100 to 1125, was a great patron of the arts and himself a painter of considerable accomplishment. In his garden-making he was a great collector of stones. The Chinese attribute the invention of the art of using stones in gardens to Yohan Koan Han, who constructed artificial hills of rocks one hundred feet high and conducted running water from a distance of many miles for ornamental purposes. Hui Tsung was a worthy successor since it is recorded that for his Ken Yu garden he collected stones with such enthusiasm that, for a time, 'they blocked all other traffic on the canals round the capital'. The Chinese loved mountains that were wild, rough, towering and picturesque, and it was after such effects that they strove in their gardens. They particularly liked old, water-worn masses of limestone that had been eroded into weird and fantastic shapes. T'sao Hsueh-c'hin described them in 1792 as 'like goblins or savage beasts, lying crossways, horizontal or in the upright position and having on their surface moss and lichen with mottled hues, or parasitic plants.' Many such stones were dredged up from Lake Tai Hu: a seventeenth-century writer said of Tai Hu stones that 'they have been collected since time immemorial and are now very rare'. They were sold, like works of art in the West, for very high prices and for this reason many were faked. Finders of good stones were accorded considerable honour.

The placing of the stones was an operation requiring great care. They were displayed in such a way that the play of light and shadow on their hollows and rough surfaces gave the maximum picturesque effect. A stone of specially remarkable quality might be set up singly. They were often used to form grottoes. Not only were they of grotesque shape, many of them were also honeycombed with holes and varied in colour from the normal white of limestone through deeper shades to slate blue, some even being black. The largest ones were more than six feet tall. The *Yuan Yeh* suggests how the gardener might use the stones like a painter:

'The white wall serves as paper and upon this one paints with stones. Those who perform such works should in the first place pay attention to the furrows and lines on the stones, and then dispose them in the light of the old masters' ideas. One may then plant Huang-Shan pines and firs, old plumtrees or beautiful bamboos. If one contemplates such a painting through a round window, it is like wandering in a mirror.'

Gardening in China had, indeed, had a long association with painting. To recapture the experience of the countryside at times when they could not revisit it, artists recorded favourite scenes in landscape paintings, often making their representations in the form of scrolls which revealed a succession of views. The Chinese tried to get the same effect in gardens as they did in the scrolls, constructing the former so that they presented a variety of scenes. As the visitor walked through he was continually confronted and surprised by some new and pleasant experience. Although they avoided symmetry not found in nature, the Chinese delighted in complementary situations, mountain and plain, rocks and water, upright and horizontal, rough and smooth, and male and female, and their creations were therefore always balanced. Their outlook, deriving from their philosophy, was conditioned by a refined aestheticism, and all their arrangements were carefully calculated to produce the desired effects. Seats, shelters, kiosks and pavilions were provided at particular places where such effects could be enjoyed. Nothing was neglected that could contribute to the experience, every path, slope or tree being laid out or planted to suit the circumstances, so that the garden became a highly sophisticated complex of related sensations.

The buildings in Chinese gardens were of a great variety of design, being suited to a particular situation rather than to any formal style. The characteristically curved lines of the beautifully tiled roofs were applied to a multiplicity of edifices, from a replica of a fisherman's hut, as in the garden of Hsi-ma-Kuang, to highly ornamented pavilions. The latter often had an open side revealing a beautiful mosaic floor and were provided with ornamental balustrades in attractive geometrical designs. Doorways were also sometimes geometrically patterned but the design of these could also be more fancifully based on lotus petals, gourds, shells or vases. Windows, too, were highly ornamental, being decorated with stylized leaf or flower shapes or elaborate geometrical designs.

Walls and fences were also made in geometrical designs, but bridges, although they could be ornate in the more splendid situations, were often rustic, being made of rough timber or stone slabs harmonizing more effectively with the scenes representing wild nature in which they were placed. From the buildings or other set vantage points such as the bridges, the visitor could watch in comfort the scene set for him, the colours of the foliage or flowers, the tumbling of the cascade, the moonlight on the rippling water or the dawning of a new day; he could listen, too, to the wind soughing through the pines or making music in the bamboos, or hear the slap on the water of a fish's leap. All these things, and others like them, gave infinite pleasure to the refined and sensitive Chinese.

The emperor Hui Tsung was more than a collector of stones: he had a great interest in the culture of flowers, sending a special officer, Chu Mien, with extraordinary powers, to collect plants and trees in the southern provinces. The Chinese have always shown, from the very earliest times, a great interest in and love for flowers, perhaps because of the great richness of the flora of China, which is part of the temperate and sub-tropical flora of south-east Asia, a flora which exceeds in number of species the total of the whole of the rest of the countries of the northern hemisphere put together. The Chinese valued plants for their distinction of habit and grace rather than for their colour, scent and form being more important than anything else; they preferred white flowers to any others although their most popular plant, the chrysanthemum, was yellow. The chrysanthemum is

first mentioned in the Li Chi or Book of Rites, which is a product of the Chou dynasty, 1122 to 249 B.C. A little later, in the *Shi Ching* or Book of Odes, the Shaoyao, the herbaceous paeony *(Paeonia albiflora)* appears, together with the peach *(Prunus persica)* and the day-lily *(Hemerocallis fulva)*. The paeony, sometimes called the 'Chang Hi' or 'Farewell Flower', was passed between boy and girl as a token of love. The day-lily was popular with the women, who wore it in their girdles because it was supposed to favour the birth of sons.

Chinese civilization expanded to the south until it reached the Yangtse river. Here Ch'u Yuan wrote the *Ch'u Ssu* or the Eulogies of Ch'u in which, in the part called 'Li Sao', he mentioned some of the beautiful orchids indigenous to the area, the sweet-scented *Cymbidium and Dendrobium* species and *Bletilla hyacintha*. The *Êrh Ya,* or Literary Expositor, which was compiled to assist in finding the meaning of obsolete literary words in the classics and was twice revised, in the fourth and tenth centuries A.D., mentions the hollyhock *(Althea rosea)*. Other flowers known to the

ABOVE *Paeonies, peach blossom and magnolias, flowers greatly loved by the Chinese shown in a Chinese painting by Chang t'ing Hsi.*

RIGHT *The gardens and buildings of Canton, painted in 1877, showing what resembles a western-type garden in this international port.*

Chinese from early times include the crape myrtle (*Lagerstroemia indica*), the tiger lily (*Lilium tigrinum*), the lilac, water-lilies, hydrangeas and various species of rose indigenous to China. With the advent of Buddhism the Sacred Lotus (*Nelumbo nucifera*) became important. The most aristocratic and gorgeous flower in Chinese eyes, however, was the moutan or tree paeony (*Paeonia suffruticosa*), whose enormous and splendidly decorative flowers are most striking. The poet Chou tun-i had something to say on this in the eleventh century A.D. 'Since the beginning of the T'ang dynasty it has been the leading fashion to admire the paeony,' he wrote, 'but my favourite is the water-lily. How stainless it rises from its bed of mud. How modestly it reposes on the clear pool, the symbol of purity and truth. It emerges symmetrical and perfect in its spotless chastity; its subtle perfume is wafted far and wide . . . something to be reverently admired from a distance and not profaned by familiar approach.' 'In my view,' the poet says, 'the chrysanthemum is the flower of retirement and culture; the paeony a symbol for high rank and wealth; and the water-lily the matchless lady of virtue. But few

have loved the chrysanthemum since T'ao Yuan-ming and none now loves the water-lily like myself, whereas the paeony is a great favourite of all mankind.'

Of the trees that the Chinese planted in their gardens the plum was the most important, thousands of poems, paintings and treatises being produced in its honour. The timber trees, *Catalpa ovata* and *Catalpa bungei*, were always planted, together with the mulberry, around Chinese homes. *Paulownia fortunei*, the T'ung tree of the classics, has been planted for more than three thousand years, the clusters of its foxglove-like tubular flowers, white spotted with purple, making a brave show in early summer. The Japanese apricot (*Prunus mume*) is frequently mentioned in early literature, being held to symbolize a good future, and there are four species of crab apple that have long been cultivated. Other trees planted in Chinese gardens included *Sophora japonica*, the Pagoda Tree; *Gleditschia sinensis*; *Ailanthus glandulosa*, the Tree of Heaven; and *Ginkgo biloba*, the Maidenhair Tree.

In the second half of the thirteenth century A.D. the Venetian Marco Polo reached the court of Kublai Khan, the Mongol successor of the Chinese emperors, and on his return recorded his adventures, including a description of the Great Khan's palace at Khan-balik (Peking), which was surrounded by outer walls:

'Between the inner and the outer walls . . . are stretches of park-land with stately trees. The grass grows here in abundance, because all the paths are paved and built up fully two cubits above the level of the ground, so that no mud forms on them and no rain-water collects in puddles, but the moisture trickles over the lawns, enriching the soil and promoting a lush growth of herbage. In these parks there is a great variety of game, such as white harts, musk-deer, roebucks, stags, squirrels and many other beautiful animals. All the area within the walls is full of these graceful creatures, except the paths that people walk on.

'In the north-western corner of the ground is a pit of great size and depth, very neatly made, from which the earth was removed to build the mound of which I shall speak. The pit is filled with water by a fair-sized stream so as to form a sort of pond where the animals come to drink. The stream flows out through an aqueduct near the mound and fills another similar pit between the Great Khan's palace and that of his son Chinghiz, from which the earth was dug for the same purpose. These pits or ponds contain a great variety of fish. At the farther end of the pond there is an outlet for the stream, through which it flows away. It is possible to pass from one palace to the other by way of a bridge over this stream.

'On the northern side of the palace, at the distance of a bowshot but still within the walls, the Great Khan has had made an earthwork, that is to say a mound fully 100 paces in height and over a mile in circumference. This mound is covered with a dense growth of trees, all evergreens that never shed their leaves. And I assure you that whenever the Great Khan hears tell of a particularly fine tree he has it pulled up, roots and all, and has it transported to this mound by elephants. No matter how big the tree may be, he is not deterred from transplanting it. In addition, he has had the mound covered with lapis lazuli, which is intensely green, so that trees and rock alike are as green as green can be and there is no other colour to be seen. On the top of this mound, in the middle of the summit, he has a large and handsome palace, and this, too, is entirely green.'

The grassy areas watered by trickling streams, the pools, the fish, the high mound and trees and the pavilion in Kublai's palace garden are all familiar features of the Chinese garden as it has always been made. Six centuries later, in the nineteenth century, Prince Kung made a new garden at the palace called Kung wang-fu. Immediately at the entrance to this garden there were bold rock formations, one of which was a tall gateway, the whole being carefully arranged to provide contrast of light and shade with the surrounding greenery. Inside the first big court was a pond fed by a canal in a setting of rough stone blocks, some of which were stepping stones. Willows and *Gleditschia sinensis* overhung the pond. On a stone platform behind it was a long pavilion with a pretty veranda. Sloping galleries on either side connected to other long galleries at right angles; the whole was reflected in the water.

A broader court behind was dominated by a high mound made of jagged stones full of holes; in the middle of the mound was a grotto. Water seeped down from a basin on the mound into the grotto and then into a little pond in front of the mound, giving the latter its name of Ti t'sui Yen or Gorge of Dripping Verdure. The grotto itself was called Pi yung Ting or Grotto of the Secret Clouds and was regarded as one of the most successful effects in the garden. Tunnels on either side of it led through the mound and sloping galleries beyond to the hall behind the mound. The latter was the summit of the whole garden, which included many other rock and water features and an open air theatre. The large pieces of water had soft bottoms so that water plants could be grown in them and the garden required so much water that a water wheel pump driven by asses walking round had to work ceaselessly to maintain the supply.

The description of this garden of almost modern times shows how little Chinese gardens have changed since they were first made, probably more than three thousand years ago. Among the palaces of the Emperor in Peking was one that bore the name of 'the Palace of the Long Springtime'. For the Chinese garden, formed as the nation moved out of the winter of barbarism into the spring of civilization, it has, indeed, been a 'long springtime'. The Chinese garden represents a tradition entirely independent of the West, but the veneration shown to natural objects and their endowment with human attributes shows that it is based on the same primal quest for one-ness with nature. From the Chinese garden sprang the Japanese garden, in which this basic idea is even more evident.

5
Gardens of the Spirit

A lonely pond in age-old stillness sleeps,
Apart, unstirred by sound or motion till
Suddenly into it a little frog leaps . . .

Basho (1644-94), tr. Page

To modern western man, Japan conjures up a picture of a hi-fi or television set, or a sleek and efficient car of notable reliability, products of a thrusting upstart commercial nation, active and vigorous all over the world. If he happens to be a knowledgeable gardener interested in plants, he might be aware that some of his best-loved plants originated in Japan, but he would be unusual if he knew anything about Japanese gardens even though, scattered up and down the countries of the West, there are attempts to create them. Nor, in most cases, is he likely to know anything about the basic notions of the Japanese mind, which have almost nothing in common with those of the West and cause the Japanese to approach the formation of a garden from a standpoint very different from his own.

To an older generation there is also another factor: the shadow of the brutality of the Second World War hangs over the Japanese. It is hard for those who were involved in that war to comprehend that Japanese beliefs set a far gentler standard of personal conduct than those of the West and that the behaviour of the Japanese reflects these beliefs, catastrophic though that behaviour may be to their enemies, but such is the case. Their cities are a strange mixture of the two, and in art there are those who have accepted modern western ideas and reject the traditional values of their nation, but it is with the latter we are concerned, as the Japanese style of gardening is based upon them. The Japanese are a people of extreme sensitivity of spirit. Their ideas of the beautiful are very precise. Something of these must be understood before their gardens can be appreciated.

The bright colours and patterns of the kimonos of the geishas are one face of beauty, the one the tourist sees: the face, indeed, put to the outside world. They recognize too a beauty in things which are clever, stylish and sophisticated: the quality expressed by the French word *chic*. There is a beauty also in right deportment, in being properly correct in an unobtrusive way, behaving soberly and sedately, even though

LEFT *Part of the lake at the Silver Pavilion, Ginkakuji, Kyoto, which was designed and built by the garden-designer So-ami for the Regent Yoshimasa. It is noted for its fine pine trees and rare water-rocks, both of which can be seen in the picture.*

ABOVE *A tree in a container as a dominant feature in a tour garden at Kamakura; stone lanterns, clipped shrubs and stepping stones complete the scene.*

dull to western eyes. These are, however, comparatively low levels of beauty. They value more, along with the unobtrusiveness they admire so much, the patina of age. In the abstract they look for a piquant quality, an astringency, combined with tranquillity, self-chosen abasement and solitariness, the whole to be harmonious but not quite balanced. The last quality is very important. Whatever is presented to others must be incomplete so that the other may mentally complete it and thus experience it in full. But even this is not

51

enough. There are no words in the English language which express exactly their highest conception of beauty. In that conception is included all that we mean by quiet taste and elegance, refined simplicity, culture, consideration for others, serenity, modesty, formality, restraint, nobility and the courteous incompleteness they feel to be so necessary. Applied to gardens, such an outlook relegates the western taste for masses of colour, except as seen in nature (as, for example, the cherry blossom they love so much) and the preponderance of showy flowers, to a very low level. Indeed, the pursuit of western breeders for ever larger and brighter flowers of each species is incomprehensible to a traditional Japanese gardener. To be larger and brighter is not to be more beautiful and may, indeed, be the reverse. Each product of nature has its own inherent beauty which is already perfect, which man may change but cannot improve.

The Japanese did not attain to the fullness of their conception all at once. Even so, before they were affected by outside influences, they had progressed far along the road. The Shinto religion, the original faith of Japan, saw all animate things and many inanimate as possessing their own spirit, so that ordinary daily life entailed reverence for even common things. Thus, when Buddhism came to Japan from China in the sixth century A.D. it did no more than add a new dimension to the old faith without destroying it. The Japanese, just as they have done with western ideas in modern times, seized on the Chinese culture with which it came, which was then the most civilized in the world, absorbed it and transformed it through their splendid artistic gifts into something which equalled, if not transcended, the original. They developed very quickly an art of the highest quality. By the eighth century A.D. they had a wide national culture penetrating through all

ABOVE *Part of a Japanese garden, seen from the house, devoted to beautifully rounded clipped shrubs.*

ABOVE RIGHT *Part of the garden of the Heian shrine at Kyoto, showing the pool and stepping stones. Gardens of the Heian period were comparatively simple creations of still water and islands with symbolic meaning.*

levels of life. The introduction of Zen Buddhism in the thirteenth century A.D. further widened and stimulated this culture.

The Japanese love and flair for beauty has its roots in their beautiful country: long sea coasts and mountain scenery inland. In spite of the large population, which lives mainly in the coastal lowlands of the islands of which Japan is composed, much of the country is still forested. Streams tumble down the mountainsides into the rivers, leaving lakes and pools on their way to the sea. Attractive scenes abound. The Japanese do not attempt to copy these in their gardens on their natural scale but are adept at capturing their essence. Indeed the great art of the Japanese gardener lies in suggestion. Their gardens are not, as in the West, to be taken merely on the face value of the plants or ornaments within them arranged in a pleasing and harmonious fashion. They contain trees, rocks, sands, pools, running water, cascades, woodwork (always unpainted), stone lanterns, pagodas, tortoises, cranes and Buddhas, often superficially attractive to the western taste as individual objects or groups, but such appreciation is a surface reaction only. Considered against a background of Japanese belief, culture and symbolism, they take on a deeper and more serious spiritual meaning.

Gardening in Japan is thus an art of considerable

refinement; there is a scrupulous attention to aesthetic rules. Considerations of unity, balance, congruity and particularly scale and proportion, together with all that tends to produce harmony and repose, are carefully observed throughout every design. The aim is to represent the natural scenery of the country as seen by the people who inhabit it. Following this line, the designer is not tempted to reproduce scenes with which he has no acquaintance, and exotic views or plants are thus not found in Japanese gardens. As a result, these gardens have a consistency not often found in the West. Even the structural ornaments suggest the real landscape of Japan or that of China. Bridges, pagodas, shrines and shelters are reduced reproductions of the larger rustic buildings that are part of every rural scene. There is, it is true, a great deal of clipping and training of shrubs and trees but this is rarely for any other purpose than to recreate favourite types of growth observed in nature. Not only do the Japanese exercise infinite care in such detail, they match the standard of the finish of the whole with the situation in which it is placed. The garden of a person of distinction would be characterized by the highest finish and attention to detail, that of the more rustic retreat by the roughest and sketchiest treatment. There are many gardens in between these extremes that merit an intermediate approach, so that the garden harmonizes in style with its surroundings. Japanese gardens are, in fact, more than a representation of nature. They are a poetical conception embracing all the factors bearing on the garden as an expression of beauty.

Japanese writers condemn in their own country what is a highly respected aspect of British gardening, the taste for filling the garden with plants rare or difficult to grow, and in their own case, with expensive rocks, as if there were some particular virtue in rarity or high cost.

Ostentation of this kind is detrimental in their view to the highest aims of garden art, which they think should be inspired by a love of nature and not a desire to impress. Gardens should be arranged, so they believe, in order that the different seasons may contribute in rotation to their artistic excellence. The Japanese garden being a retreat for ease and meditation, it should, they feel, accord with the temperament, beliefs and occupation of its owner. The gardens of priests dedicated to virtue and self-denial will therefore differ from those of owners with more worldly interests. They go so far as to attribute particular sentiments — peaceful retirement, modesty, prosperity, old age, happiness in marriage and similar qualities — to some of their historic gardens. This is not so fanciful a practice as might appear. Nature herself in different moods arouses varying emotions in man which are allied to such sentiments and many of the themes of Japanese garden decoration have come to express moral virtues. Islands, lily-pools, pine trees, plum trees, bamboos and even the tortoise and crane have all some significance in helping to convey such ideas.

The most important features in a Japanese garden have names suggestive of historical, romantic or religious connections and their surroundings are arranged to conform with these associations. A river bridge, for example, may have its neighbouring maple trees or iris beds to convey a feeling of the river scenery at Tatsutu, a rural spot famous for maples along the river banks, or Yatsubashi, a place in the province of Mikawa noted for its beds of iris crossed by a curious bridge. A clump of pine or *Cryptomeria* trees close to a garden monument or stone may suggest a familiar temple grove. Everything has a name of its own ('Torrent-breaking stone', etc); the evocative names used for both the structures and natural objects in the

LEFT *A general view of the lake in the garden of the Shogakuin Palace at Kyoto showing a turtle-backed island in the foreground, a beach of stones in the middle distance and 'borrowed' woodland scenery in the background.*

BELOW LEFT *A bridge over the pool in the garden of the Buddhist nuns at Hokkeji, among waterside rocks and clipped shrubs.*

in design. Each room must have a desirable outlook and the need to provide this dictates how the buildings shall be made and placed. A single garden in one enclosure may therefore need to make provision for several different complete scenes each viewed from a different direction from different rooms, but all must combine to preserve the overall unity. This is not all: in every garden there are viewing-points away from the residence — stones, bridges, arbours and summer-houses for which similar provision must be made. As if this were not enough, the Japanese in their later designs often incorporate features outside the garden, such as mountains or wooded hills, as part of their scene, 'borrowing', in effect, to enlarge the canvas and the picture they have painted on it.

Japanese gardens did not, of course, reach this highly sophisticated state of artistic planning at the beginning. Unlike the Chinese garden, Japanese gardens went through a continuous process of development with several well defined stages before they reached their perfection. They have often in the past been classified into three types: the hill garden, the flat garden and the tea-house garden, but it is more instructive to classify them, as a recent Japanese writer has done, into divisions that may be taken chronologically. Japanese writers have attributed the source of ideas on garden composition to India. Such ideas may possibly have come via the Chinese from their studies of Buddhism in the first century A.D. Even up to quite recent times the historical associations of mountains, lakes and rivers connected with the life and religion of Sakya Muni served as models for the gardens of Japanese temples and monasteries. When, in the sixth century A.D., Buddhism came to Japan, gardens were made at the early monasteries of Biodo-in at Uji and Todaiji and Kofukuji at Nara.

Gardens were, however, in existence in Japan before the advent of Buddhism. Matsunosuke Tatsui, in *Japanese Gardens*, published in 1934, states that 'the origin of Japanese gardens may be traced to the era of the Empress Suiko [A.D. 592 to 628] when, according to a document remaining today, there already existed well-designed gardens with artificial hills and ornamental ponds . . . Soga-no-Umako, a high functionary of that period, was the possessor of a beautiful garden.' To this period may also be added garden styles mentioned by other writers. In the Shinden-shiki, or Imperial Audience Hall style, a large lake had been formed in a quadrangle in the middle of the buildings used for Imperial receptions. In the centre of this an islet was made which was reached from the banks by a picturesque bridge. A plum tree and orange tree were planted on either side of the entrance hall. Another style was a nostalgic creation which would not in the

Japanese garden enhance the appeal of the garden, adding to the pictorial element the charm of the poem. Plants are always grown with their natural associations; the right plants in the right place add to the authenticity of the scene. There are at least six different rivers named Tamagawa in Japan, each noted for a different flower that grows on its banks. The growing of such flowers, *Kerria japonica* and *Lespedeza bicolor* for example, near a shallow stream would immediately suggest one of those rivers. The mountains of Arashiyama near Kyoto are noted for their cherries in spring and reddening maples in autumn. The planting of a garden hill with these would immediately also convey an idea of association with these mountains.

In making gardens the Japanese have full regard to the nature of adjoining buildings. These differ greatly from those of the West. Japanese buildings, except in the modern cities, are neither symmetrical nor compact. Their houses are light, low buildings in several separate blocks connected by passages sometimes quite intricate

RIGHT *A diagram taken from* Landscape Gardening in Japan *by Josiah Conder (London, 1893) of the principal stone shapes used in Japanese gardens; they may be placed singly or in groups of two, three or five stones together.*

BELOW RIGHT *The dry landscape garden of the Temple of Ryoan-ji, Kyoto, a Zen garden of the Muromachi period, which is said to have been designed by So-ami as an ocean scene, and to have been made without trees so as not to obscure the view from the monastery of a distant shrine on Yawata mountain.*

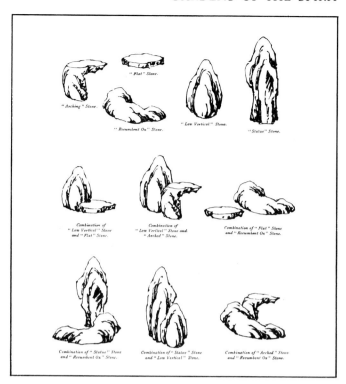

West have been regarded as a garden at all as it was composed of rocks sculptured by the waves set in the white gravelled courtyards of the houses of important people to recall distant scenes of the seafaring days of the race.

Direct intercourse with China dates from the Nara period (A.D. 645 to 781). Chinese things being new and fashionable, gardens made during this period probably reflected Chinese influence, but none of these gardens has survived, although there are occasional references to them in contemporary poetry. These gardens were followed by the 'island' garden of the Heian period (A.D. 781 to 1185). Nobles began to lay out estates, mostly in the vicinity of Kyoto, including garden pools with one or more islands of symbolic meaning, the quiet waters of which brought repose to the scene. These island and water gardens achieved considerable refinement and were often set on sites that commanded beautiful views, but they lacked one thing that the Japanese later began to regard as of supreme importance: they did not yet blend into the natural scene as if they were part of it.

Islands have always been important in Japanese gardens containing water. As they developed there were four main types. The first, the *Horai jima,* represented a sea island carrying vegetation, one of the happy isles of which, according to Chinese legend, there were three in the China Sea. This island was usually in the centre of the lake, had no bridge to it and in shape usually resembled a tortoise. Its beach was sandy and gravelly as befits a sea island. A second type, the *Fukije jima,* also represented a sea island and was without a bridge to the land, but this time there was no vegetation, the island being bare and windswept. The remaining two were usually associated with one another, one being the 'Master's Island', *Shujin-to,* and the other the 'Guest Island', *Kiakuju-to.* The former contained an arbour and was located in the foreground near the bank, to which it was connected by a bridge, while the latter was a more humble affair in the background. Other islands were often added to represent various things of interest, many of them having poetic names such as, for example 'Cloud-shaped', 'Misty' and 'Pinebark' islands.

Some of the gardens or parts of gardens of the Heian period have survived, including the ruins of one at Biodo-In at Uji mentioned above. There was no set design to these gardens; as well as the pool and island, features included a hill to the south of the pond and a stream that came in from the north and divided into two, one branch feeding the lake and the other a

waterfall on the hill. Streams had always to flow from north to south and from east to west, these courses being dictated by Chinese beliefs: four deities governed the four quarters, the east being the source of purity and the west the outlet for impurities.

During the Kamakura period (A.D. 1186 to 1393) garden design changed again. The strengthening of religion that followed civil war stimulated the creation of gardens reflecting Buddhist ideas of Paradise. Metaphysics entered the garden and the contemplation of the natural cycle of living things deepened into symbolism of life and death and speculation on nature and man. Some of the most beautiful gardens in the world have been created by Zen priests. They were much influenced by the paintings of the Sung and Yüan dynasties (A.D. 963 to 1367) in China. Gardens of the Heian kind became more reposeful under the influence of the Zen outlook, the prominent features now being stones, water and evergreens, with little change through the four seasons. Dried-up water scenery was introduced at this time: dry river beds and lakes full of pebbles and stones such as could be seen in any mountain area. More skilful use was now made of the site than formerly.

The style developed further during the Muromachi period (A.D. 1335 to 1573) which followed. Although he did not commit anything to writing, a priest called Soseki established the first rules. Another priest called Muso-Kokushi made some famous gardens at Kyoto. A fine example, preserved almost unchanged, is the Jisho-ji or Ginkaku-ji, the Silver Pavilion, at Higashiyama, Kyoto. This was designed by So-ami about A.D. 1480. It has an extensive lake backed by a magnificently wooded hill. There is a cascade, several islands, numerous granite bridges, and a number of garden stones of unusual shapes, each distinguished by its own name. The foreground was originally spread with white sand ornamentally raked into patterns and there existed a circular sanded plateau called the Kogetsu-dai, used for viewing the moonlight on the landscape. The garden also possesses a spring, pine trees and evergreens of interesting shapes, and on the west azaleas and reddening maples. A number of other gardens of this period may still be found in Kyoto.

A more remarkable expression of Zen ideas may be found in the other type of garden which began to be made in the Muromachi period. This had no water and thus became known as the 'dry' garden. The most famous example of this is the garden of Ryoanji in Kyoto which consists, apart from the buildings and surrounding trees, of fifteen stones set in an area of level raked sand, with a little moss around each stone. This garden was also designed by So-ami. His patron, who lived in the monastery, did not want trees to obscure the view of the distant shrine on Yawata mountain and So-ami therefore chose a design which did not require trees. Grass and clipped shrubs are sometimes also used in these dry gardens. It seems almost incredible to western minds that mere stones, sand, moss, shrubs and trees can be used to convey complex ideas, but even in photographs of such gardens some of the magic of the effects can be seen. These gardens mean different things to different people. So-ami is said to have had an ocean scene in mind at Ryoanji, but the garden could be a representation of a coastal landscape, a range of mountains, a chain of islands or even a cloud scene. Whatever the onlooker sees will be associated, because of the symbolism which the Japanese attach to almost everything, with some specific belief or ancient legend. Lafcadio Hearn writes:

'In almost every province of Japan there are famous stones supposed to be sacred or haunted, or to possess miraculous powers . . . There are even legends of stones having manifested sensibility, like the tradition of the Nodding Stones which bowed down before the monk Daita when he preached to them the word of Buddha; or the ancient story of the Kojiki, that the Emperor O-Jin, being augustly intoxicated, smote with

his august staff a great stone in the middle of the Chasaka road, whereupon the stone ran away!'

Stones play a large part in the art of the dry landscape garden. Those that are grey, weathered, sea-worn and moss-covered achieve, placed rightly, the highest beauty the mind can conceive. The Japanese believe that stones are superb natural works of art. Their approach to them, like that of the Chinese, contains an element of the anthropomorphic. Each stone to them has a face and limbs and must be placed so that these are in their natural positions. Their facial expression must be studied and their wilfulness humoured so that they may be rightly located. A master gardener will talk to a stone as he deals with it and commiserate with one that has been badly dealt with by an unskilled predecessor, sympathizing with it for the trials it has undergone. The apparent simplicity of the dry garden is therefore

deceptive. It hides a sophistication of imagery, belief and contemplation far beyond anything expressed in western gardens.

The dry garden could not exist without its stones. Their role in other gardens is also very considerable. Stones are chosen for each garden of a size suitable to that garden and placed as if they had lodged naturally on the site. They have always been given religious names in monastery and temple gardens and formerly those in other gardens were supposed to include the nine spirits of the Buddhist pantheon, five stones standing vertically and four being recumbent. It is still regarded as necessary to have a 'Guardian stone', a 'Stone of worship' and a 'Stone of the two deities'. Many kinds of stone are used, including granite: deep red jasper; blue, white and yellow limestone, some with compact white veins standing out like grain in woodwork; large slabs of grey and green slates and schists with ragged edges; and volcanic stone with cavities. Pebbles of granite, sandstone and flint are used for streams. As in China, there was great competition for the best, such high prices being paid in the Tempo period (1830 to 1844) that a legal limit had to be placed on them.

Five radical shapes are used, two being vertical, the first tall, having a bulging middle and cone-shaped top and the second of medium height. Of the three horizontal shapes, one is a low broad irregular flat stone, rather higher than an ordinary stepping stone; the second, the 'arching' stone, a stone of medium height bending over at the top; while the third has the form of a recumbent ox, being a long curved boulder higher at one end than the other.

These five stones may be used in combinations of two, three or five. There are situations traditionally associated with particular combinations. The tall

developed further into what was to be, in effect, the final flowering of the ancient Japanese styles. The changes at this time were bound up with the development of the tea-house garden. Monastic life of the thirteenth century A.D. in Japan had made much of the tea ceremony, investing it with precise minutiae of procedure and observance. A separate building began to be set aside for the ceremony with a garden attached. Both garden and tea-house soon became highly stylized, bringing into the lives of ordinary people some of Zen thinking: quietness, respect for others, purity and harmony.

The principal early designers of tea-house gardens each had their own conception of the aim for which he was seeking. Rikiu saw the garden as reproducing the 'lonely precincts of a secluded mountain shrine, with the red leaves of autumn scattered around'. Enshui tried to create 'the sweet solitude of a landscape in clouded moonlight, with a half-gloom between the trees', while Oguri Sotan sought to make a 'grassy wilderness in autumn with plenty of wild flowers'.

The tea-house garden as it finally developed is in three parts. The guest enters first a very small and simple area which leads after a short walk into the second or middle garden, which is a waiting area provided with a sheltered bench. Here he waits for the host to lead him, via a path of stepping stones, into an inner garden. The path may simulate a wooded walk or mountain track, its most important function being to plant in the mind of the guest a feeling that he has left the outside world and shed its cares. He must pause and meditate before he proceeds, in order to achieve the calmness of spirit requisite for the tea ceremony. The inner garden, containing the tea-house, is a comparatively small enclosed area provided with a water basin and a stone lantern. The guest washes his hands and mouth in a symbolic cleansing gesture before discarding his footwear and entering the small low opening which gives access into the building.

The tea-house itself, although ostensibly a simple dwelling of the poor, is a carefully constructed part of the garden scene, often using materials which would not be found in houses of the poor, and contributing to the air of tranquillity essential to the tea ceremony. As the Japanese became accustomed to the walk through the garden to the tea-house, with its stops en route, the idea suggested itself to them that pleasure and spiritual profit would also be derived if it were possible to walk through other gardens in the same way. Thus the

vertical stone and the flat stone, for example, are often used on the edge of a stream while the two vertical stones and the arching stone are used together at the mouth of a cascade to screen the outlet: the two vertical stones and the 'recumbent ox' stone may be found in a group on the slope of a hill. There are many similar combinations each right for particular sites and each having its special name according to position, function or principal resemblance. Stones with tops bent or distorted are regarded as 'diseased', vertical stones lying flat are known as 'dead' stones and those scattered at random as 'poor' stones.

Stepping stones are extensively used in Japanese gardens because, in the absence of lawns and with the use of sand or gravel raked into patterns and kept moist at all times, Japanese clogs would cause much damage. They are sometimes called 'flying' stones, being thought to resemble birds in flight. There are rules for their placing so that they are easy to use. This gives them the appearance of irregularity, but there is nothing random about their positioning, which is the product of close study. Larger slabs are used for ease of access to verandas or in front of flower-beds. These are sometimes made up from smaller pieces like western 'crazy' paving but again their construction is planned.

The comparative restraint of the Muromachi period was succeeded by a period when the style became almost grandiose, the Monoyama period (1573-1603) when many large castles were built. The general tone of landscape gardening was transformed. Hugh stones and plants such as the palm-like cycads were preferred as decorative features. This style continued on into the first fifty years of the Edo period (1603-1868) but then

Tour garden of the Katsura Imperial Palace, Kyoto, showing a beach of small stones, larger stones grouped by the pool, an island approached by boat and, across the water, a stone lantern lighting the waterside path of stepping stones leading away into the trees: the best planned of all historic Japanese gardens still in existence.

landscaped garden began to be made with increased attention to providing a series of viewpoints, so that the enjoyment of the viewer could be successively enhanced by stops to appreciate and admire particular effects and the meditations they suggested. The changed style of Japanese garden which began to be made from this time has been called of late years the 'tour' garden.

In the 'tour' garden the Japanese gardener, concerned now with providing as many striking views as possible within his garden, began to strive for a new objective. He ceased to study only his garden area, but looked beyond it to the distant mountains, and tried to assimilate his garden into that natural scene so that there was no perceptible boundary between it and his own work, but all was an artistic united whole. If he had to be content with an adjacent hill rather than a distant background, then he strove for the same effect, and many outstanding gardens of this kind have been made. Failing this as well, he did not change his aim, but brought all the native ingenuity of the Japanese to bear, creating the same scenes without the help of the 'borrowed' scenery. If mountains were not available, then an impression of distant mountains was created.

As is proper with things far away, no detail is visible in the further parts of the Japanese gardener's design,

the illusion of distance and size being created by the subtle use of open spaces and the hiding of the contours. The careful placing of trees and shrubs, individually or in mixed hedges, together with low clay walls and mounds, prevents the whole being seen at one time, each glimpse being calculated to suggest that there is much more to be seen. There are nearer hills more clearly defined with detail of rocks and plants, bringing one's eye down to the stream and pool in the foreground. This middle ground is the most important feature in creating the illusion of distance and size by contrasting both with the far-off scene and the objects near the viewer. There is always at least one island in the pool, planted with a carefully trained pine tree of such size and shape that it too suggests scale and distance in harmony with the mountain scene, so that the modest garden pool appears to be a large lake.

The bridge across the water is also an important factor in creating the impression of size. It may, in fact, be very small but, in the context of the rest, appears of proportions exactly fitting the scene presented. Mortimer Menpes in *Japan* commented that 'it is only accidentally that one discovers the illusion, the triumph of art over space', in a Japanese garden. 'I saw a dog walk over one of the tiny bridges, and it seemed of enormous height, so that I was staggered at its bulk in proportion to the garden; yet it was but an animal of ordinary size.' Bridges are made in a variety of ways. Sometimes they are a single stone slab, sometimes two such slabs overlapping side by side. Zigzag wooden bridges are often made to cross iris beds. Other primitive bridges are made from bundles of faggots and earth, with a turf edge to retain the latter. In larger gardens several stone slabs may be used for a bridge, carefully made and provided with moulded parapets and posts jointed together like woodwork. Similar large wooden bridges are roofed and take several right-angle turns to provide viewing-points, wistaria often being allowed to trail over them, making a charming picture. In some gardens the high arched style of Chinese bridge may be found.

There is usually a cascade, the source of which is shielded from view by tree branches and foliage so that an appearance of remoteness and depth is created. There are a number of kinds of cascades, classified according to the way the water falls, e.g. 'stepped fall' or 'spouting fall'. Elaborate gardens often represent a much-loved waterfall in the south of China known as Rozan, opposite to which is the mountain Ruimon, which is represented in the garden by a hillock opposite the cascade. In temple grounds a noted landscape in the Himalayas is often imitated. This is renowned in Buddhist lore for its cataract and lake with four rivers issuing from the latter. Once again, far removed from the original Garden of Eden, we find the four rivers.

Cascades are often the source of lakes. The latter are classified by their shapes, the important point about them being that their outline must never be completely visible from any one point, plantings of trees and shrubs or combinations of stones being used to conceal it at various points and add to the air of mystery and grandeur. The source of supply and the outlet for the water must be represented, as the Japanese abhor stagnant pools. A favourite classical model for the lake is the extensive lagoon 'Chi Chang' in China, 'Seiko' in Japanese, which is found in many monastery grounds. The China sea with its three Chinese mythical Elysian isles is also often represented.

Water basins for pure water are provided at strategic points, which may be used for the symbolic washing away of uncleanness from the soul. These have many shapes and names. Garden wells are also common, with a great variety of designs for their surface works, which may be in wood or stone. Stone lanterns, which are in every garden, are of very ancient lineage, their origin being attributed to Prince Iruhiko as far back as the seventh century A.D.; he placed the first one at a favourite lakeside spot for robbers in the province of Kawachi. They have been much used as presents to shrines, some of which possess several thousands. There are many shapes, all again with different names, most of them being made of granite or syenite; some have pedestals or legs and some are without. Whatever shape is chosen for a particular garden must harmonize in scale with that building or garden. The usual positions chosen for siting lanterns are at the base of a hill, on an island, on the banks of a lake, near a well, or at the side of a water basin. They are not really provided for the purpose of illumination since when lit they provide only a glow, but they add to the beauty of the scene, particularly when reflected in the water.

Stone pagodas, four or five feet high, which are also a common feature of Japanese gardens, appear at their best on water-side sites where their reflection may be seen in the pool or stream. There are many variations on the characteristic shape of these ornaments, which are very valuable in design because, resembling the much

TOP *A stone bridge among rocks leading to stepping stones on the lakeside at Sho Kin Tei, Katsura Rikyu.*

ABOVE *A painting by Tsukioka Yoshitoshi from* Flowers of Japan and the Art of Floral Arrangement *(London, 1892), showing Japanese entering a tea-house.*

larger temple buildings, they may be made to suggest scale. As well as these, sculptured Buddhas and household deities appear, particularly the jolly fat Hotei, symbol of the happy family life; and effigies of the tortoise and crane, symbols of longevity. Summerhouses or arbours are made to a variety of designs, the simplest being like a large umbrella, a central post holding a thatched or shingled roof.

It is not unusual to see, as the outside boundary of a Japanese garden, thick hedges 15 or 16 feet high of closely planted Kaname (*Photinia glabra*), Sugi (*Cryptomeria japonica*), Maki (*Podocarpus macrophylla*), Tsuge (*Buxus japonica*) or Kashi (*Quercus*

TOP *An impression of a large lake garden from* Landscape Gardening in Japan *by Josiah Conder (London, 1893) showing the cascade that feeds the lake, a rocky channel leading to the water, stones on the water's edge and among the grass, and bridges to an island with a single pine tree.*

ABOVE *The east garden of Heian shrine, Kyoto, showing lantern and roofed 'Taihei-kaku' bridge, which was built by Jibei Ogawa in 1895.*

laevigata). Those that lack branches near the ground are usually surrounded by a 6 foot bamboo fence. Camellias are sometimes used in country parts. Natural enclosures of this kind are carefully clipped, usually to a square form, sometimes being pierced with arched openings fitted with a square timber framework holding ornamented recessed wooden gates. Tea-house gardens usually have short clipped box hedges 6 feet high with wooden gates and gateposts. Kuromiji (*Ilex integra*), which has a sweet cedar-like scent, is occasionally used, lighter hedges being formed from the throny Kikoku (*Citrus fusca*) growing over open bamboo work. There are always two gateways to the garden, the principal entrance and the 'sweeping' gateway at the back through which the garden refuse is brushed. There are a number of designs for gates, roofed gateways like the English lych-gate being very

common; a pine tree is often trained to overhang the gate. Tea-house garden gates are of a special design, supposed to be old and primitive. Fences for enclosures within the garden are of natural wood, the more ancient and exposed looking being regarded as the most beautiful. They were first employed in the Kamakura period and taken up as an essential part of the tea-garden. There are many designs, close fences of bamboo in a variety of patterns being common, but there are also open bamboo fences. Short ornamental lengths are made for use as screens to cover up particular objects.

With the passing of time the tea-house garden gradually ceased to be a religious garden in the full sense and began to be made for its own sake. Its evolution, to some extent, therefore, led to a break with the earlier wholly religious conception of garden design. Allied to the tea-house garden, and an offshoot from it, is the secular courtyard garden of the town. This corresponds with the arrangement often found in suburbs or country towns of the West, where the shopkeeper carries on his business in the front of his premises and lives in comparative seclusion behind, the garden being at the back. In the Japanese case, space is too limited to permit of the establishment of a full tea-house garden, but much may be done by borrowing some of the techniques and ornaments of that garden: the division into sections, the lantern, stepping stones and water basin. Most of these gardens are arranged on the basic plan of leading the visitor through a dark passage from the shop in front into a bright garden, so as to make the most of the contrast, then to the main living quarters, whence another corridor, beside which is another bright garden, leads to the rearway of the house, which is separated from the storage building at the back of the site by a third garden. Many of these courtyard gardens still exist, but, under the influence of imported western ways, numbers have been converted to other uses, and a substantial portion of those remaining are neglected.

Although the Japanese flora has supplied many superb plants to western gardens, the Japanese, because of the nature of their gardening styles, make less use of these than might be expected. Bamboos, camellias, cryptomerias, the Japanese native pines, azaleas, maples, *Podocarpus*, ferns, moss and water-lilies are ubiquitous in the 'tour' gardens and some others are found less frequently. The love of the Japanese for cherry blossom is well known, but their almost equal passion for the iris is less familiar. A favourite plant, particularly for the courtyard garden, is *Nandina domestica*, a small shrub with red berries, which fits very easily into the small space available. An old belief of the Japanese about this shrub, which perhaps in part may have accounted for its popularity, is that if you have an evil dream, a dream which bodes ill luck, you should whisper it to the 'Nanten', as the shrub is called, in the morning, and then it will never come true. The list could be extended but would fall far short of what can be found in comparable western gardens.

The Japanese excel, as is well known, in the art of 'bonsai', that of dwarfing trees and shrubs so that,

while they are minute in size, they are perfectly proportioned and complete in every detail. Less well-known is their ability to apply this technique to whole gardens. So skilful are the Japanese in the art of suggestion that effective gardens both of the 'dry' and 'tour' styles are produced in the smallest space and there is a whole section of the art devoted to the production of landscapes on trays which, although perfect in every balanced feature, from mountains to plants, are so small as to serve as a table centrepiece.

Josiah Conder who, in 1893, issued the first comprehensive study in English of Japanese gardening under the title *Landscape Gardening in Japan*, commented that the Japanese 'treatment of a landscape garden not merely as an artistic medley of pretty colours and choice vegetation but as a single composition abounding in suggestions of natural spots and favourite fancies, is one which seems to give the Japanese art a rank and importance unsurpassed by any other style.' Although sparing in the range of species that they use, it is hard to escape the conclusion, when examining Japanese gardens, that Conder's judgement was right. The ideas around which Japanese gardens are formed, the craftsmanship that enters into their construction, and the effect they convey, are in conception and appreciation of real beauty centuries ahead of the ideas and practices shaping the gardens of the western world.

ABOVE *Ritsurin Park, Shikoku, which was completed in 1747. The planted pines, dramatically trimmed, harmonize with the natural pines of the mountain, which forms the background of the garden. The garden is arranged to have a similarity of scene throughout, because of its flatness.*

BELOW *The Sangen-in cloister at Daitoku-ji, Kyoto: a pleasant raised walk among beautiful shrubs, covered from the weather so that the monks may enjoy it at any time in comfort.*

6
Though Strong the Sun

Though strong the sun on Babylon's crumbled clay
And shattered stones of cruel Assyria;
Though toppled both are Athens' walls
And Rome's high-pillar'd citadel,
Four-square the ancient rivers flow
'Neath arching spray and trailing vine
Through tree-dark shade to Paradise.

The gardens of China were in later times to have a great influence on those of western countries but those of Japan, due to the continuous operation of a policy of exclusion of foreigners, did not become known to the West as did those of China, where for a time this policy was partially relaxed. Moreover, Japanese gardens were so sophisticated and strange to early western eyes that they would doubtless have remained an enigma even if detailed knowledge of them had been available to the West in earlier times. Nevertheless, the gardens of Japan, a prominent part of the national culture, based on well understood principles, and bound up with religious beliefs, have a parallel elsewhere. Almost at the same time as Chinese ideas first came into Japan in the sixth century A.D., the conquering Arabs were carrying the sword of Islam across North Africa and into Spain and to the East into Persia, so that the old gardens of Persia felt a new influence and were brought under the sway of the Koran and the ideas of Mahomet.

There were, broadly speaking, three forms of Persian garden. The garden of the small town house behind its high walls seemed from outside to be a dense bosquet of trees and only inside under the shade could the ancient pattern be seen, marked out with shallow intersecting irrigation channels, kept small to conserve precious water. The wealthy, however, made bigger gardens where the channels were lined with avenues of trees and the supply of water copious enough to be called a canal. The central pool, lined with blue tiles, often acquired a pavilion in the middle and was itself split into four sections around the building. Palaces outside the town somewhat distorted the ancient plan. These were sited on slopes with a background of mountains. A pavilion at the top looked over terraces, watered by a stream which flowed down to fill the pool at the foot of the slope, an avenue of trees leading to the gate from which one could see the city a mile or two away.

Closely bound up with Persian garden design is an ancient craft for which that country has been famous for a very long time, the making of rugs and carpets. The

LEFT *The Arab Garden of the Pool, called also the Patio de los Arrayanes and the Court of the Myrtles, in the Alhambra is one of the most beautiful of the Moorish courtyard gardens. The cream marble pavements, graceful colonnades with a dado of iridescent tiles and the shallow marble basins and fountains are superb examples of the Moorish style.*

ABOVE *This splendid tomb at Naishapur was made for Farid od-din Attar, a Persian poet of the late twelfth and early thirteenth centuries, one of the greatest Muslim mystics and thinkers. Here is shown the narrow canal of the Persian garden and, above all, the profusion of roses, meeting in an arch overhead, expressing the great Persian love for that flower.*

A carpet, made in Persia in the seventeenth - eighteenth century, showing the standard design of the Persian garden. The four rivers of Eden still flow from the centre. The cartouche in the middle stands for the pavilion at the heart of the garden and in the broad border may be seen the boundary row of cypresses and fruit trees, symbolizing death and immortality through rebirth.

primitive shepherd tribes began to make these for their comfort and the art, which probably originated in central Asia, passed down to Assyria, Egypt and Babylon. The Romans were particularly fond of Babylonian rugs which, according to Metellus Scipio, they used for table coverings. Pliny also praises them in his *Natural History*. When Cyrus conquered Babylon in 538 B.C. the Persians acquired the art and very soon became supreme. A few fragments of these ancient carpets have survived. In ornament of beasts and flowers and religious and military symbols they presented a varied picture of the passing of the centuries.

Rugs served in Persia not only for floor coverings but for coverings generally and also for wall hangings and partitions. One of the most common designs was that of the garden. These designs showed the central tank, the 'four rivers' leading from it and sometimes a bordering canal; others showed the terrace garden. The former design must have been very popular with the Arabs, for the border of Arabian carpets was until recent times still

called by the Arabic word for water, and the foundation or ground by the Arabic word for earth, which was the same in old Persian. Marie Luise Gothein, in her *History of Garden Art,* draws a pleasing picture of the love of Persians for their gardens, carpets and miniatures. 'The Persians were delighted', she says, in reference to their carpets, 'with this illusion of a garden, helped out as it must have been by the sweet scents of their artificial perfumes. On these carpets we can realise a picture, though a conventional one, of the pleasure gardens and those surrounding the houses.' The pictures of gardens in the miniatures look like carpets. 'The love of trees', she adds, 'is an inheritance of all Persians; they still love to have little rooms fixed up among the branches.'

The Sassanids, who ruled Persia from A.D. 224 until the Arabs came in A.D. 637, had their capital at Ctesiphon, where the mighty ruins of their principal palace may still be seen. The throne room of this building is reported to have been 300 yards long by 120 broad. In the days of Chosroes I, who ruled from A.D 531 to A.D. 579, a wonderful carpet was made for this palace which was 100 feet square. This is the old description:

'The ground of this carpet represented a pleasure garden, with streams and paths, trees and beautiful spring flowers. The wide border all round showed flower-beds of various colours, the flowers being red, blue, yellow or white stones. The ground was yellowish, to look like earth, and it was worked in gold. The edges of the streams were worked in stripes, and between them stones bright as crystal gave the illusion of water, the size of the pebbles being what pearls might be. The stalks and branches were gold or silver, the leaves of trees and flowers made of silk, like the rest of the plants; and the fruits were coloured stones.'

The Arabs of the desert swept over Persia like a tide, and like a tide they receded. They found in the country a virile race, sensitive and artistic, which they did not displace, but to which they gave their religion. The traffic was by no means one way: they received much in return. The Koran promised those who feared God 'two gardens, planted with shade trees. In each of them shall be two fountains flowing. In each shall there be of every fruit two kinds . . . Besides these there shall be two other gardens of dark green. In each shall be two fountains pouring forth plenty of water. In each shall be fruits, and palm trees, and pomegranates.' There is a familiar ring about this. Taken together the whole comprises a garden divided into four parts by four flowing streams: once again the ancient pattern recurs. In Persia the invaders from the hot and thirsty deserts, where the blown sand rises to choke the traveller, found many such gardens and learnt how to make them, modified to meet the needs of their religion.

Although the basic dependence on water continued to be the central feature of the gardens, as it must always be in arid countries, and high boundary walls were still needed to keep out the encroaching desert, Muslim symbolism changed to some extent the internal design of the garden. It was now divided into eight instead of four parts, to represent the eight divisions of the Koran. The water tanks must now always be brimming level with the surround to conform with the Muslim rules of ablution before worship, which also dictated the size of the tanks. The whole garden acquired the geometrical symmetry characteristic of the art of Islam, which showed the burning conviction of its practitioners of the idea of the unity of God.

The new conception did not carry with it, as did the Japanese garden, an obligation to prune and persuade the vegetation to create particular effects, and in that respect exhibits less garden craft than its eastern counterpart. Persian practice was indeed rather the reverse, and there was no change in this after the Arab conquest. The formality of the architectural aspects of the garden contrasted with the freedom allowed to the vegetation. Climbing roses, reflected in the water as they hung over the tank, continued to delight the Persians as they had done for many centuries, flinging their arching sprays wherever they wished, while the trees grew into the shapes that nature gave them, casting their precious shade at will. Only in the regular alternate planting of fruit and cypress trees along the water-channels to symbolize death and the renewal of life at the annual flowering did the idea of symmetry enter into horticultural practice.

The Persians grew a variety of trees in their gardens. Those planted for shade were the 'lofty pyramidal cypress, tapering plane trees, tough elm, straight ash, knotty pine, fragrant masticks, kingly oaks, sweet myrtles and useful maples'. Others grown for this purpose were willow, poplar, alder, beech, juniper and walnut. Fruit trees included the apricot, date, fig, olive, orange, apple, pear, plum, peach, cherry, nectarine, mulberry, quince and pomegranate. Flowers were also used in considerable variety, Persia being the home of many of the flowers commonly grown in European gardens. The Persians have a great love for the narcissus, which grows everwhere, as well as the rose, of which they grow a number of varieties, some reaching a great size. The beauty of the rose stirred the thirteenth-century poet Sa'adi to entitle his beautiful collection of moral stories, the 'Golestan', which means the 'Rose Garden'. Hafez, the great Persian lyric poet of the next century, wrote an ode on the rose, a stanza of which appears as part of the design of a rug in the Victoria and Albert Museum:

Call for the wind and scatter roses; what dost thou
    seek from Time?
Thus spake the rose at dawn: O nightingale, what
    sayest thou?
Take the cushion to the garden, that thou mayest
    hold the lip and kiss
The cheek of the beloved and the cup-bearer,
And drink wine and smell the rose.
Proudly move thy graceful form and to the garden go,
That the cypress may learn from thy stature how to
    win hearts.
Today while thy market is full of the tumult of buyers,
Gain and put by a store out of the capital of goodness.
Every bird brings a melody to the garden of the King:
The nightingale songs of love, and Hafez, prayers for
    blessing.

A variety of Rosa damascena *as portrayed by the famous French artist P. J. Redouté in his book* Les Roses. *An old tradition asserts that this rose was first introduced into western Europe by Crusaders who planted it in their castle gardens on return from the Holy Land. A specimen grows on the grave of Omar Khayyam, and it may have been one of the roses used at Shiraz for the production of the celebrated rose-water and thus probably an inhabitant of old Persian gardens.*

But it was Nezami, who wrote in the eleventh century, who captured the heavenly essence of the Persian Paradise:

Now when once more the night's ambrosial dusk
Upon the skirts of day had poured its musk,
In sleep an angel caused him to behold
The heavenly garden's radiancy untold,
Whose wide expanse, shadowed by lofty trees,
Was cheerful as the heart fulfilled of ease.
Each flow'ret in itself a garden seemed,
Each rosy petal like a lantern gleamed.
Each glade reflects, like some sky-scanning eye,
A heavenly mansion from the azure sky.
Like brightest emeralds its grasses grow,
While its effulgence doth no limit know.
Goblet in hand, each blossom of the dale
Drinks to the music of the nightingale.
Celestial harps melodious songs upraise,
While cooing ring-doves utter hymns of praise.

Persian rugs and carpets were well-known in Rome but by the time King Chosroes' great carpet was made,

LEFT *The Court of the Lions at the Alhambra showing the irrigation channels dividing the court into four in the ancient tradition of the Persian garden.*

TOP *The Fountain of the Lions in the court of that name in the Alhambra. There are twelve of the marble lions supporting the alabaster basin; the design of this fountain has been copied in concrete for modern gardens.*

ABOVE *A garden at the Alhambra in which formality is attained by clipped shrubs instead of architecture.*

the Roman Empire in the West had gone down into darkness under the attacks of the barbarians. Although Rome was barely visible in the dimness, the light of civilization still burned in the eastern empire, centred on Constantinople. Roman ways were a major factor in influencing Byzantine styles at the beginning but they soon began to be transmuted into something more splendid and elaborate under Oriental pressures, which were characterized by a taste for costly and glittering materials, ostentatiously displayed to impress the onlooker with the rank, wealth and pomp of the possessor. There were doubtless many beautiful gardens around the palaces of the emperor and the nobles, but although such gardens are mentioned many times in romances they are never described, so that nothing is known about them.

The caliphs of Islam fixed their capital at Baghdad, which became a city of marvellous wealth and wonder, inseparably linked for ever in the minds of people of the western European countries with the *Tales of the Thousand and One Nights,* stories told for the great Harun al Rashid. In the ninth century one of his sons founded a town at Samarra on the Tigris which exceeded even Baghdad in luxury. The first step in creating the town was to build an extensive irrigation system to bring water from the river. Encouraged by their ruler, the nobles created palaces and gardens of a fairyland quality. A grandson built a second settlement not far away, which excelled even the first. The principal palace covered one and a third square kilometres and doubtless there were gardens to match. Unfortunately, within a year the builder was murdered and afterwards this settlement and the original were abandoned. The court returned to Baghdad and many fine palaces were built there the gardens of which reached down to the river.

One of the most famous palaces of that day was called the 'House of the Tree'. It stood in the midst of lovely gardens and took its name from a tree of gold and silver standing in the centre of a large round pond in front of a large room of the palace surrounded by trees. This artificial tree had eighteen boughs of gold and silver, and innumerable branches and twigs covered with all sorts of fruits which were in reality precious stones. Gold and silver birds perched on the branches. When a breeze passed through these birds whistled and sighed in imitation of real bird-song. There was apparently a fashion for these trees as the Sicilian poet Ibn Hamdis describes another and there was a third in the emperor's palace at Constantinople. Which tree was the first and set the fashion is not known but it would be consistent with the ostentation of the Byzantine court for the original to have been made in that centre of luxury. These trees recall the artificial tree made in honour of the Buddha in Ceylon more than a thousand years before.

Near the 'House of the Tree' was another palace called the 'Kiosk' which had a very fine garden attached to it. In the middle was a pewter-lined tank (pewter was more valuable than silver at that time) and there was also a canal lined with the same material. The tank was thirty yards long and twenty wide. The grounds contained four grand summerhouses with golden seats. In the gardens all around the buildings grew 700 dwarf date palms, each about eight feet high. The unadorned trunks of these were disliked, so they were entirely covered with teak wood, held in place by gilded copper rings. In a similar garden at Cairo water pipes were installed under the wood encircling the dwarf palms so that each of them could be turned into a fountain. This was a particularly fine garden, full of roses and sweet-smelling plants. There were many grafted rarities, e.g. different grapes on one vine, and many trained and clipped plants, with birds and beasts encouraged in great numbers and provided with special buildings.

The Arabs took the knowledge of making gardens they had gained from the Persians into all the countries they conquered, making such gardens to the north up and beyond Damascus, where they were so fine that they were often copied, and to the west in north Africa and Sicily, and then in Spain. In the last-named country the Persian garden developed a beauty and character that has rarely been equalled. As the Arab culture bloomed to which western Europe was to be indebted for the transmission onward of much of the knowledge of ancient times, and for an extensive original contribution of its own, so did the art of the architect and the garden designer flourish, until the gardens of Spain outstripped those of the East.

Interest in gardens in Moorish Spain began with the first Omeyyad Emir, Abd er-Rahman, in the eighth century A.D. After the conquest of Cordoba he began to

build a garden modelled after a garden at Damascus, and sent emissaries to the East, even as far as Turkestan and India, to obtain plants and seeds. Succesive emirs sustained the interest, the third Abd er-Rahman building the celebrated palace and suburb of Cordoba called Az-zahra, high up on the slopes of the Sierra Morena, the terrace gardens of which were made by Byzantine designers. The splendid palace at the top, rival of anything at Samarra or Baghdad, looked out over the extensive gardens lower down to the attractive mountain scenery of southern Spain. There can have been few palaces more impressively sited or garden localities fitter for their purpose, but again we know nothing of their detail.

As time went on the original Persian ideas were refined and adapted. The simple tank and fountain became at Toledo a lake having a water pavilion of stained glass ornamented with gold. The Sultan could not only rest here in the heat in the middle of the day but could enjoy its beauty by lamplight in the dusk. At its peak the city of Cordoba was twenty miles across, most of it taken up with the gardens of the houses of the nobles. Little of this remains today but there is to be found at Cordoba the oldest garden in Europe still largely in its original form. The Patio de los Naranjos was laid out by Al-Mansur in A.D. 976. Each row of orange trees leads up to one of the arched openings of the mosque and is, in effect, a continuation of the line of a row of pillars within and thus preserves a perfect illustration of the continuing preoccupation of the Islamic architects and garden designers with the integration of the garden and the building. The courtyard is 400 feet long by 200 feet wide and its orange trees are divided into three plots, each with a fountain

FAR LEFT *The Patio de la Riadh at the Generalife showing the narrow canal which runs the whole length of the court.*

LEFT *Some of the many fountains in the Patio de la Riadh at the Generalife, the sound of which is pleasantly cool in the hot sunshine.*

BELOW *A fountain in the garden of the Generalife set in a circular pool in a parterre with carefully clipped box edgings. Pot plants stand on the rim of the pool. The view is taken looking down from the Pabellon Norte.*

the usual Moorish fashion, through narrow twisted passages in the thickness of the walls. Coming out into the glow of the courtyard at the end, bathed in a warm amber light reflected from the cream marble pavements, is to experience what the Japanese tried to capture in their courtyard gardens, coming from the corridor into the bright garden, but here on a grander scale amid superlative architecture and decorations. The graceful colonnades at each end with their dado of iridescent tiles and the shallow marble basins and fountains are particularly beautiful.

The Court of the Lions at the Alhambra is also gracefully arcaded and has a magnificent central basin held up by the noble but only remotely lion-like beasts. The area that used to be planted with orange trees in four plots (once again the foursquare division of the Persian garden survives) is now gravelled and thus does not appear as it used to do in Moorish times. The Patio de Daraxa (Court of Linderaja - Boudoir of the Sultana) is, however, still set with cypresses and orange trees in the traditional fashion, although the fountain basin is not the original, but one moved by Charles V from the Mexuar Patio. An archway leads from the Patio de Daraxa to the Patio de los Cypreses, a modest court which gets its name from the four cypresses which rise from cut stone bases.

Above the Alhambra stands the Generalife (House of the Architect) constructed in the fourteenth century, the gardens of which have a fair claim to be the most beautiful of the surviving Moorish gardens, partly because of their delightful situation on the slopes of the hill. Here may be found the Patio de la Riadh, the only garden remaining in Spain where the stone-edged

in the centre and a palm tree in its usual position at the corners of the design. The irrigation channels, which are small and stone-edged, run from tree to tree and it is probably the need to maintain these that has kept the garden intact.

Another garden at Cordoba that retains some of the features of Moorish days is that of the Alcazar. Although the cypress avenues have gone, the planting is probably otherwise still much as it used to be. Below the first patio there is a paved terrace with two large ornamental tanks to supply the fountains, but the most interesting things in the garden are probably the 'glorietas', arbours of rose and jasmine. Glorietas are found in almost all Spanish gardens, but in this garden they appear to have been arranged to represent the eight pearl pavilions of the Muslim paradise.

It is perhaps at the Alhambra in Granada that the Moorish atmosphere may be felt most strongly because it is here that the remaining Moorish gardens are so closely integrated with the buildings that they are architecturally one. Although it has lost much by destruction, neglect and restoration (the original Alhambra complex probably resembled Az-zahra, with the park on the lowest level), four of the Moorish garden courts of the palace remain. The finest and most important is the Court of the Myrtles, so called from its myrtle hedges. This is the principal court of the palace, being 125 feet long by 75 feet broad. A canal runs through the whole length of the court, terminating at each end in a fountain. The sides of the court are arcaded.

Persian gardens usually had magnificent gateways, but this feature disappeared in the Moorish courtyard gardens. The Court of the Myrtles is approached after

canal, four feet wide, runs the full length of the garden.
Here, too, are lotus flower or bud fountains, a link with
the East, where they are often set up on the edge of the
canal, as in this case, and perpetuate the homage to the
sacred flower. There are other gardens and courts, each
in themselves beautiful, and some with enchanting
views of the surrounding countryside.

A Venetian nobleman visited the Generalife in 1526
and left a description of it as it was then:

'One leaves the encompassing walls of the Alhambra
by a door at the back, and walks into the lovely garden
of a pleasure house that stands a little higher. This,
though not very large, is a striking building with
wonderful gardens and waterworks, the finest I have
seen in Spain. It has many courts, all abundantly
supplied with water, but one in particular with a canal
running through the middle and full of fine orange trees
and myrtles. One gets a view outside from a loggia, and
below it the myrtles grow so high they almost reach to
the balcony. The foliage is very thick and the height so
nearly the same that it all looks just like a green floor.
There is water flowing through the whole palace, and
even at will in the rooms, some of which are joined to a
grand summerhouse.'

Moving into another court he finds it 'full of greenery
and wonderful trees, with a good conduit: if certain
pipes are closed up', he says, 'a person walking on the
green lawn sees all of a sudden that there is water under
his feet and that everything threatens to be swamped,
but he can turn the water off quite easily and without
being observed.' The narrative continues:

'There is another remarkable court, though not a large
one, which has ivy growing so thick that the walls
cannot be seen: this court stands on a rock and has
several balconies, from which one looks down into the
deep valley where the Darro runs — a charming,
ravishing view. In the middle of this court there is a fine
fountain with a very large shell. The pipe in the middle
shoots the water more than ten fathoms into the air; the
amount is astonishing, and nothing could be more
attractive than the appearance of the waters as they fall.

'On the very highest part of the castle grounds, in one
of the gardens, there is a wide stairway leading up to a
little terrace; from it there falls out of a rock the whole of
the water that is distributed over the palace. There it is
held back by a great number of taps, so that one can let it
out at any moment, in any manner, and in any amount
one pleases. At the present time the stairs are so made
that often every four steps there comes a wider one
which has a hollow place in the middle for the water to
collect in. The balustrade on either side of the stairs also
has a depression in it like a small gutter . . . . Above
there are taps for each of these divisions, so that one can
at pleasure turn the waters into the gutters of the
balustrade, or the hollows of the wider steps. Also at
will one can so increase the flow that it escapes all
restraints and overflows the steps, wetting anybody
who happens to be there; many little jokes are played in
this way.'

Owners of large estates in Renaissance and
Elizabethan times, as we shall see later, took an

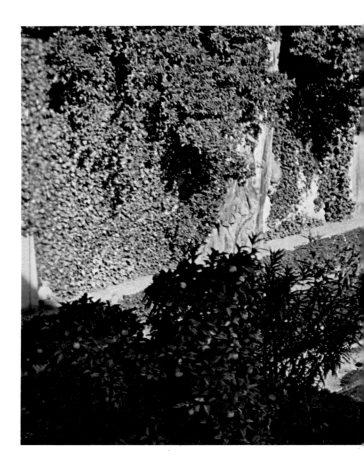

TOP *A pool in the Generalife with fountains and orange trees
in fruit.*

ABOVE *The flowers in the foreground of this part of the garden
of the Generalife are modern varieties, but their colour, set off
by the tall dark vertical lines of the cypresses in the background
and the contrasting horizontal lines of the garden
architecture, makes a charming picture in this fourteenth-
century garden.*

RIGHT *Pot plants around the edge set off an ornamental pool in
the Generalife which is enclosed within clipped hedges.*

innocent delight in catching visitors to their gardens in these water traps, particularly the ladies. In the warm climate of Spain the experience was more often pleasurable than not, but there might be doubt about this in the more northern countries. The water stairway described here was not the first of its kind, such waterways being known to the Romans.

The splendours of the Generalife, the Alhambra and other gardens already mentioned obscure to some extent the lesser garden works of the Moors which may still be seen. Many of these are to be found in Granada. Though often remnants only, here and there the authentic style and feeling is still evident, prompting the imagination to reconstruct those long-ago days when the Moor enjoyed them.

Written description can do only weak justice to these Moorish gardens of Spain. Photographs capture more of their exotic elegance and beauty, even though what can be seen is but a fragment of the past, and that often altered. On all these gardens the sun beats down, as it did in ancient Persia, so that even the hardy native longs for water. Coming from the coolness of the dark corridors and colonnades of their buildings, themselves extraordinarily beautiful, he is entranced by the long blue-tiled tanks and canals filled to the brim with the sparkling fluid, constantly agitated by the fountains always playing. The coolness enhances his physical comfort, and the garden itself, laid out like the Paradise of the Koran, reminds him of the eternal truths of his religion. As he meditates in the shade of a 'glorieta', itself a representative of one of the promised pavilions of heaven, he looks out upon the dark cypresses, emblem of death, to the orange trees, whose blossom reminds him of the renewal of life, and to the other flowers such as the iris, whose purple-blue was a favourite of the Moors, and whose brightness heralds the joys of the world to come. Like the Japanese, the Moor derived far more from his garden that the superficial pleasure of the aesthete. His garden, too, drew inspiration from the deep recesses of the spirit.

The ancient Persian garden, which came to Spain via Baghdad and Damascus, spread also to Byzantium and Sicily, and when the emirs of the latter island were conquered by the Normans, its influence, as we shall see, penetrated into western Europe even as far as England, though all the western countries were, for most of the period with which we have been concerned, still wrapped in the barbarism that followed the destruction of the Roman Empire. At home in Persia, the rulers grew weaker until that country also fell like a rotting fruit into the path of the invading conquerors, first the Mongols, then the Turks. Like the Arabs, they rolled over the country like a tide. When the tide retreated it carried with it the faith of Islam. It took also Persian culture, including the making of gardens, and where the conquerors settled, they began to make such gardens in imitation of those they had left. Thus, by way of Samarkand, the Persian garden moved east across all that high land that joins Persia to India to its final triumph in the days of the Great Mughals when, many thousand miles and several hundred years distant from the Moors in Spain, it gave rise again to gardens of beauty, luxury and magnificence.

ſez y fenr et
ſurtay.
Et maintteſſoé
Je eſcou[n]tay
Se le voiroix ſcauɾe mulle anne
Le touche qui eſtoit de charme
Jlle onme vne pucellette
Qui aſſez eſtoit comte et nette
Cheuaulx eut blonc cõe vng baſſĩ
La cher plus tendʒe q̃ nul pouſſin

front reluiſant ſour[r]aꝰ vouſtr[e]
Lentreoul ſi neſtoit pas petite
Anie fut aſſez maniɛ y ineſnre
Le nez eut bien fait a droiture
Les yeulx eut vre cõe faulcon
Pour faire enuie atoue ſionne
Doulce aleine eut et ſauouree
La face blanche et coulouree
La bouche petite et groſſette
Et au menton vne foſſette

7
Cloister and Castle

Fenced early in this cloistral ground
Of reverie, of shade, or prayer,
How should we grow in other ground?
How can we flower in foreign air?

When the Roman empire in the West went down under the attacks of the barbarians, the Roman villas and their gardens fell into ruins. By the end of the fifth century A.D. there was one dim light only burning in the darkness, that of the comparatively new faith of Christianity, which had been adopted as the official religion of the Roman Empire in A.D. 313. Great doctors of the Church such as St Augustine of Hippo were working and writing where, for a time, peace could still be found. Holy men like him prayed and taught quietly in many places of the goodness of God, which must have been so hard to see in those times of rapine and pillage. They taught also of the need to live as he had commanded, trying themselves to live like this.

Such men sought out men of like belief, to learn from them and to give them support in return. Communities began to form to live a common life, and were often donated places to live by wealthy followers. St Augustine himself was the object of such a gift. 'I assembled in a garden that Valerius had given me', he says, 'certain brethren with intentions like my own, who possessed nothing, even as I possessed nothing, and who followed after me.' The men who formed these communities found that, for their mutual benefit, it was desirable to organize their daily lives into a routine so that the community functioned in an orderly fashion. St Benedict of Nursia was the first to codify and record such a rule. He did it so well that the rule of St Benedict is still followed today.

The lover outside the garden where the Rose grows, from the Roman de la Rose. *The picture shows almost all the parts of a mediaeval castle garden, the stout stone enclosing wall, the trellis fences of the internal divisions, fruiting trees, individual beds of herbs, a fountain and pool in a 'flowery mede' the stream discharging from the garden in a rivulet that passes out through a channel and grating in the wall, and the wild-flowers in the background beyond the trellis.*

The Benedictine communities had to be self-supporting. The rule of the founder required that the monks, when not at services, food or rest, should engage themselves in useful work, either manual labour, study, copying books or teaching. There was no lack of manual labour in cultivating the land and tending the crops which they had to raise for food or starve. They usually had several separate kitchen gardens among their buildings, some of which were allocated for special purposes such as supplying the needs of the prior or abbot, or those of visitors. The buildings themselves were centred round an area which was enclosed with a roofed pillared walk on all four sides, which greatly resembled the atrium and portico of Roman houses, perhaps because, in early days, they were given such houses by patrons or took over derelict Roman property. The church, being the tallest building, was usually placed on the north side. Apart from the time spent in church, the life of the community centred around this enclosed central area, which was called a cloister, because it was here that the monks came to meditate and study. There was a natural wish to make it pleasant and thus the central portion was often treated as an ornamental garden. In this small way the spirit of such gardens lived on in western Europe through the dark times.

The centre of the cloister garden often had a well, or at least a tub of water, but in some cases a tree stood in the middle. The rest of the area was used in various ways. Sometimes fruit trees or flowers were grown in grass plots, and sometimes there was a herb garden. It was the monks who through these times kept the knowledge of the medicinal value of plants alive in the West. By a survival which seems extraordinary, the name 'Paradise', derived from the ancient Persian hunting garden, and first used by Xenophon a thousand years before, lingered on into these times. It had become attached as a name to the entrance court of churches. There was generally a portico, always planted as a garden, adjoining the ancient basilicas,

ABOVE *The cloisters at the monastery of St Mark in Florence showing a large tree as the central feature. Cloisters such as this provided shelter for the monks in bad weather.*

RIGHT *Clipped hedges enclose this simple central stone trough in the cloisters of Fossanova Abbey.*

where sinners had to go before entering the church itself, and it was to this that the name was applied. The cloister, having the church for one of its sides and being itself a garden, seems to have inherited the name. It is said to have referred to the grass plot in particular, 'signifying to the monks', said Wycliffe, 'the greenness of their virtues.'

Many women accepted community life. Among those who did so was St Radegunda, the wife of Clotaire I, who, becoming disgusted with the dissolute life of the sixth-century Merovingian court, founded a convent at Poitiers to which she herself retreated. The poet Venantius Fortunatus, two of whose beautiful hymns, 'Sing my tongue the glorious battle' *(Pange lingua)* and 'The royal banners forward go' *(Vexilla regis)* are still sung, came to Poitiers and, impressed with the holiness of Radegunda, himself became a priest and then bishop of Poitiers. Radegunda often sent gifts of food to Fortunatus, almost always sending flowers with the gift. Once she had him to a meal where the tablecloth was strewn with roses, the dishes were wreathed and garlands hung on the wall in the old Roman fashion. Fortunatus thanked her always in poetic words. It is clear that the Roman love of flowers had not at this time finally perished and perhaps, in convents rather than monasteries, it lingered on through the dark times yet to come.

As monasteries grew larger the simple layout of the early days grew more complex. One plan has survived which shows among other things the gardens for which provision should ideally have been made. The plan was drawn about A.D. 820 or 830 by a Benedictine monk of St Gall in France. It is not a plan of the actual monastery as it existed then but of how such a monastery ought to be designed. The cloister garden on this plan was as described above. There was a separate medicinal garden next to the hospital building which was to be planted with sixteen different types of herbs in four beds surrounded by a border. The great emperor Charlemagne issued a list in A.D. 812 of the herbs to be grown in his garden. This list probably included the greater part of all that then would be grown anywhere. The list on the St Gall plan is obviously taken from Charlemagne's list. The same may be said of what was to be planted in the large kitchen garden also to be found on the plan. This provided eighteen long narrow beds each furnished with a different vegetable. There was also an orchard, which did duty as a cemetery as well, planted with the fruit trees on the list.

There was a variation from the usual plan in the monasteries of the enclosed order of the Carthusians, where each monk lives like a hermit in silence and solitude in separate cells around the cloister. Each cell has its own small garden attached to it. The Certosa in the Va di Ema still keeps its mediaeval appearance. The individual cells are set round the court like buttresses. In this case the monks enjoy a wonderful view from their gardens.

Charlemagne's plant list included two flowers only, the lily and the rose, and in the early monasteries, except where the Roman influence may have lingered on, flowers played a small part only in the lives of the monks. Roses and lilies were, in fact, at first condemned by the early Christians because they had been such a feature of pagan celebrations, but they soon acquired a new symbolism, the rose being the flower of Mary and lilies standing for the reward of martyrdom. By the first half of the ninth century there is evidence that, although flowers were not as yet freely used, the monks took considerable pleasure in their gardens. The young abbot Walafried Strabo wrote a peom entitled 'Hortulus' which describes the little private garden he had at his monastery at Reichenau on the islet in Lake Constance. The garden was on the east of the house, close to the porch which protected it from the weather. A wall on the south side sheltered it from too much sun. Strabo grew 23 different kinds of plants in his garden, including the lily, the rose and the violet. The poem was addressed to the abbot of the monastery of St Gall and concluded pleasantly by saying, 'If you are sitting in the precincts, in your green garden, under your shady apple tree with its swelling fruits, where the peach tree parts its foliage to cast a dappled shade . . . then read my gift.'

So fond did the monks become of their gardens that it was considered that they could become a temptation drawing them from the path of virtue. In a work by Herrad of Landsperg, called *Hortus Deliciarum*, the author tells of a monk who had climbed to the very top of the ladder of virtue but then looked behind him. There he beholds his flower garden, is seized by strong desire, and plunges headlong down, because he has preferred the earthly to the heavenly paradise.

In some of the larger monasteries there was a large outer garden as well as those among the buildings. The Abbey of Clairvaux possessed one of these which was described by a contemporary of St Bernard of Clairvaux. 'Behind the abbey', he said, 'and within the

wall of the cloister, there is a wide level ground: here there is an orchard, with a great many different fruit trees, quite a small wood . . . Where the orchard leaves off, the garden begins, divided into several beds.' William of Malmesbury paints a similar picture of Thorney Abbey, near Peterborough. In later times the abbey garden of St Germain-des-Pres had such a garden, sections of which were shown as 'knots', indicating an ornamental interest which probably meant that the garden contained a good number of flowers. The overall care of all the monastery gardens must have required considerable attention, particularly when comparatively large areas of this kind were added, and a separate office of gardener was instituted in quite early days. In the plan of the monastery of St Gall the gardener is allocated a house of his own. During the ninth century a separate flower-garden seems to have evolved for the use of the sacristan in decorating the altar, mint and thyme being used with rushes on special occasions.

As time went on the monasteries acquired larger estates, including vineyards and fruit-gardens. King John of England, for example, gave Llanthony Abbey twelve acres of fruit-garden. A plan of the abbey at Canterbury made in A.D. 1165 shows fruit-gardens and vineyards outside the walls. In spite of the extra land an interest in flowers seems, however, to have remained limited until quite late. Alexander Neckam, who was the earliest Englishman to write on gardens, included in his manual of the scientific knowledge of his time a section 'on herbs, trees and flowers which grow in the garden'. This mentioned a few, roses, lilies, heliotrope, paeonies and violets being the only flowers included. His work was compiled around the year A.D. 1200. John de Garlande, who lived in Paris in the first half of the thirteenth century, adds the marigold to this list. Le

Menagier of Paris of 1393 has a slightly more extensive selection, including along with those already mentioned the gillyflower (the clove pink). It is not until the first gardening book in English, John Gardener's fourteenth-century *The Feate of Gardening*, that a more comprehensive list appears. Among the 97 plants he mentions he includes the daffodil, daisy, catmint, cowslip, foxglove, gentian, iris, hollyhock, lavender, lily, periwinkle, primrose, red and white rose, the violet and white or yellow water-lily.

Albertus Magnus, the great Dominican whose learning earned him the title of Universal Doctor of the Church, not only studied plants scientifically in the thirteenth century but, if a story about him is to be believed, achieved a high skill in their cultivation. On January 6th, A.D. 1249, King William II of Holland, the

LEFT *The garden in this cloister of the monastery S. S. Quattro Coronati in Rome contains a central fountain and pool, and is so beautifully planted that many house-owners would be glad to have it as a garden.*

ABOVE *Gardens in the cloisters of the monastery of the Certosa di Pavia. Carthusian monks live like hermits in silence and solitude in separate cells round the cloister.*

King of the Romans, was travelling through Cologne, and was received by Albertus and entertained in his monastery. The guests were amazed when he took them to the cloister garden and showed them fruit trees bearing ripe fruit in the middle of winter and other flowering growths, bought on out of season by the use of gentle heat. Unfortunately the story does not specify which plants were dealt with in this way.

Monasteries flourished until the Reformation, when in the north of Europe they were largely suppressed. Their contribution to gardening forms therefore a continuous thread from the courtyard of the Roman villa to the gardens of the Renaissance, but there were other efforts at gardening during this period. Domesday book mentions gardens in England during the tenth century but these were doubtless filled with vegetables and herbs; it seems unlikely that any could be classed as pleasure gardens. Elsewhere peasants' gardens are mentioned in the songs of the wandering minstrels, the land in the front of the house being used for social gatherings and the vegetables and herbs grown at the back; again it seems unlikely that any could be regarded as pleasure gardens although perhaps a few flowers were grown. Gardens at the back of the house, such as are known to have existed in the twelfth and thirteenth centuries in the centres of Paris and Rouen, were obviously to be preferred; where gardens could not be provided due to lack of space in towns sheltering behind defensive walls, they began to be made outside the walls, even though they were liable to interference because of the unsettled times. William Fitzstephen, who wrote a life of St Thomas à Beckett in the time of Henry II, the second half of the twelfth century, says that a situation of this kind prevailed in London, where 'on all sides outside the houses of the citizens who dwell in the suburbs there are adjoining gardens planted with trees both spacious and pleasing to the sight.'

Landulph of Carcano, Archbishop of Milan in the tenth century, had made much the same kind of remark about Milan. It was in Italy in the twelfth and thirteenth centuries that a beginning was made in the provision in towns of public parks. The Prato existed in Florence in A.D. 1290 and that in Siena was established by statute in A.D. 1309. The half-military, half-religious brotherhoods that were set up to encourage archery also practised horticulture, their produce being given to the poor. In none of these situations or pursuits, however, did ornamental gardening and the growing of flowers play very much part. It is to the estates of the wealthy that attention must be turned for such progress.

reditas dñi filii merces fructus Ventris.
Sicut sagitte in manu potētis : ita filii ex:
cussor. Beatus Vir qui impleuit desideriuz

In the earlier centuries of what are called the Dark Ages even the great people of western Europe were concerned more with survival than with niceties of life. The Roman villa, where it remained, was transformed into a fortified settlement and where it did not, those in power built stout castles on higher ground with natural defence advantages. Cultivation outside the walls of these castles was always liable to interruption by marauders and within the walls space was very limited. The small area set aside for a garden was probably near the women's quarters so as to be under the eye of the lady of the castle, for the garden was chiefly the preserve of the ladies. In it, guided by lore learnt from the monks, vegetables would be grown together with herbs to heal the sick and wounded. There would probably be a fruit tree or two and perhaps a central well and an arbour, and even a small stretch of flower-spangled turf if space allowed.

Contact between western Europe and the eastern civilizations was not wholly severed. Charlemagne had diplomatic relations with Harun-al-Raschid in Baghdad and received some plants from him which he added to his list. Embassies began to be sent to the Byzantine court, where they saw wonders beyond their imaginings. Bishop Liutprand of Cremona brought back an account of the emperor's golden tree with its singing birds in A.D. 968 and in A.D. 1167 a German embassy saw some of the wonders of the Sultan's palace at Baghdad, being particularly impressed with the marvellous fountain courts, with all their splendour of Islamic decoration. The alliance of Frederick II, Holy Roman Emperor, with the Saracens and Moors brought Islamic influences even closer. The golden tree seems to have fascinated poets of the West and more than one included such a tree and its attendant singing birds in his work.

Ornamental gardening on any scale larger than the internal castle garden had little chance of revival until somewhat more settled times arrived, but even as early as A.D. 1000 flower-gardens where 'roses, marigolds and violets grow' were mentioned. By the twelfth century all castles probably had a 'herb' or 'kitchen' garden within their walls. It became possible during

ABOVE *A girl spinning and a youth emerging from an arbour in a herb or vegetable garden of rectangular beds enclosed by a lattice fence: from a* Book of Hours *c.1522.*

RIGHT *A stylized version of the 'flowery mede', one of the features of castle gardens, from a mediaeval manuscript.*

that century to establish 'orchards' ('hort-yards'), though these were not confined exclusively to fruit trees, which is the meaning of the word 'orchard' today. These were usually situated at the back or side of the castle, often being separated from it by a moat with a drawbridge and surrounded by a crenellated wall with towers and battlements. Entrance was obtained through a narrow door or gate. Some castles had a second orchard in the courtyard itself, but this was usually separated from the courtyard proper by a narrow moat of its own.

What is known about the orchards of castles is derived in the main from two sources: the beautiful and carefully executed pictures drawn and painted by the monks in their devotional works such as the 'Books of Hours' (daily services of the church), many of which have survived, and the verbal description and pictures in the poetry and romances which were so popular between the twelfth and fifteenth centuries, both of which sources doubtless idealize their subject to some extent. Originally the orchard was simply a shady place or 'pleasaunce' turfed to form grass plots and planted with shade and fruit trees mixed together. There were no lawn-mowers then to make it easy to keep the grass short, so that the turf was not like a lawn in the modern sense. People of those times would, in fact, probably have thought such an unbroken green expanse uninteresting. They preferred the 'flowery mede', in which the wild-flowers grew among the grass, creating a scene very much like that depicted in the carpet-like patterns of the Persian miniatures.

It is very likely, in fact, that the taste in western Europe for the 'flowery mede' was acquired from the countries where such gardens were first made. The Arab emirs who conquered Sicily in the first great headlong expansion of Islam were, like those who

Ib icenis pratum sive campus rex ubi granum
D ar folamen hake quia nomen ferr fine tube.
Virgines fient opime ubi femper fioneres
Her est Flaceum rebolencag colorers Letum.

and monastery gardens of their home countries in the north, and, when they got home, they began to imitate what they had seen.

Roger, who became known as the 'Great Count', had walled in an area of countryside of four to five miles radius round Palermo and dotted it with pleasure pavilions so that to an Arab visitor in the second half of the twelfth century A.D. it seemed that the gardens of the ruler surrounded the town like a necklace on the neck of a young girl. Water was brought into the area by underground conduits to fill lakes and canals, and ornamental buildings were erected among the waters. These buildings owed nothing to the northern origin of the Normans, being quite Islamic in character. The only one to survive in some semblance of its original condition is the Ziza. Leandro Alberti saw it in 1526 when its gardens were still in existence. He described the small pavilion in the midst of a pool and the sweet-scented groves of oranges and lemons among the ruins of the gardens. Oranges and lemons were already well established in Sicily in the twelfth century, prototypes, introduced by the Arabs, of the groves that were later to be such an attractive feature of Italian gardens. Hugo Falcandus also saw these fruits there, as well as date-palms and blue water-lilies. He says that the royal palaces and gardens were furnished not only with pavilions and kiosks but also possessed courts surrounded with porticos. One of these had a central fountain with lions and may have resembled the Court of the Lions at the Alhambra. The gardens were provided with such devices as stalactite vaults and water staircases to please the curious.

The ingenious use of water in these gardens was one of the things that greatly impressed the returning Crusaders. One knight who was influenced in this way was Robert of Artois, who had returned from the Crusades by way of Palermo in A.D. 1270. He created at Hesdin in Picardy a garden containing automata and water-tricks which was quite unlike anything previously seen in the north. The garden became very well-known but it was before its time and an isolated aberration in northern Europe, where such gardens were not to be created generally for several centuries yet. There was, however, one feature almost certainly derived from this source which was now universally adopted in castle orchards. One of the principal objects in the Persian garden, and the Islamic garden derived from it, was the central water-source or fountain from which channels divided the garden into the traditional fourfold or eightfold pattern and thus irrigated the plots. Such fountains and water tanks now appeared in every orchard garden. The water was so attractive that it soon became an established custom for ladies to wash their feet in this central tank before social occasions and there are pictures extant which show them seated on the edge of the tank, their skirts decorously arranged, doing this, a fashion perhaps less agreeable in the colder climates of northern Europe than in the hot and dusty lands where the Crusaders had fought their battles. There are also other illustrations, somewhat less decorous, which appear to show mixed bathing!

The gardens of hotter lands were enclosed by high walls to prevent the encroachment of the drier lands

settled in Spain, inheritors of the Persian garden tradition and made magnificent gardens around their palaces. They were, in their turn, attacked by a conqueror. Robert Guiscard the Norman had carved himself out a dukedom in southern Italy and had got a foothold in Sicily at Messina. His followers, under his younger brother Roger, completed the conquest of the island, and in A.D. 1091, the emirs were destroyed. Though conquered physically, their influence continued. The Normans, with little culture of their own, took on the culture of the lands they conquered. They absorbed it so thoroughly in Sicily that they came to be known as the 'baptized sultans'. The ravaged gardens of the emirs were restored and improved, reaching new heights of beauty and grandeur. By geographical accident these gardens were on the route that many Crusaders took on their way to and from the wars with the Saracens. Their splendour must have been a revelation to the knights and their retainers accustomed only to the narrow confines of the early castle orchards

A wall hanging of about A.D. *1500 representing the Biblical story of Susannah at the bathing pool. The picture shows the custom of using the garden pool for bathing (in this case very decorously). Part of the 'flowery mede' with large violets, strawberries and other flowers can be seen at the bottom of the picture. The tree bearing red apples shows the scars of pruning to encourage the top to grow out and shade the pool.*

outside. Castle orchards were similarly enclosed but in their case for defence purposes. Strongly fortified castles which were designed with an austerity fitting them wholly for battle and for nothing else ceased to be built after the end of the thirteenth century. Although there was probably still an outer wall not featured in the pictures, it would seem from the illustrations to the romances that the orchards also ceased to be so strongly enclosed. Many of those shown are surrounded by no more than a wattle fence. Lattice fences appear and also brick walls, these sometimes being turf-topped.

Seats under the trees or under specially made shelters were probably an early feature of castle orchards, as the ladies doubtless liked to sit out in the garden on fine days, enjoying their pleasant surroundings, which contrasted greatly with the starkness of the rest of the castle. Many of the gardens in the pictures have seats with brick or stone walls supporting a turf top. Flowers are sometimes shown growing from these turfed seats, which perhaps is the reason why in some cases the people in the illustrations are sitting on the grass in front of the seats rather than on the seat itself. As soon as gardens began to be made away from the main castle buildings there was a greater need for

shelters as it would no longer be so easy to slip back into the castle if there was a sudden adverse change in the weather. The garden arbour, therefore, is likely to have been an essential garden feature almost from the beginning. The earliest form of arbour was a pergola or trellis-work covered with greenery provided either by honeysuckle or by roses. A rose tree was often grown to great size for this purpose. 'So broad and thick that it can give its shade to twelve knights together; wound evenly and bound into a hoop, yet taller than a man' is the description of one such arbour, adding that 'under the same thorny bush there is gold mullein and lovely grass.' Some summerhouses were substantial enough to be used, like the building in Pliny's Tuscan garden, as sleeping places: John Lydgate, a prolific poet who wrote at the end of the fourteenth century, describes an arbour of this kind in 'The Nightingale'.

There was often within the orchard a kind of inner retreat, which was a separate feature within low trellises, fences or walls. It was not covered like an arbour and was not related in plan or arrangement to the main garden around it and was sometimes enclosed on three sides only. It has been customary to give the name *hortus conclusus* to this small enclave, which seems to have been designed to provide a small private area, which could have a variety of uses. This conception of a 'garden room', i.e. an outdoor area cut off to provide privacy and intended to be used in suitable weather as a place where all the normal pastimes of daily life could be carried on outside as they were in the indoor rooms, had great appeal and constantly recurs as a theme in garden design.

As time went on, cultivated flowers began to be used in beds in the orchards. The chief sources of information as to what plants were grown in these beds are the romances. Several Latin and French love tales of the twelfth and thirteenth centuries are set in gardens but it is the 'Roman de la Rose', part I of which was written about A.D. 1237 by Guillaume de Lorris and Part II by Jean de Meung (called Clopinel) about forty years later, which more or less standardizes the description of the castle orchard. The garden in this poem is by 'a castle wall hemmed round'.

The wall was high and built of hard
Rough stone, close shut and strongly barred . . .

Entry to the garden was through

. . . a wicket, strait and small,
Worked in the stern forbidding wall . . .

The garden is described as square, being 'nigh broad as wide', and well supplied with water:

Within the glades sprang fountains near
No frog or newt ere came anear.
The waters gently sounded . . .

The water was carried away from the fountains (springs) in 'small channelled brooks' which the poet describes in delightful terms; the streams would

. . . fling
Their waves with pleasant murmuring
In tiny tides. Bright green and lush
Around these sparkling streams did push
The sweetest grass . . .
As though 'twere bed of down . . .

The poet says, with regard to flowers:

. . . my feet
Bruised mint and fennel savouring sweet . . .
'Twere no light task some flower to name
That was not found thereon, each came
To lend its beauty, blue periwinkle
'Twixt rose and yellow broom did twinkle,
With violets, pansies, birdseye blue
And flowers untold of varied hue
Sweet-scented roses red and pale . . .

To this he adds later in the poem:

. . . ever here
Things bud and burgeon through the year
The violet, sweet of scent and hue,
The periwinkle's star of blue,
The golden kingcups burnished bright,
Mingled with pink-rimmed daisies white
And varied flowers, blue, gold and red
The alleys, lawns and groves o'erspread.

The flowers mentioned are all that might be found in western European gardens, but the same cannot be said of the trees and shrubs listed in the poem which included 'every tree from out the land of Saracens'. These begin with pomegranates, nutmegs, almonds, cloves, dates, figs, liquorice, aniseed, grain of Paradise, cinnamon and zedoary, almost all exotics not to be grown in colder lands. There follows, however, cherry, pear, quince, medlars, plums, apples, chestnuts, peaches, sorb-apples, barberries, fruit of 'loti' and

ABOVE *A picture from a Flemish* Book of Hours *(1450-75) of the Virgin and Child sitting on a brick-based turfed seat in a 'flowery mede'.*

BELOW *The lover and Bel Acueil approaching the garden where the Rose grows, from a fifteenth-century version of the* Roman de la Rose; *only part of the garden is shown, a simple 'flowery mede' enclosed by a wall and terrace.*

olives, most of which are the customary inhabitants of western orchards; as were all the shade trees which complete the list. These are holly, laurel, holm oak, yew, hornbeam, cypress, pine, beech, silver birch, aspen, maple, ash, hazel and oak.

The trees were carefully spaced to allow free growth yet provide continuous shade:

. . . such skilful art
Had planned the trees that each apart
Six fathoms stood, yet like a net
Their interlacing branches met,
Through which no scorching rays could pass
To sear the sward and thus the grass
Kept ever tender, fresh and green
Beneath their cool and friendly screen.

The poet made the final beauty of his garden a fountain, or rather a spring, underneath a single pine tree, recalling the ancient nymph-haunted places revered by the Greeks. 'I lastly came', he says

ABOVE *The lover in the* Roman de la Rose *stands in the lush grass by the water's edge in front of a lady emerging, richly dressed, from a flower-covered* berceau *(ornamental alley of plants trained on a framework).*

BELOW *The lover in the* Roman de la Rose *finally reaches and kisses the Rose growing in a stout basket-work container among rocks in a stone-walled enclosure.*

> . . . to where I found
> A fountain 'neath a glorious pine . . .
> A pine so tall, straight-grown and fair
> And in a stone of marble there
> Had Nature's hand most deftly made
> A fountain 'neath that pine-tree's shade.

Geoffrey Chaucer, great poet though he was, added nothing to this description of the garden in his version of the story, which he wrote in the latter part of the fourteenth century. Nor did John Lydgate in the garden he described in 'Love's Chessboard'. In the anonymous 'Flower and the Leaf', however, an arbour is mentioned which is like a room, the roof and walls being cut out of a hedge, which is described as thick as a castle wall and smooth as a plank, the seats inside being turfed with short, thick, freshly cut grass.

One feature of some mediaeval gardens was a maze or labyrinth cut out of the turf or delineated by hedges. The labyrinth is an idea that has intrigued men since very early times, being known to the ancient Egyptians. The most famous example in antiquity is the labyrinth made by Daedalus for King Minos of Crete, which led Theseus to the Minotaur. The labyrinth was used as a sign or decoration in Roman times and was afterwards adopted by Christians; it may still be found in mediaeval churches. When mazes were first made in gardens is not known, but Henry II of England kept his mistress 'Fair Rosamond' in a 'House of Daedalus' in the twelfth century and this has been taken to mean that she was kept in a lodging which was approached

through a maze. References to such 'Houses of Daedalus' occur also in French sources.

Some of the Crusaders must have been impressed with the size of the gardens they saw in Sicily although conditions in their home countries did not as yet permit of the making of large gardens. As time went on, however, the influence of these gardens began to spread in another way. The son of the Great Count, Roger II, consolidated Sicily and southern Italy into one kingdom, reigning with the splendour of an oriental potentate, and large gardens began to be developed in southern Italy. In the time of Frederick II of Hohenstaufen, who reigned in the first half of the thirteenth century, and spent much of his life in Italy, the gardens of the south became well-known.

Petrus Crescentius of Bologna wrote a book on husbandry in the thirteenth century in which he distinguishes between the small garden and that of the wealthy, indicating that larger gardens were coming into being. The small garden he describes is an unpretentious affair almost entirely utilitarian, with a boundary consisting of a trench and a hedge of red and white roses and sometimes a pergola. The larger garden is enclosed with a high wall. 'Towards the north', says Crescentius, 'there should be a thicket of tall trees where wild beasts are kept and to the south a palace with shady trees and an aviary.' In other parts of the ground there should be shrubberies in which the tamer animals were kept but these should not be placed so as to obscure the view from the palace. There should be summerhouses made from trained trees, over which vines could be allowed to trail. The ground should be ornamented with evergreens carefully placed and there should also be clipped trees cut out as walls, palisades and turrets.

As early as A.D. 1300 Giovanni Villani had said of Florence that, approaching from outside, a visitor might mistake the costly palaces with their walled gardens for the actual city itself. As the fourteenth century advanced gardens elsewhere began to become more elaborate. The stone-built castle was replaced as a residence for the great by the fortified house or château. The gardens of these were no longer comparatively small plots with a few plants but now comprised

cultivated areas which included beds arranged in ornamental patterns. The parterre, which was to become so important a feature of future gardens, had begun to evolve.

These changes and the ideas of Crescentius were a long way from the orchard garden, but the older notions still reigned for some time. Even Giovanni Boccaccio, author of the universally known 'Decameron', describes an orchard garden exactly like that of the 'Roman de la Rose', with a fountain, birds, flowery mede, rivulets and flowering trees, in his 'Vision of Love', written in A.D. 1345. In the 'Decameron' itself, however, written five years later, there is a change. There are still many elements of the orchard garden in the design but there is a new feel about it.

The house to which the 'Decameron' garden was attached was on a hill, surrounded by meadows and approached by a path which itself had been made attractive. The house also possessed an inner court with a loggia furnished with flowers, recalling the atrium of the past. It was here that the guests were received. The garden, to which they went afterwards, was situated at the side of the house and was enclosed with walls. A very wide path took one round the boundaries of the garden and there was a similarly wide path through the middle. Scattered along these paths were many vine-clad arbours, the sides of the path being marked with red and white rose hedges. The centre of the garden, says Boccaccio, was occupied by

Cultivating an enclosed garden of herbs or vegetables: from a mediaeval calendar.

'a plot of ground like a meadow; the grass of a deep green, spangled with a thousand different flowers, and set round with orange and cedar trees, whose branches were stored with ripe fruit and blossoms, at the same time affording a most pleasing object to the eye, as well as a grateful odour to the smell. In the centre of this meadow was a fountain of white marble, beautifully carved; and (whether by a natural or artificial spring I know not) from a figure standing on a column in the midst of the fountain, a jet of water spouted up, which made an agreeable sound in its fall.'

Boccaccio adds that 'the sight of this garden, its form and contrivance, with the fountains and springs proceeding from it, pleased the ladies and gentlemen so much, that they spared not to say, if there was a paradise on earth, it could be in no other form, nor was it possible to add anything to it.' Once again, the ancient word 'paradise' recurs.

In spite of the persistence of the older ways, change could not be denied. Almost at the same time as Boccaccio was writing, the Florentine artist Andrea Orcagna was painting his 'Triumph of Death' in which he depicts a larger and more elaborate garden and it is clear from this that change had already begun. A letter from the great Italian poet Petrarch written in A.D. 1336 from Vaucluse in France shows that he at least was not bound by tradition. He says:

'I have made two gardens that please me wonderfully . . . One of these gardens is shady, formed for contemplation, and sacred to Apollo. It overhangs the source of the river, and is terminated by rocks and by places accessible only to birds. The other is nearer my cottage, of an aspect less severe and devoted to Bacchus; and what is extremely singular, it is in the midst of a rapid river. The approach to it is over a bridge of rocks; and there is a natural grotto under the rocks, which gives them the impression of a rustic bridge. Into this grotto the rays of the sun never penetrate.'

These gardens seem a long way in conception from the formality of the orchard gardens.

Towards the end of the fourteenth century the powerful prince Gian Galeazzo Visconti, who was strongly influenced by Petrarch, created a great walled park around Pavia. With the entry of Petrarch into the story, we enter also the Renaissance, since no one did more than he to restore knowledge of the ancient world and to provide the impulse that was to bring to life in his own and succeeding generations the best of that world. Even before this could come about, however, the skill of the Italians as gardeners had become widely known and the influence of Crescentius had spread throughout the West, so that requests were received for Italian gardeners to exercise their skill in other countries. In their own country the ideas of the Renaissance worked like yeast, bringing to gardening, as to everything else, great changes, which produced some of the finest gardens the world has ever seen, the influence of which went far beyond Italy and their own time. Gardens were enlarged and transformed, but may still trace their lineage back through the Sicilian emirs to the ancient gardens of Persia and express, in new terms, the inexorable urge to recreate the lost serenity of Paradise.

8
A New World from the Old

Knowst thou the land where the pale citrons grow,
The golden fruits in darker foliage glow?
Soft blows the wind that breathes from that blue sky
Still stands the myrtle and the laurel high.

Coleridge

In mediaeval times the sun which had shone on Pliny's villa still bathed a Tuscan landscape which, like the sturdy people who won their living from that lovely countryside, had changed little since Roman days. One family of that stock, the Medici, shrewder than the rest, saw new opportunities in the urban life of Florence and, moving in from the country, probably in the twelfth century A.D., settled near the church of San Lorenzo, just outside the walls of that town. By the fourteenth century they had become wealthy and Cosimo de Medici, born in 1389, entered a world in which the name of his family was already well-known. Caught up in the intellectual ferment of the new learning, Cosimo employed Michelozzo Michelozzi in 1457 to replan a villa he had inherited at Careggi and to create round it a garden with a classical flavour. In this villa and garden he brought together the most learned men of his time to form the Platonic Academy in which the basic ideas of the Renaissance were formulated and discussed. Modern historians tend to discount the notion that the Renaissance was a sudden growth that sprang up overnight and trace its origins much further back than Cosimo's academy, which they regard as one of the fruits of a process already long in existence. It may be that in the making of what are called Renaissance gardens some such long development could also be traced were the evidence available. In its absence the Careggi villa garden must be regarded as the first to be influenced by Renaissance ideas.

The apostle of the new vogue in gardens was Leon Battista Alberti who, in 1452, produced the treatise *De Re Edificatoria* which, ostensibly about buildings, contained much about gardens. It is based almost wholly on the ideas of classical times and, indeed, lifts whole chunks out of the classical authors. The main ideas, which must have seemed fresh and new at the time, are the notion that the house and garden should be treated as an integrated whole and that the garden should be wedded into the landscape. Alberti is still, however, somewhat mediaeval in his outlook. He has

LEFT *Statuary in the amphitheatre of the garden of Isola Bella on Lake Maggiore.*

ABOVE *The magnificent view from the terraces of the Villa Medici at Fiesole across the countryside to the mountains in the distance. Sites for Renaissance gardens were deliberately chosen to afford such views as this.*

little idea of the use of statuary, which became such a feature of later Renaissance gardens, nor, indeed, of the use of architecture generally as a garden adjunct. Similarly, he seems to have no conception of an overall design and does not, in fact, give any really precise indications about layout. While Alberti was writing his book, Poggio Bracciolino had been methodically describing and cataloguing, for the first time, the ruins of Rome. In his book *De Varietate Fortunae* he dealt with them from an aesthetic as well as an antiquarian standpoint and thus provided a reliable reference work which must have been a valuable aid to garden design, although in Rome little was yet being done in this direction.

In 1446 Alberti had designed a palace for Giovanni Rucellai in which the first use in Renaissance times was made of the classical orders of architecture. A few years later, in 1459, he was asked to design for the same patron the Villa Quaracchi on the outskirts of Florence. The house was surrounded in mediaeval fashion by a moat and fishponds, which were viewed from a balustraded terrace. A pergola ran from the front of the house down the centre of the garden. On either side of this there were walks edged with breast-high clipped box, the arms of the family being suspended above in a festoon. This part of the garden ended in a *giardino segreto,* a small intimate garden like the *hortus conclusus* of earlier gardens. Immediately beyond this the garden was bisected by a road. Across the road, the line of the pergola was continued through an avenue of trees to

LEFT *The magnificent Neptune fountain made by the Carlone brothers in 1601 for the gardens of the great statesman and admiral Andrea Doria at Genoa.*

ABOVE *A pavilion at the Villa Medici, Fiesole, showing a painted garden scene, to give the illusion of greater space by creating the impression of a path leading further on; this was a common Roman device called* topia.

the Arno so that from his dining room Rucellai could see, in the distance, the passing river traffic. This part of the garden consisted mainly of hedged orchards between paths shaded by evergreens. There were also arbours of evergreens, an aviary and a rose garden. Topiary was a feature of the garden, with shrubs cut into fantastic shapes. While still mediaeval in some respects, the hedged orchards, for example, the whole struck a new and more expansive note which brought many visitors to see it.

Michelozzi laid out other gardens for Cosimo at this time: that of Il Trebbio, the hunting lodge for the Villa Cafaggiola in 1451, and that of the villa at Fiesole, which he laid out between 1458 and 1461. The garden of the Villa Cafaggiola itself was also laid out for Lorenzo de

Medici after Cosimo's death in 1464. All three designs were, in the main, mediaeval. An opportunity was missed at Fiesole which was exactly the kind of site in which later Renaissance garden designers did their best work. The formation of a garden on this precipitous site was a difficult undertaking. To be truly Renaissance the terraces would have been reached by architectural means, stone stairs or ramps sweeping boldly up through the centre, but they were, in fact, approached by much less impressive cypress walks. The garden was, nevertheless, still well in advance in design of what was being done at Rome, where the ambitious plans of Pope Nicholas V, who reigned from 1447 to 1455, for the Vatican garden had been shelved when he died. Pope Paul II's Palazetto Venezia, made in 1466, was designed like a cloister and showed no trace of Renaissance influence.

In 1467 the Dominican monk Francesco Colonna wrote an allegorical romance under the pseudonym of 'Polyphilius' called the *Hypnorotomachia*, a combination of three Greek words that was aptly rendered in the English translation of 1592 as 'Love's Struggle in a

ABOVE *A beautiful sunken garden at the Villa Cicogna at Bisuchio near Lake Lugano.*

RIGHT *Colossal figures at the entrance to the* giardino segreto *in the Villa Madama on Monte Mario just outside Rome.*

Dream'. Much of the story is laid in a series of gardens, of which the 'garden of the heart's desire' is the most important. This garden comprised a circle of level ground surrounded by a clipped hedge of myrtles and cypresses. Concentric circles inside the main circle were divided into segments, each of which was given over to a different type of planting. Some sections were woods, each wood being of a different species. Some of these were scented, such as those planted with juniper, cypress and rosemary. Others were evergreens, such as the bay and laurel woods. There were also woods of various kinds of oaks, nut trees and pines.

The woods gave way to meadows, which were divided by covered trellis walks on which grew familiar climbers, clematis, jasmine, honeysuckle, convolvulus and others. The corners of the meadows were marked by apple trees which were trained to form circles. These grew on ornamental platforms rising by steps, on each of which was planted a different fragrant herb. Some of the meadows which were surrounded by trellis-work had central marble baths in the mediaeval style. In contrast to these there was a peristyle garden with Corinthian columns in the new Renaissance mode

Pool and grottoes at the Villa Cicogna, where the house was provided with gardens which were Roman in conception.

which was planted with scented shrubs and herbs, including box, marjoram, lavender cotton and small clipped junipers in tubs, so that the garden was a mixture of the old and the new. This garden enclosed a rose garden in which all the roses mentioned by Pliny were planted, including the famous roses of Paestum, as well as Praenestine, Campanian, Milesian and Damascene roses.

A flowery mede ran down from these gardens to an ornamental water and the flowers that Colonna mentions show that he was not a copyist but quite familiar with the actual plants. In the grass he placed gladioli, white and purple hyacinths, lavender and herbs like mint and marjoram; down by the water's edge were narcissi, orchids, gladioli, iris, buttercups, mare's tails, pansies, balsam and forget-me-nots. His names had a great variety of origins, some being in the local vernacular while others were in Greek and Latin. The ornamental water enclosed a formal garden which was laid out in a series of elaborate parterres which are illustrated in woodcuts. It is evident from these that the art of making such parterres had progressed very rapidly and that designs had already reached a high level of complexity. A variety of herbs were used in contrasting shades of green. Among them were southernwood, rue, marjoram, germander, thyme and lavender cotton. The intervening spaces were planted

with primroses, love-in-a-mist, white and yellow pansies and purple and white violets. Clumps of hollyhocks and hyssop clipped into a ball-shape were placed among them at regular intervals. Each alternate parterre had a large urn or Roman altar in the centre under a cypress tree surrounded by flowers. Sometimes a complicated design in box was used, such as peacocks drinking from a basin. Colonna was clearly used to a high standard of skill in topiary.

A chapter later on in the book describes another kind of garden, a flower-garden made within a Roman ruin like an amphitheatre. In the 'steps' or 'seats' around it grew cyclamen, cornflowers, melilotus, pinks and yellow and white narcissi. Covered walks or galleries shaded by roses and clipped myrtles and cypresses filled the centre. These were flanked by a host of other plants, among which were hyacinths, columbines, white and orange lilies, wallflowers, lilies-of-the-valley, yellow immortelles (everlasting flowers), carnations, primroses, love-lies-bleeding, red anemones, and yellow ranunculus.

Colonna's book is important for several reasons. There seems little doubt that, although the story is a flight of the imagination, the surroundings in which it is set are based on real gardens and represent very fairly the state of garden art at the time the work was written, a period of transition when mediaeval ideas were lingering on but the new notions were still only developing. The work is the only source available which tells us which flowers were used in Renaissance gardens before the influx of those discovered and

91

brought in by plant collectors in the age of discovery just about to start. No other work is so specific in this matter, most referring, as Boccaccio does, to 'a thousand different flowers', or some such phrase, in the flowery mede. The work was in advance of its time both as regards gardens and architecture. The amphitheatre and peristyle gardens, the antique classical reliefs shown in the illustrations, the references to statues and herms, altars and amphorae in a landscape of classical ruins are pure Renaissance, but in 1467 their use had barely entered the minds of most people. Even as late as 1483 Poggio Bracciolino was laughed at by his friends because he put classical statues in his garden, but by then the wheel was turning. Lorenzo de Medici had begun to collect statues for his garden in the Piazzo San Marco in Florence

where he displayed them for artists, among them Michelangelo, to study. Colonna's book must have been very influential in furthering the ideas of the Renaissance.

Immediately after the book was written, political and financial troubles slowed down development but in 1485 Pope Pius II rebuilt his home village, renaming it Pienza, and erected for himself the Palazzo Piccolomini in a superb situation affording magnificent views; he provided it with a garden some of which, including a fine octagonal well head with sculptured reliefs, has survived. The garden of the Villa Cigliano at San Cassiano illustrated well Alberti's precept that the garden should be integrated with the house; its whole length could be seen from the main courtyard entrance through the loggia on the far side. The Renaissance in

FAR LEFT *The terraces at the Villa Imperiale at Pesaro in the Marche on the Adriatic, showing the courtyard as the lowest terrace and the second, the lemon garden, on the top of the villa buildings. The woodland, to which pathways lead from the top terrace, may be seen in the background.*

ABOVE *Giambologna's colossal statue of the Apennines in the Medici garden at Pratolino near Florence, the only thing now left of this once-famous Renaissance garden.*

LEFT *Sculptured animals in the grotto of the Medici garden at Castello, still as fresh and lifelike as they were when Montaigne saw them in the 1580s.*

Rome, so far as gardens were concerned, still lagged behind Florence. Not until the time of Pope Julius II did the change gain momentum. The first garden with which Julius was concerned was attached to a palace by San Pietro in Vincoli, his titular church where, in 1486, he created a garden from a walled and wooded tract of land behind the church. This garden became well-known, not so much as a garden, but for the statuary which Julius collected and placed in it. After he became Pope in 1503 he decided to move the collection to the Vatican, but was faced with the problem of where it could be housed.

For a number of years Donato Bramante had studied the ruins of Rome and his knowledge and abilities were widely respected. When Julius fixed on the Villa Belvedere as the best future home for his statues and the question arose of providing covered access from the Vatican to the Villa, it was to Bramante he turned for a design. The Villa Belvedere was slightly out of line with the palace and separated from the Papal lodgings by a wide stretch of rising ground. Bramante's brief, apart from the sheltered connection between the two buildings, was to give a worthy setting for the statuary and a garden that not only provided a private retreat for the Pope but also a stage for the pageantry of the Papal court. Julius' instinct had not erred: Bramante was the man to do it. Thoroughly soaked in the classical spirit, his imagination was fired by the task laid upon him. He produced a masterpiece which set out the principles of Renaissance gardening for all to see with such success that the results are reverberating yet.

ABOVE *The Botanic Garden at Padua, the first of its kind to be made in Europe; the plants in the garden have changed many times since it was first planted in 1545 but the garden itself has remained unaltered.*

ABOVE RIGHT *The amphitheatre behind the Pitti Palace in the Boboli garden at Florence.*

BELOW RIGHT *The water-garden called the 'Isolotto' created by Alfonso Parigi in the Boboli gardens, Florence, showing, in the centre, Giambologna's splendid Fountain of Oceanus.*

Gone was the garden of the early humanists like Colonna on level ground. Bramante boldly adopted the Roman notion of moulding the terrain to an architectural form so that, with supreme art, the architecture seemed to grow out of the site. He related his garden to the axis of the house and linked it with the landscape, so that all was open to the outside world. Two enormous loggias were built enclosing the area within the axis of the palace and the Belvedere. At the lowest level these were triple, changing to double and then finally single as they matched the series of terraces that gave the hill architectural form. He levelled a large area of ground in front of the palace to provide the 'stage' of a theatre for the display of pageants and jousts, which the audience could watch from a vast half-circle of steps against the palace wall. On the far side of this level ground rose the terraces, linked together by monumental stairs and ramps which rose to

a climax in a niche at the Belvedere end which was approached by a final series of semi-circular steps.

The Renaissance ideals of symmetry and proportion were at once firmly established by this garden. The view from the level ground at the bottom up through the terraces, which spread away at right-angles, to the niche at the top, was the dominating feature, affording a commanding central perspective which was now seen for the first time in a Renaissance garden. It astonished Bramante's contemporaries by the majesty of its conception. The inspiration for this design was formerly supposed to have come from the gardens of Lucullus on the Pincian Hill, but the Temple of Fortune at Praeneste, which was built over but has become more visible since the bombing of the last war, has a similar layout of terraces connected by ramps and stairs and a semi-circular sanctuary at the top. This may have been visible in Bramante's time. Bramante died in 1514 while the work was in progress and the design at the top was somewhat altered from his original plan. Pirro Ligorio completed the task. A later library building erected on the lowest level against the terraces has since destroyed Bramante's perspective.

The adaptation of the approach to the Villa Belvedere behind the garden terraces was carried out with similar vision and skill. The Venetian ambassador visited it in 1523 and left a description of it:

'One enters a very beautiful garden of which half is filled with growing grass and bays, mulberries and cypresses, while the other half is paved with squares of bricks laid upright, and in every square a beautiful orange tree grows out of the pavement, of which there are a great many arranged in perfect order. In the centre of the garden are two enormous men of marble, one is the Tiber, the other the Nile, very ancient figures, and two fountains issue from them. At the main entrance to this garden on the left there is a sort of chapel built into the wall where, on a marble base, stands the Apollo . . . Somewhat further on, also on the same facade which runs along the side, in a similar place on a similar base as high off the ground as an altar, opposite a most perfect well, is the Laocoon . . . Not far from this, mounted in a similar fashion, is the Venus . . . On one side of the garden is a most beautiful loggia, at one end of which is a lovely fountain that irrigates the orange trees and the rest of the garden by a little canal in the centre of the loggia.'

At the other end, through a small door, one passes out into two even more beautiful loggias, high on the top of a hill with a marvellous view. From one side of these loggias the visitor could look back over Bramante's terraces while from the other he looked down on the large walled stretch of woodland in which the Villa Pia was afterwards built.

The placing of statues in niches in the Villa Belvedere was the first occasion on which this ancient Roman practice was used in a Renaissance villa and started the fashion that is still with us. The statues sometimes stood on bases, but at other times were turned into fountains. Sometimes the niche was plain, sometimes ornamentally painted, and sometimes it was disguised

LEFT ABOVE *One of the chambers in the grotto made by Bernardo Buontalenti for the Boboli gardens.*

LEFT BELOW *The Neptune fountain designed by Stoldo Lorenzi in the pool in the upper part of the Boboli garden; water flows out through the three jets of Neptune's trident.*

ABOVE *The loggia at the Villa Papa Giulio, showing a view through to the gardens beyond.*

as a grotto. With the revival of this fashion water was restored to an integral part of garden architecture, as it was with the Romans and always had been with the Persian gardens and those that stemmed from them, unlike the mediaeval or early Renaissance gardens, where it had been merely a nodal point in the flowery mede.

In 1516 work commenced on the first truly Renaissance villa to be built outside the walls of Rome. On Mont Maria, a site similar to that of Fiesole, Cardinal Giulio de Medici began to build the Villa Madama. The design was by Raphael but the villa was not built by him. It was somewhat different from other villas in that it was not designed to be used as a residence, but consisted of a series of open courts and loggias solely for entertaining, the rooms serving merely as an enclosing framework. The outstanding feature was the inter-penetration of the house and garden, which were married together in intimate perfection emulating perfectly such examples from ancient Rome as

Hadrian's Villa. Passages led from the central court to each of the four loggias. The south loggia opened on to the entrance court, the east had a view over the terraces and the Tiber valley, the north led into the *giardino segreto* and the west faced a semi-circular theatre cut out of the hillside. This villa is usually regarded as inferior to Bramante's work because, although there was again a series of terraces lying along the slopes of a hill, there was no central perspective in the design to pull the conception together. Similarly, although the grottoes and fountains around the pool in the garden were very fine, they were an isolated unit not integrated with the remainder. Sculpture was used on an extensive scale, including the elephant fountain made by Giovanni da Udine. There was also another fountain, now disappeared, which was of considerable importance as it was the first in the Renaissance placed in a woodland setting to imitate nature. The fountain stood in a natural hollow some distance from the terraces. Vasari says that it 'was surrounded by a wood . . . and was made to fall with fine artifice over rough stones and stalactites dripping and gushing so that it really appeared natural, and above it among the grottoes and rough stones he composed a great lion's head garlanded with maidenhair and other water plants.'

Renaissance influence was now being felt in gardens away from Florence and Rome. The Villa Imperiale built for Francesco Maria in the Marche at Pesaro on the remote Adriatic coast owes much to the Villa Madama. Like that villa the buildings were not designed primarily as a residence but served as a screen which surrounded a garden court on three sides, the fourth facing the hillside terraces. Immediately around the court were grottoes, porticos and shell-decorated rooms which were connected with the terraces by spiral staircases. The court itself was the first terrace level. The middle terrace was a lemon garden and the top terrace was on the same level as the roof, being connected with walks on the roof of the building. This terrace was a spacious walled garden with semi-circular loggias at the corners away from the house leading out into the woods. It contained a substantial amount of topiary and there were espalier oranges on the walls. The paths were shaded with iron pergolas and bays formed into pleached alleys. There were low rose hedges, parterres of box, myrtle and rosemary, and citrus trees regularly spaced in pots, the whole forming a most attractive setting from which to enjoy the lovely views. The Villa Imperiale was often used as a model for other gardens in the Marche, but it was never equalled or surpassed because the wealthiest families did not build in that

BELOW *The Fountain of the Moors in the Villa Lante at Bagnaia, in which Montaigne saw the small marble boats, slightly obscured in the picture by vases, with 'two arquebusiers and a trumpeter' shooting volleys of water. The parterres in the foreground are of the simple geometrical design typical of Italian gardens of the Renaissance.*

RIGHT *The magnificent pool and statues of the River Gods at the Villa Lante.*

region. It has survived in almost complete form and is probably the best Italian sixteenth-century garden still in existence which remains much as it was first laid out.

North of the Marche, in Veneto, there was much less to show at this time. Venice had obtained control of Padua at the beginning of the fifteenth century and by 1460 fine gardens were being made. In 1490 an observer records the existence of villas but the area was sacked by the League of Cambrai in 1509 which for a time retarded development. Cardinal Bembo describes a garden of this period at Asolo Castle. He says that in this garden

'a wide and shady pergola of vines ran down the centre and the walls on either side were concealed by thick hedges of box and juniper, while bays arched overhead and afforded a most pleasant shade, and were so carefully cut that not a single leaf was out of place . . . [There was] a little meadow at the end of the garden. Here the grass was of as fine a colour as an emerald and all manner of bright flowers sprung in the fresh greensward and just beyond was a shady grove of bays not clipped or trained like the others but allowed to wander at will. In the midst was a beautiful fountain . . . from which rills flowed all over the garden.'

This description evokes a picture of an almost wholly mediaeval garden to which Renaissance ideas had not yet penetrated. It was probably typical of gardens in the Veneto at this time, even those in the mountains. As they contained few architectural elements none has

survived. Renaissance changes were slow in coming in this area.

They were similarly slow along the west coast, the first Renaissance garden in Genoa being that of Andrea Doria, construction of which did not begin until the late 1520s. The merchants of Genoa still lived in mediaeval palaces in the narrow streets of the old town. Andrea Doria absorbed the new ideas and decided to build a new palace outside the walls at Fassolo. The buildings already on the site were not symmetrically related to the hillside which he had chosen. A loggia was built to remedy this defect and the buildings incorporated into the design, which was based on a scheme of terraces covering the whole side of the hill from the top down to the seashore. A central perspective of stairs linked the different levels. The main facade looked out over a level enclosed garden to the sea. The terraces above, which ran up the hillside, have vanished, but the lower terrace garden remains. The gardens were furnished with fountains, parterres and pergolas in the older style, but the attractive loggias designed by Montorsoli which ran out into the gardens from the buildings were more modern in conception and there was a novel feature in the access provided through a pillared arcade under the lower terrace to the sea. At its peak the whole must have had an imposing grandeur hard to equal.

There were other gardens in northern Italy in which, as the sixteenth century progressed, the Renaissance began to be felt, particularly in the vicinity of Ferrara and Mantua, centred round the Este and Gonzaga courts in those towns. Judging by the comments of

LEFT *One of the River Gods overlooking a pool at the Villa Lante at Bagnaia.*

ABOVE *The Organ Fountain of the Villa d'Este at Tivoli, near Rome, is a remarkable example of the 'water-tricks' beloved of Renaissance garden designers and their patrons; it greatly impressed Montaigne, who described it. Water from the river filled large cisterns providing pressure in a round, vaulted recess to supply wind for the pipes and to drive a wheel with teeth like a musical box which struck the keyboard, making various sounds from ordinary organ tones through the blare of trumpets, the reports of cannon and the fusillades of arquebusiers.*

Charles V and his courtiers they must have been worth seeing, but few relics have survived. More remains of Lombardy gardens. There is one, indeed, that retains its sixteenth-century character almost intact. This is the Villa Cicogna at Bisuchio near Lake Lugano. The house is northern in style, but Roman in the loggias and gardens. The latter contained two main features, a water staircase and a terrace at right-angles to it connecting a sunken garden adjacent to one side of the house with a terraced garden on the other side of it. The latter served both as a walk and to conceal a gallery beneath which was a cool retreat such as was often made to render tolerable the hotter climate of the south. Above the water staircase the garden shaded off into woodland.

Around Florence development now occurred on the grand scale. As the Medici family had grown in wealth and influence so it had acquired great estates and by this time there were eleven Medici villas and gardens around the town. The garden at Castello, which was laid out for Grand Duke Cosimo I by Il Tribolo in 1540 was, however, more conservative than might have been expected considering the time that had elapsed since Bramante had begun his work and the Villa Madama had been designed. It still bore more evidence of the influence of Alberti than of the Roman designers. As in the Villa Quaracchi, it was originally intended that an avenue of trees should lead from the Arno up to the house. The centrepiece of the arrangement was a square walled garden which sloped gently down behind the house in the middle of which was Giambologna's 'Venus', a circular fountain which was one of the masterpieces of this gifted Mannerist sculptor, surrounded by trees. It is now at Petraia.

The main garden was separated by a wall adorned with fountains from the lemon garden on the upper terrace. Out of this led a grotto which became very famous for its surprise fountains, shell mosaics and animal sculptures. There were two smaller gardens on either side of the main one, that on the east containing a tree house. An ivy-covered stair concealed the mechanism of the surprise fountains in this garden and the copper tubes that gave out musical sounds and other noises. The west garden was a herb garden. Vasari described Castello as the 'most rich, magnificent and ornamental garden in Europe' and it must therefore have been very well stocked and cared for even though not of the most advanced design. Montaigne visited it about forty years after it was made and commented on 'several galleries [pleached alleys] . . . very thickly interwoven and covered with all kinds of aromatic trees, like cedars, cypresses, orange, lemon and olive trees, the branches [being] so mingled and interlaced, that it is easy to see that the sun at its greatest strength could not penetrate them. The trunks of the cypresses and those of other trees are planted in rows so close to one another, that only three or four people could walk abreast.' He was also impressed with the fountains:

'There is a large basin, amongst others, in the midst of which is to be seen a natural or artificial rock, which seems all frozen over at the top, by means of the sam

The famous Hundred Fountains at the Villa d'Este at Tivoli, one of the water effects for which this villa is famous.

material with which the Duke has covered his grottoes at Pratolino; and above the rock is a great copper medallion, representing a very old hairy man sitting down, his arms crossed, from whose beard, forehead and skin, water drips incessantly drop by drop, representing sweat and tears, and the fountain has no other conduit but this.'

In another grotto he found a fountain where 'every kind of animal is represented materially, emitting streams of water either by the beak, the wing, the claw, the ear or the nostril.' Of the topiary in the garden he was struck by 'a tree . . . so thick by artificial cutting that it seemed to be a circular ball, massive and trim, about a man's height', and by 'coats of arms over the gateways formed from the branches of trees fostered and strained in the natural growth by certain ligaments and by pruning and tying.'

Another magnificent Medici garden near Florence was Pratolino, mentioned by Montaigne in the quotation above. This had a superb central alley, fifty feet wide, bordered by fountains and water-courses and, like the Castello garden, was full of surprise fountains and automata, which Montaigne greatly enjoyed, more than perhaps the beauty of the garden, which had the reputation of being one of the greatest Medici gardens. Nothing now remains of it but a grotto and Giambologna's colossal statue of the Appenines.

One attractive garden made at this time was, although minute in size compared with the gardens of princes, nevertheless a product of Renaissance ideas. Alongside the interest in gardens had grown an interest in plants for their own sake and a movement not only to revive the ancient knowledge about them but to study them afresh, particularly the new plants that were coming in from the New World and other countries which now began to be visited by travellers. The university world was stirred by these opportunities to acquire knowledge and in 1545 the University of Padua established in that city the first botanic garden in Europe. This small garden still exists and has fulfilled its function faithfully for more than 400 years. Circular in shape, the contents have changed over the years many times, but the garden remains as it was first laid out. It was in due course copied in every town in Europe that had any pretensions to a scientific interest in plants. The function of these gardens influenced their design and, in general, an attempt was made to provide for this function within the framework of ordinary ornamental garden practice, often with interesting results.

Four years after the founding of the botanic garden at Padua the most spectacular of the Medici gardens of Florence was laid out for Eleanora de Medici at Boboli. Il Tribolo was commissioned to carry out the task. The garden, on which work began in 1549, is sited on a steep hillside extending to the south and west behind the Pitti Palace. The garden, which is open to the public, still exists today.

Boboli as the visitor now sees it is more splendid and impressive than when it was first completed. Although the hillside was considerably excavated and lent itself to architectural treatment in the Bramante manner, more than half the horseshoe-shaped valley was taken up with 'plantations', which were small woods planted regularly along the terraces. Only a smallish square lawn at the bottom with a central fountain was left unplanted. From this an alley led up the hill between the plantations to a rectangular tank at the top. The view from the principal apartments of the palace was over the lawn, the parterre being placed at the side of the palace. In its day, the layout was probably regarded as fully effective, particularly as it was designed as a setting for the spectacles of which the Florentines were very fond, but Il Tribolo and Ammanati, who finished off the design after Il Tribolo's death in September, 1550, are now generally thought to have missed an opportunity.

Gradually, in the years that followed, the faults were rectified. The amphitheatre was cleared of the intrusive plantations and surrounded by a wall with six tiers of stone benches for the spectators. A laurel hedge beyond these set off the steeply rising ilex-clad slopes of the upper garden. At the foot of the alley which divided the garden Alfonso Parigi created a striking oval-shaped water-garden called the 'Isolotto' for which in the 1570s Giambologna designed the splendid 'Fountain of Oceanus' which has sometimes been described as the finest fountain in Europe. The tank at the top of the hill was replaced by a fountain comprising a figure of Neptune aiming at a fish, the water issuing through the three jets of his trident. The canal was guarded by

ABOVE *The fountain called 'Little Rome' at Villa d'Este, so named from the children Romulus and Remus who founded Rome, seen in the picture portrayed in stone with the wolf who suckled them.*

RIGHT *The stairway approaching the mound in the garden of the Medici Villa on the Pincian Hill in Rome.*

twelve watchdogs carved in stone, and water gushed from the heads of winged dragons.

The central alley was made easier to negotiate by conversion of the steep slope to a double series of shallow sloping steps which also enhanced its impact on the scene so that from the amphitheatre the grand perspective of the Renaissance garden could be seen, the contrast of the ascending vertical line with the right-angle crossing of the garden terraces. Buontalenti, the great stage designer and theatre architect, exerted his talents to make a grotto which consisted of a series of chambers leading one into another and ornamented in a most impressive way with statuettes, shell mosaics, animal sculptures, paintings and artificial rockwork. Vasari commented that the Boboli gardens were in his time 'adorned with innumerable statues both old and new as well as many streams'. One of the statues was Giambologna's 'Venus of the Grotticella', which was housed in a grotto with pergolas and little birds painted by Pocetti. Another was a colossal statue that began as a representation of Francesco I's wife but was converted by Ferdinando II

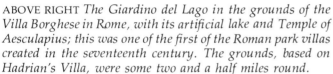

ABOVE RIGHT *The Giardino del Lago in the grounds of the Villa Borghese in Rome, with its artificial lake and Temple of Aesculapius; this was one of the first of the Roman park villas created in the seventeenth century. The grounds, based on Hadrian's Villa, were some two and a half miles round.*

RIGHT *A view up the cascade of the Villa Torlonia at Frascati, near Rome, formerly one of the most attractive of the Frascati villas. Its charm has now been marred by a trunk road.*

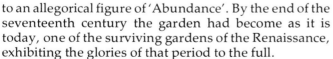

to an allegorical figure of 'Abundance'. By the end of the seventeenth century the garden had become as it is today, one of the surviving gardens of the Renaissance, exhibiting the glories of that period to the full.

The developments around Florence were paralleled in Rome. Pope Julius III, elected in 1550, began to develop the Villa de Papa Giulio at a site on the via Flaminia, about a mile outside the walls. The large grounds extended to the banks of the Tiber. Julius filled them with fountains, fishponds, grottoes, statues, aviaries and pavilions, planting 36,000 trees and other plants among them. The central feature of the garden was the magnificent horsehoe-shaped court divided by a porticoed screen from a nymphaeum through which the central perspective continued through another loggia to a small garden. The villa, like the Villa Madama, was an enclosing framework for the gardens and like that villa is an example of the interpenetration of the house and garden for which the Renaissance gardeners strove, in this case, with very great success. Pope Pius IV who succeeded Julius found the Belvedere gardens too public and in 1560 built the Villa Pia in the woodland overlooked from Bramante's loggia. It is still, though altered, a beautifully quiet and sequestered retreat.

In 1566 building began of the Villa Lante at Bagnaia, which was almost certainly designed by Giacomo da Vignola, who had been concerned also with the Villa de Papa Giulio. The garden that he created for Cardinal Gambara is regarded by many as the most beautiful garden in Italy and has fortunately survived almost unchanged. It has all the ingredients of the Renaissance garden harmonizing with one another superlatively, but there is one highly significant change. The paths from the gates that come almost immediately upon

PROSPETTO DEL TEATRO, E CASCATA DELL ACQVE DELLA VILLA LVDOVISIA À FRASCATI CON VARII

Giambologna's 'Pegasus' not only lead on into the walled gardens and villa but diverge the other way to penetrate naturally into the woodland. Similarly the top terrace above the house merges unobtrusively into the background of trees. Man is no longer the supreme master as he was believed to be in early Renaissance times and his garden no longer a man-made creation glorifying man. The first glimmerings of the rebirth of the consciousness of man's insignificance may be perceived in the Villa Lante garden where the formal layout for the first time merges naturally with the wild.

When Montaigne visited the Villa Lante in the 1580s, however, his thoughts were not on this level. He was intrigued with a fountain he saw there in which a pyramid gushed water in 3,000 jets into four magnificent basins. Each of these basins had a small

ABOVE RIGHT *A seventeenth-century print made by G. B. Falda of the cascade of the Villa Torlonia at Frascati showing the statuary that used to fill the now empty niches.*

BELOW *A view of the pool and cascade at the Villa Torlonia at Frascati.*

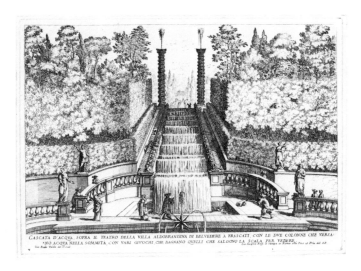

Cascata d'acqua sopra il teatro della villa Aldobrandina di Belvedere a Frascati, con le due colonne che versano acqua nella sommità, con vari giuochi che bagnano quelli che salgono la scala per vedere...

ABOVE *A print made about 1683 by G. B. Falda of the cascade at the Villa Aldobrandini at Frascati.*

BELOW LEFT *The fine nymphaeum and cascade at the Villa Aldobrandini at Frascati near Rome. This is the best-preserved of all the Renaissance villas at Frascati.*

BELOW RIGHT *A view down the cascade and pine avenue at the Villa Caprarola, not far from Rome; this is the reverse of the view which, from the bottom of the pine avenue looking up the cascade, has been described as the most beautiful 'surprise' in Italian gardens.*

boat of marble, very finely carved, and was furnished with a crew of two arquebusiers and a trumpeter who were able to shoot back a volley of water at the pyramid as if in a naval battle.

Other villas and gardens in Rome or its vicinity were under construction at the time. The garden of the Villa d'Este at Tivoli, about 20 miles from the city, which still exists, largely unaltered in design, is usually regarded as one of the peaks of the High Renaissance. It shows no trace of the future foreshadowed by the Villa Lante. It contained, like that villa, all the ingredients of the Renaissance garden superbly executed, but is distinguished by the use of water on a scale and with a grandeur unequalled by any previous garden. The villa was on a superb site — the top of a hill commanding a view of the Sabine Mountains — and the waters of a river were available for diversion to serve the garden. There were fishponds at the base of the terraces, water staircases as the visitor climbed, great fountains in separate enclosures and then the unsurpassed 'Promenade of a Hundred Fountains' before the great open terrace in front of the villa was reached. One of the most impressive sights was the great water organ. Montaigne describes how water built up a wind pressure in a round vaulted recess so that the organ was able to play the same tune over and over again. The programme could be varied by another stream which turned a wheel fitted with teeth. These teeth struck the keyboard and could imitate, among other things, the blare of trumpets. Montaigne writes:

'In another plan one may hear the song of birds, which is produced by small bronze flutes such as are seen at feasts, and give a sound similar to that produced from those earthen vessels full of water into which children blow with a mouthpiece; and by another device an owl is made to appear on the top of a rock, whereupon all the harmony ceases at once, the birds being terrified at his presence. Then the owl retires and they sing again. Elsewhere a noise like the report of a cannon is produced, and again, other sounds, less loud and very frequent, like the fusillade of arquebusiers.'

The fountains also produced effects of mist and rainbows, giving a welcome coolness in the climate of Italy. There were even grottoes equipped with imitation seaweed. The garden of the Villa d'Este at Tivoli is still one of the sights of Italy.

The Villa Medici on the Pincian Hill in Rome itself where Lucullus had his gardens in Roman times was bought and developed by Cardinal Ferdinando de Medici about 1580. It was a town villa notable for its collection of statuary and an obelisk set up in the centre of a number of square flower-beds. It had one feature uncommon in Italian gardens but often found in northern European gardens. Evelyn described this as a mound circular in shape and enclosed with cypresses, being cut in the shape of a fortress with a pavilion. There was a fountain on top approached by a path winding to the top in the form of a spiral. This garden was the subject of pictures by Velasquez which capture

One of the rustic fountains at the Villa Aldobrandini at Frascati; the line of these fountains leads upwards from the formality below to the natural woodland above. This kind of transition is typical of the later style of Italian baroque gardens.

RIGHT *A view up the cascade at the Villa Caprarola, part of the 'surprise' seen through the pine avenue.*

BELOW *A terrifying giant mouth open to swallow the unwary in the garden of the Villa Orsini at Bomarzo.*

FAR RIGHT *The centre of the impressive terraces of the Villa Garzoni at Collodi, a splendid baroque garden near Lucca.*

FAR RIGHT BELOW *The interior of the grotto garden at the Villa Gamberaia at Settignano. The original Renaissance gardens of this villa were replaced by an eighteenth-century garden of great beauty of which this is part.*

for ever the essence of the reaction of the Italian people to their Renaissance gardens.

The gardens of the Villa Borghese, which were also on the Pincian Hill, were distinguished by their size. The wall around the estate was three miles in length. Most of the grounds were open to the public and contained menageries and aviaries, the private gardens reserved for the owners being round the edge. These were planted with orange trees and flowers. The Villa Pamphilj on the Janiculum was another Roman garden with a distinctive feature. Here trees were planted so closely together that they made a hall roofed in green with the trunks of the trees as the pillars. There were also lakes, canals and bridges, with a water theatre and a menagerie and also parterres. This garden was even larger than that of the Villa Borghese, being six miles in

circumference and, being made later, was somewhat freer in design. It was one of the few gardens in Italy large enough, when the eighteenth century came, to be satisfactorily adapted to the English landscape style. Most of the original layout of the Villa Farnesina on the Tiber is gone, but there is a pleasant walk of pleached bay trees in the part that survives.

Outside Rome itself there were a number of fine villas and gardens at Frascati. The earliest of these, the Villa Muti, dates from about 1579 and is one of the most charming small gardens in Italy. All but one of its original box parterres still exists, showing, in its slight elaboration, traces of French influence. The gardens of the Villa Falconeri are not now in the original design and a road has been driven through those of the Villa Torlonia destroying, among other things, the fine view from this villa. The garden of the Villa Mondragone, an enormous building with 365 rooms, was noted for its water effects, particularly a water game in which combatants manipulated leather hoses. The finest garden remaining at Frascati is, however, that of the Villa Aldobrandini.

Imperceptibly, as the years went on, the gardens of the High Renaissance were changing into those of the Baroque. The gardens of the Villa Aldobrandini illustrate this change. Adoption of the new style did not alter the basic principles of Renaissance gardening. Near the house Baroque gardens remained much the same as their predecessors although architectural features were more elaborate. As, however, the garden receded from the house these features disappeared, giving way to less vivid contrasts of light and shade.

The woodland closed around the clipped alleys and absorbed them into the landscape. The change foreshadowed in the Villa Lante was carried to its logical conclusion. Man accepted the role allocated to him. In the formal part of the garden of the Villa Aldobrandini there is a magnificent semi-circular nymphaeum. This part and the water staircase are framed in clipped ilex and if the Renaissance style had been followed would have continued upwards in formal terraces. The grand perspective in this case, in contrast, leads into woodland, the terrace above the water staircase being quite small and containing only a rustic fountain. There is a second fountain in the trees above this and the vista terminates in a third and larger rustic fountain gushing naturally from the mountainside through the trees. In three steps, formality has dissolved into forest. This is typical of the Baroque style.

The Villa Ruspoli at Vignanello not far from Rome contains the most magnificent box parterre in Italy still in its original Renaissance form. As it was made in 1612 it preserves an accurate picture of the comparatively plain geometrical designs that remained current in Italy even up to as late as 1650. The Villa Caprarola built for Cardinal Alessandro Farnese a little further away from Rome was the finest ever built in Italy. Pentagonal in shape and built in a typical Renaissance situation on a hilltop it has two gardens separated by plantations of trees. One of these leads the visitor up into a wood beyond which he emerges suddenly on to a beautiful grassy avenue bordered with pines leading to a vista of fountains and cascades which is probably the most

beautiful 'surprise' scene to be found in Italian gardens. The garden of the Villa Orsini at Bomarzo also near Rome built for Vicino Orsini belongs to no known school and portrays perhaps the superstitious underside of the Roman civilization that the Renaissance sought to recreate. Although the villa is sited on a precipitous hill, Orsini did not build terraces but made his garden among the rocky outcrops in the woods of the valley bottom, filling it with monsters and giants which create a sinister atmosphere of mystery. They are seen at their best in the half-light of dusk or moonlight, or the dimness of a misty day, when they suggest worse horrors lurking in the dark patches of the woods behind them. Bomarzo at such times is not a place for the nervous. It has often been said that these creations are unique but Georgina Masson in her *Italian Gardens* has pointed out that some of the features of the Bomarzo

creatures may be found in other gardens of the area and that there was another Orsini garden near Pitigliano which has relics of gigantic figures and small gazebos carved out of the rock of a gorge.

Gardens continued to be made in the vicinity of Florence, the Villa Capponi at Arcetri, made in the 1570s, being a perfect example, still in existence, of the smaller Renaissance garden. The original garden of the Villa Gamberaia, near Settignano, has been replaced by a later garden of great beauty dating mostly from the eighteenth century and containing a superb water parterre. The Villa Bombicci at Colazzi is notable for its magnificent cypress avenue and spacious terrace with a splendid view. Boccaccio framed the 'Decameron' round the garden of the Villa Palmieri but this was completely altered in 1657 so that the garden about which he wrote cannot now be traced. The present

In the nightmarish world of the garden of the Villa Orsini at Bomarzo, quite unlike in ornament and feeling any other Renaissance garden, there are savage dragons and lions, a majestic elephant swaying through the woods, terrible giants tearing each other limb from limb, and other frightening things starting out of the undergrowth and from behind the rocky outcrops in a wild valley.

design includes a pleasant oval lemon garden. It was unusual for Renaissance gardens to be made on a completely flat site but the first garden at the Villa Corso Silviato at Sesto, which was on such a site, was made as early as 1502. It was a very simple layout occupying a small area only which was greatly augmented in 1644 and altered again in 1738 to a Baroque form.

A number of fine gardens were also made around Lucca. The gardens in this area had a particular characteristic. They almost always took the form of a number of separate but connected 'garden rooms' within a woodland surround. The earliest garden in the area was that of the Villa Bernardini at Saltocchio of which the modern garden still contains a surviving *giardino segreto,* to which curving pools and staircases add some grandeur. The Villa Marlia at Fraga is the most famous garden in the area, its chief feature being a large Baroque pool in wooded surroundings. The castle

111

of Celsa also has a charming pool in the woodland. The Villa Torrigiano at Camigliano possesses an outstanding 'Garden of Flora', but the most spectacular of the gardens near Lucca is the Baroque garden of the Villa Garzoni at Collodi, which was made in the seventeenth century. This is an exception to the rule. It is not split up into 'garden rooms' but built on a precipitous hillside and laid out in terraces in the Roman manner. These terraces are linked by staircases that provide the line of the main axis. The final garden of parterres, stairs and open terraces gradually merges into walks shaded by clipped trees. The central axis is still marked but by a much less formal water staircase eventually leading to a statue of Fame, where the perspective finally fades out into the woodland. It is a skilful transformation from the formal to the wild.

Further north on the west coast, a notable garden was made in Genoa at the Palazzo Podestà in the via Garibaldi. Here the garden backed against a steeply rising hillside, the culminating point of the perspective being a shallow grotto and fountain built against the retaining wall of the upper terrace. The arrangement of the fountains, parterres, terraces, trees and paths is cleverly worked out to provide light and shade in various parts of the garden as appropriate at various times of day.

In 1630 Count Carlo Borromeo decided to convert an island in Lake Maggiore into a vast pleasure galley. Two-thirds of the island were given over to gardens which were completed by 1670. At one end he made what may be called the 'poop' of the vessel, ten terraces

TOP *The upper pool and niches at the Villa Garzoni at Collodi, above which the ascent fades into the woodland in the manner characteristic of Italian baroque gardens.*

ABOVE *Terraces and parterres of the spectacular garden of Isola Bella on Lake Maggiore, which was converted by Count Borromeo from a barren rock into a summer residence and garden in the seventeenth century.*

rising 100 feet above the surface of the lake. All the garden was given over to elaborate parterres but to modern eyes the planting is too spare. The Isola Bella, as it is called, is, however, an object of beauty and wonder as it sails in magnificence on the lake. Another interesting garden in the north of Italy was that of Il Bozzolo at Casalzuigno, a dramatic seventeenth-century layout intended to be seen from the road. It is built in the grand Roman manner against a hillside but the house is offset so as not to obscure the view from the highway. A notable feature of the garden is a large octagonal sweep of lawn above the terraces before the final architectural feature merges into the woods above. The Villa Sarni Picenardi resembles Il Bozzolo but the garden is on a smaller scale and the house is part of the scene. Of the Villa d'Este at Cernobbio, made in 1570, which has for long been a hotel, only the water staircase remains. The Castello Balduino at Montalto di Pavia, a mediaeval castle on the highest peak of the Apennines, possesses a remarkable survival. The original topiary garden, of which the date of origin is unknown, still exists and is an impressive and highly finished example

RIGHT *The remarkable topiary garden of Castello Balduino at Montalto di Pavia, a mediaeval garden set on the slopes of the highest peak of the Apennines. The date of origin of this highly finished example of topiary work is unknown.*

BELOW *The Garden of the Villa Rotonda near Vicenza, designed by Andrea Palladio about 1550-51. Palladio's architectural style has since been copied all over the world.*

of this kind of work. Even the flowers stand out like sculptural reliefs, being massed in colours and slightly raised in an evergreen setting above the gravel.

While these magnificent gardens were being created in the west and north of Italy, Andrea Palladio was filling the Veneto in the east, in the declining years of Venice, with elegant villas. The gardens of almost all of these consisted of a flat or slightly sloping rectangular walled enclosure laid out in front of the house, the main feature of which was a central road or vista leading from the gate to the portico of the house, often prolonged on the far side of the road to enhance the effect of the vista when looked at from the house. They tended to be old-fashioned, some having old-style fountains. The Villa Barbaro at Maser, the garden of which was entirely enclosed by the house and the hillside, showed more Roman influence than others and in consequence, though small, gives an impression of grandeur not felt in other Veneto gardens, springing primarily from the contrast of the pool and fountain with the dark green of the hillside above. The Villa Brenzone at San Vigilio, which was famous in the sixteenth century, is one of the smaller gardens, but occupies a site of exquisite beauty looking over the lake. Another survival from that time is

the Villa Cuzzano at Grezzana, the main feature of which is a superb original parterre in front of the house. The Donà della Rose at Valsonzibio, laid out in 1669, is a green garden without flowers and differs from others in that it is larger and more elaborately designed, taking advantage of a striking hillside site to provide wonderful vistas.

Gardens in the Marche on the Adriatic coast of Italy tended to be very conservative, early modes persisting there long after they had vanished elsewhere. The Villa Miralfiore near Pesaro is not unique in possessing a sixteenth-century box parterre of simple design in the

flat area round the house, but the edges of clipped thyme surrounding surviving parterres at the Villa Montegallo at Ancona, dating from 1592, are straight out of the pages of the 'Hypnerotomachia'. The sunny terraces of this villa are later in date than the parterres, being of Baroque design. This garden possesses a building which appears to be unique in Italy, a hermitage ostensibly occupied by friars and decorated on the walls with life-size pictures of friars going about their work. The water-tricks at the Villa Mosca near Pesaro, which has a series of terraces amid woodland, have been carefully preserved and it is still possible for the unwary visitor, taking a seat to admire the view, to find himself suddenly clamped to it and sprayed with water.

As time went on the situation changed. The initiative in garden design was to pass in the seventeenth century to the French, and the Italian gardens began to fade into history. The great flowering of the human spirit, which the rediscovery of the ancient classics induced in Italy, spread to all European countries. The gardens that it inspired in Italy were the equal in beauty of any hitherto seen anywhere else in the world. There is an air about them, as with all Italian art of this time, which draws those who have seen them to look again and again to recreate their magic, even though it may be only by the turning over of the pages of photograph albums of almost-forgotten holidays and savouring again in memory the scent of the lemons, the rustle of the bays and cypresses, and the pleasant music and sparkle of the fountains in the sunshine.

LEFT *Part of the gardens of Isola Bella on Lake Maggiore seen against the background of the distant Alps, which set off admirably the formality of the low-clipped box-edging, the larger clipped shrubs and the neat cypresses which are the principal constituents of the garden.*

BELOW *The magnificent box parterres of the Villa Ruspoli at Vignanello, which are still in the form in which they were made in 1612 A.D. and illustrate the comparatively simple geometrical designs used in Italian Renaissance gardens.*

115

9
Flowing Waters

Iram indeed is gone with all its Rose
And Jamshyd's Sev'n-ringed Cup where no one knows;
But still the Vine her ancient Ruby yields
And still a Garden by the Water blows.

Omar Khayyam

As the Renaissance in Italy was gathering momentum, the news came through to Europe in 1492 that, by sailing west from Spain, new land could be reached. It was not Cathay itself, but Cathay could not be far away. Columbus, the bringer of this news, had, in fact, made a landfall in the Bahamas and subsequent exploration revealed the existence, not of the desired Cathay with all its fabulous wealth, but of the wholly new continents of north and south America, which were, in the event, to prove even greater sources of riches. In 1519 Hernando Cortes and his small band of conquistadors pushed their way into Mexico and tumbled the Aztec empire into the dust. Founded on a religion requiring human sacrifice, the civilization they destroyed had a facet of extreme savagery, but at the same time there was artistic development of a high order and a love of beautiful things, including flowers, that was totally opposite to that aspect of their life.

The capital of the Aztec empire, Tenochtitlan, was approached by a causeway between lakes Chalco and Texcoco. As they moved along this causeway, the conquerors passed through Iztapalapan, which was under the governorship of the emperor Montezuma's brother. They were amazed by what they saw.

W. H. Prescott in the *Conquest of Mexico* says:

'The pride of Iztapalapan was its celebrated gardens. They covered an immense tract of land; were laid out in regular squares, and the paths intersecting them were bordered with trellises, supporting creepers and aromatic shrubs that loaded the air with their perfumes. The gardens were stocked with fruit-trees, imported from distant places, and with the gaudy family of flowers which belonged to the Mexican flora, scientifically arranged, and growing luxuriantly in the equable temperature of the tableland. The natural dryness of the atmosphere was counteracted by means of aqueducts and canals that carried water into all parts of the grounds . . . The most elaborate piece of work was a huge reservoir of stone . . . sixteen hundred paces in circumference.'

LEFT *Outdoor living in the days of the Mughals portrayed in a miniature showing a meal being prepared under tall trees and flowering shrubs.*

ABOVE *An impression by a nineteenth-century French artist, D. Lancelot, of an Aztec garden, which he has named 'Paradis de Quetzalcoatl': from* Histoire des Jardins *by Arthur Mangin (Tours, 1883).*

The Bagh i Vafa or 'Garden of Fidelity' made by the Mughal Emperor Babur at Kabul about 1508; this miniature from his memoirs shows water from a grand cascade in the background passing into a marble tank from which four streams issue.

necessary to build strong, high, cemented walls of unbelievable size, going from one mountain to another, with an aqueduct at the top which came out at the highest point of the park.'

The water went into a reservoir, from which it flowed into two basins, one north and one south. From these basins the water cascaded and 'leapt and dashed itself to pieces on the rocks, falling into a garden planted with all the scented flowers of the hot lands, and in this garden it seemed to rain, so very violently was the water smashed on these rocks.' There was a splendid palace in the park and 'the whole of the rest . . . was planted . . . with all kinds of trees and scented flowers.' The ruins of the architectural garden works may still be seen, authenticating Ixtlilxochitl's account.

Nothing is more astonishing about Aztec gardening than their scientific approach to it, which was much in advance of the nation that conquered them. Long before the botanic garden was established at Padua, the Aztec emperors had been making such gardens, a notable example being that of which the Aztec writer Tezozomoc speaks, or which Montezuma I (ancestor of Cortes' Montezuma) made when he conquered the 'hot lands' of the West and made a garden of the plants discovered there in his own home grounds. Within a few years of the Spanish conquest, unfortunately, all these gardens had vanished from the scene and remain no more than a memory of something that, in its time, captured and held its share of beauty, even though it was against a terrible background. In 1532 Francisco Pizarro attacked and conquered the Inca empire in what is now Peru. Here, too, although under less favourable conditions than in Mexico, gardens had been established. Garcilaso de la Vega mentions a favourite residence of the Inca princes at Yucay where, 'in this delicious valley, locked up within the friendly arms of the sierra, which sheltered it from the rude breeze of the east, and refreshed by gushing fountains and streams of running water, they built the most beautiful of their palaces.' This, too, and other Inca gardens like it, went down under the heel of the conqueror, so that in a few years it was as if it had never been.

The gardens of the Aztecs and Incas, with no past of which we have any knowledge, a future which suddenly ended, and no connection in style with that of any other country, were an isolated phenomenon, but their making was prompted no less by a love for beauty and a feeling of unity with nature than the others. Indeed, the fact that the making of gardens arose among a group of mankind in an isolated position is itself evidence of the deep-seated nature of the urge from the unconscious that prompts men, whatever the circumstances, always to seek to recreate the ancient paradise.

In the excitement of exploring America, those who followed Columbus forgot Cathay, but on the other side of the world very near Cathay, in Xipangu (Japan) the tea-house garden and the tour garden were at this time beginning to evolve. The Chinese garden continued in its ancient forms unchanged though dynasties rose and fell. Further west in India there had been some falling away from the standards of the earlier princedoms. In

When they got to Tenochtitlan, the amazement of the Spaniards increased. Built out on causeways over the lake like a western Venice, with floating artificial islands used as nursery gardens around it, the flat roofs of the buildings were covered with flower-gardens and there were terraced gardens between the houses. On the other side of Lake Texcoco from Tenochtitlan was the kingdom of Texcoco, reigned over by King Nezahualcoyotl. His favourite residence was at Tezcotzinco, the gardens of which the Aztec historian Ixtlilxochitl described in his *Historia Chichimeca*:

'These parks and gardens were decorated with rich and sumptuously ornamented summerhouses with their fountains, their irrigation channels, their canals, their lakes and their bathing places, and wonderful mazes, where he had a great variety of flowers planted and trees of all kinds, foreign and brought from distant parts . . . and the water intended for the fountains, pools and channels for watering the flowers and trees in this park came from its spring: to bring it, it had been the north-west of the Indian sub-continent, however, remarkable gardens were made again in the sixteenth and seventeenth centuries, stemming from the old gardens of Persia. That country lies astride the trade route from east to west, but this is also the route of the conquerors. In 1220 Genghis Khan and his Mongols swept out of central Asia and, in the course of one of the bloodiest campaigns ever fought, burnt the Persian towns and slaughtered most of their populations. The great Timur (Tamerlane) conquered Persia again, but his reign was kinder. He became a patron of the arts and Bokhara and Samarkand flourished under his rule. Bokhara had already in the ninth century enjoyed a time of prosperity under the emir Ishmael when it had been encircled with villas and palaces with orchards; under Timur that prosperity was renewed. His first care was to augment the water supply and for this purpose he made eleven large canals to serve the environs of the town. There were said to be no less than two thousand pleasure houses on the banks of one of these alone.

Samarkand was even more luxurious, as Timur made it his capital. The area devoted to gardens was very large. On the east side was the Bagh i Dilkusha, 'the garden that cheers the heart', which was joined to the town by a long avenue. Another magnificent palace garden was famed for its fine poplar avenue, which gave it the name of the 'Poplar Garden'. The favourite place of all, however, which Timur called his 'hermitage', was the Bagh i Blisht, the 'Paradise Garden'. Sheref-ed-din, Timur's biographer, describes the palace as made entirely of the famous white marble of Tabriz. It was built on a terrace with a deep trench around it, with two bridges leading over into the garden, which had a park for wild animals alongside it. Another description adds that the garden was enclosed by a high wall which was 'a full league around' and that it was full of fruit trees of all kinds. There were six great tanks, part of 'a great system of water, passing from end to end' of the garden. Five avenues of trees had been planted, 'leading from one tank to the next', these avenues having been paved 'to look like platforms'. Smaller roads led off from these avenues and, in the centre of the garden, a hill had been created 'built up artificially of clay', which had on its summit a small level space 'enclosed by a palisade of wooden stakes', within which enclosed area there were 'several very beautiful palaces'.

An eye-witness account of one of the gardens of Samarkand was given by Ruy Gonzales de Clavijo, who was sent as ambassador to Timur's court in 1403-06: 'The ambassadors', he said, 'went to see a chamber which the Lord [Timur Beg] had set apart for feasting and the company of his women. In front of it there was a great garden, in which were many shady trees and all kinds of fruit trees, with channels of water flowing amongst them. The garden was so large, that great numbers of people might enjoy themselves there in the summer with great delight, near the fountains and under the shade of trees.'

The Timurid empire went down under a welter of conflicting candidates for the succession at the end of the fifteenth century, but there emerged from the melee a man of conspicuous intelligence and gifts who was

ABOVE *The Emperor Babur giving instructions for the alteration of the course of a stream in the Bagh i Kilan, or 'Great Garden'.*

NEXT PAGE *Jahangir's tomb in the Dilkusha Bagh, Nur Jahan's 'Garden of Delight', now known as the Shah Dara.*

also a lover of gardens. Zehir ed din Muhammed, who was called Babur (the 'Tiger') was one of the competitors for Timur's shoes and twice for a short time occupied Samarkand, but when it became obvious that he could not retain the throne permanently he gave up the idea and established himself at Kabul. From this base among the Afghan mountains he made sorties into India and in 1526, at the fifth attempt, decisively defeated the Sultan of Delhi and established himself as the first Mughal (i.e. Mongol) emperor of India. Babur produced a set of memoirs which in clarity and interest rival Caesar's 'Commentaries', but he was more than a great prose-writer: he was a poet in the Persian language and an accomplished critic, being devoted to learning and art. He was a powerful man physically, described as 'a desperate warrior' and 'resolute and jovial drinker of wine', but he was also 'a great admirer of beautiful prospects and fine flowers'.

Babur grew up in an atmosphere of Persian art and culture endowed with a love of poetry and gardens. When he was young, before the days of his battles, he

ABOVE *A miniature of the Emperor Babur, seated in a flower-filled garden, distributing treasure at the conquest of Agra in* A.D. *1525.*

RIGHT *The tomb of Humayun at Delhi; this is built in red sandstone and white marble and set in a beautiful garden that retains the ancient division into four parts.*

had visited Samarkand, where his uncle was ruler. He saw there the gardens that his uncle had laid out and to which he had given such names as 'The Perfect Garden' and 'The Most-Delighting'. These made an indelible impression on his mind. He had also visited Herat in Khorasan which was then a great cultural centre; here another royal kinsman, the Sultan Husain Baquara, had laid out beautiful gardens. As soon, therefore, as he was settled at Kabul, long before he was emperor, he began to make gardens like those he loved at Samarkand, which he lists in his memoirs. He describes how he made the Bagh i Vafa ('Garden of Fidelity'):

'Opposite to the fort of Adinaphur [south of the Kabul River], to the south on rising ground I formed a great garden in the year 1508 A.D. . . . It overlooks the river, which flows between the fort and the palace . . . I brought plantains and planted them here. They grew

and thrived. The year before I had planted sugar-cane in it, which throve remarkably well . . . It is on an elevated site, enjoys running water, and the climate in the winter season is temperate. In the garden there is a small hillock, from which a stream of water, sufficient to drive a mill, incessantly flows into the garden below. The fourfold field plot of this garden is situated on this eminence. On the south-west part of this garden is a reservoir of water . . . which is wholly planted round with orange-trees; there are likewise pomegranates. All round the piece of water the ground is quite covered with clover. This spot is the very eye of beauty of the garden. At the time when the oranges become yellow, the prospect is delightful.'

The garden had the background to the south of the White Mountain of Nangenhar.

Although each garden was idiosycoratic, Mughal gardens in general had a number of features common to all of them. They were always square or rectangular in shape and, as was customary in the Persian garden, were surrounded by a high wall pierced by a lofty entrance gateway. In the larger gardens there were four such gateways, one in the centre of each wall. The angles of the garden were marked by octagonal pavilions. Almost all the gardens were divided into four by waterways at right-angles to one another, still repeating the ancient pattern of the Garden of Eden: the name 'charbagh' given to any great garden means, in fact, 'four gardens', as divided by the waterways. The main stone or brick-edged canal extended the whole length of the enclosure, the water rushing in a tumult of white foam down carved water-chutes, often flowing at the bottom of these waterfalls into a tank with many small fountains. The side canals of the larger gardens terminated in architectural features, a gateway, a raised platform, a pavilion or a summerhouse, the water being conveyed away underground. The principal pavilion was usually in the centre of the largest sheet of water where the spray of the fountains cooled the air and the roar of the cascades was pleasant to the ear. Avenues were planted around the outer walls and trees were used to emphasize the lines of the garden, the main divisions being cut up into smaller square plots by minor water-courses and filled with fruit trees or flowers. There were, here and there, open squares of turf with large trees at the corners or a central tree, usually a plane or mango tree with a surrounding raised platform of masonry or grass, used as a gathering-place; shady walks and pergolas of vines and flowers completed the scene. Mughal gardens were about 600 by 400 yards in extent, but there were a number larger and in these the flowers were limited to the water-courses, with more avenues of trees to give shade elsewhere.

Babur formed another garden at Kabul, which was named the Bagh i Kilan ('Great Garden'), in the district of Istalif, west of the town. Of this he said:

'On the outside of the garden are large and beautiful spreading plane trees, under the shade of which there are agreeable spots finely sheltered. A perennial stream, large enought to turn a mill, runs through the

TOP *A long view looking up the terraces at the Nishat Bagh, the 'Garden of Gladness', on Lake Dal in Kashmir.*

ABOVE *A junction of water-channels in the garden of Humayun's tomb, showing the narrowness of the channels, reflecting the needs of the mountain districts to which the Mughals were accustomed rather than those of the hotter gardens of the plains.*

garden; and on its banks are planted plane and other trees. Formerly this stream flowed in a winding and crooked course, but I ordered its course to be altered according to a regular plan, which added greatly to the beauty of the place . . . On the lower skirts of the hills is a fountain named Kwajeh seh yaran [Kwajeh, 'three friends'] around which there are three species of trees: above the fountain are many beautiful plane trees, which yield a pleasant shade. On two sides of the fountain, on small eminences at the bottom of the hills, there are a number of oak trees . . . In front of this fountain, towards the plain, there are many spots covered with the flowering arghwan tree [*Bauhinia variegata*] . . . I directed the fountain to be built around with stone and formed a cistern of lime and mortar twenty feet square. On the four sides of the fountain, a fine level platform was constructed.'

When the arghwan was in flower, Babur thought this garden incomparable.

When Babur conquered the Hindus he fixed his capital in the plains at Agra. He did not like the flat country, which was so unlike the mountains to which he was accustomed that he felt at first that it would be impossible to make a garden there. When, however, he is expressing his disgust at the flatness, heat, strong winds and dust of the plains he describes a garden he made there using much stone and water to achieve coolness. He does not mention its name but it has been thought that he was probably referring to the Ram Bagh at Agra on the Jumna, which is the earliest garden of the Mughals to survive until modern times, although shorn of much of its beauty. Another garden at Agra made in Babur's time was the Zuhara Bagh, which was noteworthy for a great well 220 feet in circumference, the garden having sixty wells in all.

Four miles south of Delhi is one of the greatest architectural monuments of the Mughals, the tomb of Babur's weak successor Humayun, who succeeded him in 1531. The garden surrounding the tomb still preserves the original plan, but the foursquare design is not picked out by broad canals: the main water-courses are only two feet wide, the water being distributed to the rest of the garden by a labyrinth of little channels. These are connected by tiny carved chutes down which the water ripples like mountain rivulets, the whole being fed by larger chutes through which the water rushes in from wells outside. The tiny water-courses are a feature of the earlier Mughal gardens, later gardens having larger ones, probably because experience taught them that what was adequate for the mountains was not sufficient for the hotter plains.

Humayun's successor Akbar, who reigned from 1556 to 1605, was the opposite of his predecessor, being a strong man and a conqueror. He was the first Mughal emperor to enter Kashmir, the state which became the great love of these emperors and where they made a number of gardens. Akbar made the first of these, the Nasim Bagh, on the shores of Lake Dal, not far from the town of Srinagar, which he founded. Little remains of this, so that its original plan is unknown, but it took its name from the cool breezes which could always be felt there, it being a terrace garden in an open position above the lake. Akbar, buried in a magnificent tomb at Sikandra, near Agra, surrounded by a garden of orthodox 'charbagh' design, gave way in his turn to another great emperor, Jahangir, whose empress, Nur Jahan, was equally renowned.

As a young man, Jahangir made several gardens at Udaipur. One is of interest because it appears to have been made on a plan exactly the same as the garden pattern used in some Persian carpets. In these the water from the lake flows into the space surrounding the design. The centre is occupied by a small pavilion which in the real garden would be of marble and probably house the musicians. There are platforms on which to sit and enjoy this and also the beauty of the flowers. Surrounding the garden is another platform, which would also be of marble, and beds in which trees would be planted. Pavilions on the four sides look out over the lake. There was also a zenana courtyard garden where geometric flower-beds panelled by slabs of marble surrounded a central tank; four cypresses marked the corners and there were flowers in pots enclosed by a perforated marble rail.

Across the Ravi, five miles north of Lahore, is the Dilkusha Bagh, Nur Jahan's 'Garden of Delight', now known as the Shah Dara, where Jahangir is buried. This garden, entered through a fine courtyard, is very large, the tomb being in the centre. The building lacks a dome

TOP *A view from about halfway up the terraces of the Nishat Bagh looking down to the pavilion and the lake and mountains beyond. In later European gardens in the French style it would have been considered wrong to interrupt the vista with a building in the way the placing of the pavilion in this garden blocks out part of the view.*

ABOVE *A cascade pouring down from the 18-foot wall of the top terrace of the Nishat Bagh into a transverse canal with many fountains.*

ABOVE *The final cascade, with a 20-foot drop into the lower pool, at the Chasma Shahi garden in Kashmir, made in 1632 by Ali Mardan Khan for Shah Jahan.*

RIGHT *The garden of Shah Jahan's Shalamar Bagh at Lahore, seen from the zenana terrace above the Emperor's throne, looking across the central pool with its large number of fountains and marble platform reached by a causeway. Beyond the two pavilions the water cascades on to the lower terrace and passes through the pavilion in the distance.*

and for this reason does not seem to match up with the grandeur of the garden. There is an interlocking pattern of raised causeways, canals and tanks, in which bricks are beautifully used. The narrow canals are bordered by long parterres, the raised tanks forming eight large platforms around the mausoleum. Nur Jahan also made a garden at Agra for the tomb of her father I'timad ud Daulah. This, unlike the Shah Dara, was small, four tanks on a central platform supplying the customary four water-courses. Although the garden is small, the tomb itself is one of the most beautiful of all garden tombs.

Though not created by Jahangir himself, another great garden, the Nishat Bagh, the 'Garden of Gladness', was created in his reign on Lake Dal, probably by Asaf Khan. In the lovely setting of mountains and water, this garden rises in twelve grand imposing terraces, each dedicated to a sign of the zodiac. It is the gayest and most spectacular of all the Mughal gardens. The stream rushes down carved cascades and there are fountains in every tank and water-course with many flowers in the beds. The garden consists of two main divisions, each of the terraces being slightly higher than the other, except for the zenana terrace (for the ladies) at the top, which has a larger wall eighteen feet high across the full width of the garden. The main canal is thirteen feet wide and eight inches deep and there are a number of stone and marble thrones, one across the head of almost every waterfall. Avenues of cypress and fruit trees mark out the lines of the garden and there are parterres on two of the terraces. There is a pavilion in the centre of the lowest

terrace which to European eyes, accustomed to the uncluttered sweep of the Renaissance perspective down through the terraces, seems to mar the scene.

At the far end of Lake Dal there had existed for many centuries a place called 'Shalamar', which means 'Abode of Love'. On this site Jahangir, helped by his son Shah Jahan, built a garden which was called Farah Baksh, the 'Bestower of Joy', but has come to be known by the older name of Shalamar Bagh. Francois Bernier, who was physician to the Mughal court, described this garden not long after it had been made.

'The most admirable of all these gardens is that of the King, which is called Chahlimar. From the lake, one enters it by a great canal, bordered with great green

turfs. This canal is above five hundred common paces long, and runs 'twixt two large allies of poplars: it leadeth to a great Cabinet [Pavilion] in the midst of the garden, where begins another canal far more magnificent, which runs with a little rising into the end of the garden. This canal is paved with large freestone, its sloping side covered with the same; and in the midst of it there is a long row of jets of water.'

Many other jets of water, he concluded, 'do spring up: and this canal ends at another great cabinet, which is almost like the first.'

The garden is about 250 yards wide and 600 yards long, being divided like all royal Mughal gardens into the outer public part, the emperor's private protion,

and the zenana garden for the ladies of the household. Bernier begins his description from the lake as he doubtless entered that way but it is more natural to follow the flow of the water. At the top of the garden a small river is diverted into a broad shallow canal leading to a wide rectangular basin in which the main black marble pavilion is situated, surrounded on all sides by water and the spray of fountains. This pavilion is the second 'cabinet' mentioned by Bernier. Seen through the vistas, it draws the rest of the garden together. Below it, the garden broadens and the slope drops in small contrived steps until the Diwan i Am, the 'Hall of Public Audience', is reached, where the emperor sat above the water when such audiences were being held. A wonderful effect was achieved in this garden at night,

as in other Mughal gardens, by the provision of lights behind the waterfall.

Close by the old direct road to Srinagar was made another garden, the Achabal Bagh. Jahangir described this garden in his memoirs of 1620 as a 'piece of Paradise'. Bernier was impressed with the water in it. In 1665 he wrote that what 'most adorns it is a Fountain, the water whereof diffuseth itself on all sides, round about a [pavilion] and into the garden by a hundred canals. It breaks out of the Earth, as if by some violence it ascended up from the bottom of a Well, and that with such abundance that as might make it to be called a River rather than a fountain. The water of it is admirably good, and so cold that one can hardly endure to hold one's hand in it.' The coldness was not surprising as the supply was a mountain spring that broke out naturally at the foot of a hill, the pavilion being built over it. Little remains of this building now. From the pavilion the water spilled into a reservoir whence it tumbled in a fine cascade which is the main feature of the garden. The waterfall was flanked by two summerhouses and below were wide pools with fountains and an island pavilion. Below again, water passed under a larger pavilion and down the length of the garden to fall once more at a final change of level. There were chutes on either side down which the water rushed into long canals brimming level with the ground. Bernier concluded his account by saying that there was 'a very high Cascata of water, which by its fall maketh a great Nape of thirty or forty paces long, which hath an admirable effect, especially in the night, when under the Nape there is put a great

ABOVE *The black marble pavilion which Shah Jahan built in the zenana garden at the Shalamar Bagh, Kashmir, about A.D. 1630. Surrounded on all sides by the play of fountains, it is one of the most beautiful creations in a Mughal garden.*

BELOW *The main pavilion at the garden of Achabal Bagh seen looking upstream from the canal below it.*

number of little lamps fitted in holes purposely made in the wall, which maketh a curious show.' Fast-moving water sparkling in the sunlight is the keynote of Achabal, conveying a sense of urgent movement not so marked in other gardens and absent almost altogether in the Mughal gardens of the plains.

The Vernag Bagh, which was rather more remote and whose name is derived from snake worship, is also fed by a spring which comes up in a deep pool and is the source of the Jhelum river. The pool is enclosed by an octagonal tank, with arcaded recesses all round. The water is led off from the pool to the north by a large canal twelve feet wide and 1,000 feet long to feed the river and a second smaller canal forms the crossing axis of the garden. Although the buildings have mainly disappeared and the design remaining is simple, merely the tank and a long canal, the garden still has much charm. The background hills are clothed with graceful deodars, setting off the arcaded court below, the blue-green pool full of great fish, and the immensely long canal, which holds a surprise for those who, at the bottom end, come suddenly upon the attractive diagonal view up an adjoining valley. The entrance itself is also arresting as the visitor, passing through a low dark arch, comes suddenly out into the light and the view of the pool. This garden was supposed to be the favourite of Jahangir and Nur Jahan; possibly because of its remoteness. Jahangir said of it in his memoirs that 'in the whole of Kashmir there is no sight of such beauty and enchanting character.'

There was a third garden fed by hill springs which was much admired in Jahangir's time. The Wah Bagh at Hasan Abdal, Rawalpindi, covered a space of about a quarter of a mile in length and half that in breadth, the enclosing walls now being in ruins. There were two large stone-walled tanks at the eastern end, the western end being occupied by parterres divided by a building. Gardens in Kashmir in Jahangir's time contained the two extremes of garden-making by the Mughals, the merry joyousness of the cascades of the Nishat Bagh contrasting with the quiet air of controlled leisure and repose of the Shalamar Bagh, the most subtle and romantic of royal gardens.

After his father's death, Shah Jahan became emperor in 1628 but there was no break in garden-making. Dara Shukoh, Shah Jahan's eldest son, made two memorable gardens in Kashmir. That at Bijbehara occupied a site on both sides of the Jhelum River. Traces of the parterres and canals may still be seen, but the garden fell into ruin, the site being marked now mainly by the great *chenars* (Eastern plane trees - *Platanus orientalis*) and the remains of a bridge and pavilion. The design was clearly on a grand scale. Peri Mahal, the other garden, lay across a spur of rock on a remote site on a hill immediately south of Lake Dal. It is now in ruins and overgrown, but five terraces may still be seen and traces of a number of fountains and tanks. This must have been one of the most beautiful of the Mughal gardens from its superb site looking out over the lake with the hills behind it.

In 1632 Ali Mardan Khan laid out a Kashmir garden for Shah Jahan, the Chasma Shahi ('Royal Spring'). It was not a large garden, and has been altered from its

A view through the archway of the main pavilion at the garden of Achabal Bagh across the fountains to the smaller pavilion; this is set on an island reached by raised stone causeways.

original design, which was strongly axial. The spring gushed up through a lotus basin in the floor of the upper pavilion and was led down by a little cascade and a canal to fill a wide rectangular tank, furnished, unusually for a Mughal garden, with a single jet. The remainder was rather more spectacular. The water passed through a second pavilion standing on a wall 20 feet high, and down a central chute to a tank and fountain on the lower level. This garden also commands a beautiful view across the lake to the mountains.

The next year, 1633, Shah Jahan made another Shalamar Bagh at Lahore, having the task, before he could begin on the garden, of constructing a canal to bring the water of the Ravi to it. There were three terraces, dropping down from the south about fifteen feet each time. The first and third of the terraces were laid out as standard 'charbaghs', but the middle terrace contained a great reservoir which was 200 feet across and was the principal feature of the garden. In this reservoir there were originally 152 fountains, and more than a hundred still remain. In the centre was a marble platform reached by a causeway. From the reservoir the water passed through the pavilion and cascaded down a broad carved marble chute just beyond which, at the bottom, was the emperor's white marble throne. A double path all round, with a flower parterre, was paved with the beautiful Lahore brickwork; the cascades were lit from behind at night by candles placed in pigeonholes which during the day held vases of flowers.

North-west of Shahjahanabad, close by the Grand Trunk Road at Badli Sarai, one of Shah Jahan's wives, A'Azzd un Nisa, made a third Shalamar Bagh in 1646-50 which was modelled on the orginal in Kashmir. The central canal was eighteen feet wide and ran the full length of the garden. There was a fall of nine feet between the upper terrace and the next, the change being marked by a complex of buildings with rows of fountains. Below was an octagonal reservoir in the middle of the garden and then the bottom terrace.

Magnificent gardens were made at the Forts of Lahore, Delhi and Agra. Jahangir's Quadrangle in the Lahore Fort was a large open space with a central reservoir, many fountains and a marble platform in the middle. Paen Bagh at the same fort was smaller, having a central brick platform and water tank with hexagonal pattern red brick paving, small grassy sub-divisions each side and trees and pools. The two major gardens at the Red Fort at Delhi, the Hayat Baksh ('Life-Giving Garden') and Mahtab Bagh ('Moonlight Garden'), both enclosed by rows of cypresses, formed one grand design. Both were particularly sensitive creations. The Hayat Baksh was planted with crimson and purple flowers and the Mahtab Bagh with paler flowers, jasmine, tuberoses, lilies and narcissus. The latter has disappeared, but much of the former remains. In this a central pavilion stood in a pool full of fountains. Four canals terminating in pavilions radiated from the pool. Each of these canals had three rows of fountains; there were 49 inside the central pool and 112 on the four sides, each plated with silver. Again, candles used to be placed at night in niches behind the cascades. Along the

river terrace was a water parterre, terminating in a beautiful pavilion. Agra Fort also possessed two principal gardens: the Machchi Barwan ('Fish Square') in which the fish have gone and the pool is grassed over, although it is still a magnificent garden because of the beautiful buildings and the outlook over the surrounding countryside; and the Anguri Bagh, which is a Mughal garden of the standard type described earlier.

The Taj Mahal at Agra, built by Shah Jahan in memory of his wife Mumtaz Mahal,thought by many to be the most beautiful building ever made by man, has been described as a white marble jewel in a sandstone casket, the mausoleum itself being the climax of a complex and beautiful garden layout. It is in an

LEFT ABOVE *The Taj Mahal at Agra, built by Shah Jahan in memory of his wife Mumtaz Mahal. Few will need an introduction to this building, possibly the most beautiful thing ever made by man, which seems to float above its reflection in the canal. The garden is a 'charbagh', this picture being taken from the junction of the four canals in the centre of the garden.*

LEFT *Jahangir's Quadrangle in the Fort at Lahore.*

ABOVE *Looking out from the Red Fort at Delhi over one of the canals of the former Hayat Baksh ('Life-Giving') garden. This garden, enclosed by rows of cypresses, formed a grand design with the Mahtab Bagh ('Moonlight Garden').*

immense enclosure, entered through a sandstone gatehouse, walled on three sides and open on the fourth to the river. The canal runs the length of the garden, the building being on a platform at the end. It is flanked by two other red sandstone buildings, an assembly hall and a mosque; four smaller sandstone pavilions mark the corners of the river platform. There were many parterres full of flowers and a fine raised tank in the centre of the garden with two more sandstone pavilions on the cross axis. The whole has a superb unity with many subtly planned details. It is the climax and pinnacle of Mughal gardening. A few gardens were made in the time of Aurungzeb, who

followed Shah Jahan as emperor in 1658, but only one could bear comparison with the earlier Mughal gardens. This was the garden made by Fadai Khan, Aurungzeb's foster-brother, at Pinjaur, near Simla. It was made on a magnificent site looking out across a fertile valley ringed by hills. Unlike most Mughal gardens, entrance is from the top. There is a strong central water-course, with impressive falls between each of the seven terraces. When the water is flowing and the lights are burning under the cascades the whole presents a magnificent sight, but the garden is somewhat bleaker and more open than other Mughal gardens.

In the reign of Akbar, Persia itself, away to the west from the land of the Mughals, had come under a strong ruler, the renowned Shah Abbas, who succeeded to the throne in October 1588. Persia was, at that time, in a very weakened state, the Ottoman Turks to the west and the Usbeks to the east having made considerable inroads into Persian territory. In 1598 Shah Abbas defeated the Usbeks and immediately moved his capital to Isfahan; four years later he also defeated the Ottoman Turks and regained the territory they had seized. With peace ensured, Shah Abbas turned his attention to civic improvement, laying out Isfahan anew so that it became one of the world's most beautiful cities. His works were grouped around a splendid rectangular space called the Maidan, which was about a quarter of a mile long by 150 yards wide. There were avenues around it and an encircling two-storied colonnade. One of the grand boulevards was the Tshehar-Bagh ('Street of the Four Gardens'). Between the Maidan and the Tshehar-Bagh was the wide square of the palace precincts, embracing various pavilions with gardens around them, among which the most noteworthy was the Tshihil-sutun with its forty pillars. The interior decoration of the building recalled the golden trees of earlier times. 'Over the whole field of ornamentation', says Chardin, a contemporary French visitor to Persia, 'there is a smooth raised surface, kept in place by strongly-rooted trees, on which are leaves and bunches of flowers. In the branches are set bright birds of curious appearance.' Chardin was impressed with the quantity of water flowing in the palaces and gardens, which were arranged in long avenues and had beds filled with flowers. One octagonal pavilion intrigued him because water fell down it from the terrace so that 'if one stretches a hand out of the window, it is at once covered with water.'

The Tshehar-Bagh itself mounted up by low wide terraces, with a canal in the middle which on each terrace widened into cistern, both cistern and canal being bordered by stone paving, so wide that two men could ride side by side. The tanks were of different sizes and shapes, the water falling in cascades from terrace to terrace. The ends of the street were blocked off by two pavilions set crossways. Similar pavilions at the side gave entrance to the gardens off the street, the 'Mulberry Garden', the 'Garden of the Vineyard', the 'Garden of the Barberries' and another, each of which had a gilded middle pavilion, and which were the four gardens from which the street took its name.

Of similar gardens made outside the town, one is still

recognizable, although in ruins. Ashraf, near Astrabad, on a slope of the Elburz mountains, dates from the time of Shah Abbas. Sarre described it in the seventeenth century:

'There are seven perfectly regular rectangular gardens, not arranged to correspond with one another according to any main design, but simply placed side by side as would be most convenient on the land they occupied. The gardens are separately walled in, each with its chief buildings arranged as terraces, dropping towards the north and north-west. Through a forecourt one arrives at the head garden, the Bagh-i-Shah, or Shah's Garden. This is the largest, about a quarter of a mile in length and upwards of 200 yards in width, and rises in ten terraces. A wide canal between walls cuts through from one terrace to another, falling down the middle in cascades, and streaming through the pavilion which overlooks the open pillared hall on the fifth terrace. On this, wider than the others, the canal broadens out into a rectangular pond enclosed by four flower beds, with an arm of the canal separating them crosswise.'

Most of the other gardens were laid out in the same way, including the one at the top with its domed pavilion, and the Bagh-i-Sahib-Zeman ('Garden of the Lord of the Age'), whose grand pavilion was built like a palace. The harem had its own home garden with an unusually high wall around it. There were high terraces to the east of the main garden.

Shah Abbash used the shores of the Caspian Sea as a winter retreat, making a stone causeway along it to give access to the garden retreats he made there, of which there were at least six. These gardens of the Mazanderan coastal strip were in the main of orthodox design, except for the Bagh-i-Shah (Royal garden), the 'Bahr or Eram' (the 'Sea of Paradise'), which had a very large lake with an island and bridge, and a separate pavilion in the lake, but detail of these gardens is lacking. Detail is also lacking for gardens made at Shiraz, which lay on either side of a broad avenue, each being entered through a domed pavilion, which caused one observer to complain of monotony. The day of renewal of gardens at Shiraz was still, however, to come. What Shah Abbas did for Isfahan in the seventeenth century, the Shahs of the Qajar Dynasty did for Shiraz when, at the end of the eighteenth century, they moved to that place.

Marie Luise Gothein commented, in her *History of Garden Art*, on the Persian garden; in the following quotation she describes its nature as having been unchanged over the years:

'Though flowers and many kinds of trees and shrubs have in the course of centuries given a different aspect to the gardens of western Asia, there is but little change in the general scheme of the picture. The civilization of other races seems only like a new graft of an old stem, and the scion has grown in obedience to the impulse communicated by the old sap.'

In that area men continued to make the old Paradise as if in obedience to an unalterable law.

LEFT *The garden of Eram at Shiraz, Persia, showing typical narrow canal and roses.*

TOP *The canal in the Taj Mahal garden looking from the Taj Mahal to the sandstone gatehouse in the distance.*

ABOVE *Tall cypresses and rose in pots in the Khalili garden, Shiraz.*

133

10
Parterres and Princes

A garden in old days with hanging walls,
Fountains and tanks, and rose-banked terraces,
Girdled by grey pavilions and the sweep
Of stately palace-fronts . . .

Sir Edwin Arnold

When, in 1495, Charles VIII of France marched into Italy his political gains were ephemeral but there was nevertheless a lasting outcome of his adventure. He was so impressed with the cultural achievements he saw that when he returned to France he brought back with him twenty-two Italian artists and a quantity of art treasures, including sculpture, establishing them at Amboise on the Loire. Thus began the French Renaissance: many Frenchmen in the ensuing years went off to Italy to study the new ideas. Charles resolved to rebuild Amboise but died before much could be done. Louis XII, his successor, transferred the court from Amboise to Blois, twenty miles or so up-river. Here there had been a small mediaeval garden, no more than a narrow strip originally, which had been enlarged and was now converted to the lowest parterre of a garden of three terraces. Renaissance ideas did not, however, make much impact. The terraces were each of them separate enclosed gardens and there were no connecting steps. The central terrace, to which a gallery ran from the house, was the principal pleasure garden, being surrounded by wooden galleries covered with verdure and with a central pavilion. The beds were enclosed with latticed railings and there were several smaller gardens.

About the time the Villa Madama was being built, 1516-20, when Francis I had succeeded Louis XII, Cardinal Amboise began work on the garden of the castle of Gaillon on the Seine above Rouen. As at Blois there were a series of terraces, of which the middle one, reached through a large courtyard with a lovely Venetian fountain, was the principal garden, above

which stood an orchard on the higher terrace. The beds were bordered with box, the corners being planted with low-growing trees. Some contained flowers, while others were filled with slate or terracotta. Where Italian gardens had statuary, that of Gaillon was ornamented with carved wooden animals, with what was described as 'a masterpiece of joiner's work' in the centre. There were two labyrinths, one rectangular and the other circular. The garden was overlooked by a gallery, which afforded a fine view of it. There was, however, no unity in the design, each terrace being independent and not related either to the others or to the axis of the buildings.

Political events now influenced the garden scene again. The attempt of the Emperor Charles V to attain hegemony in western Europe led to fighting in Italy. Francis I was captured by Charles in 1525 when the latter defeated him at Pavia and was later imprisoned in the Alcazar at Madrid. In the twists and turns of the struggle Charles V's troops looted and sacked Rome in 1527. These events, deplorable in themselves, did not however impede the progress of the Renaissance in Italy very much so far as gardens were concerned; elsewhere they accelerated its spread by the opportunity they gave to Francis I and Charles and their followers to see the admirable gardens that were being created in that country.

Francis I concentrated his earlier garden efforts on Fontainebleau about forty miles south-east of Paris, where he built the castle, which had a large pond at the side. The garden consisted, in effect, of a number of courts, an avenue of four rows of trees with a path on a raised bank running from the old house to the pavilion at the gate, with a garden on the side away from the pond through the middle of which ran a canal. On the other side of the pond adjacent to the castle was the *Jardin des Pins* with another wide canal extending along the facade of the buildings, which included a 'Gallery of Ulysses'. A grotto at the end of this gallery, the first grotto to be made in France, was flanked by

A restored seventeenth-century parterre at the Castle of Angers, a thirteenth-century feudal stronghold built in the form of a pentagon on a rock dominating the River Maine, a tributary of the Loire.

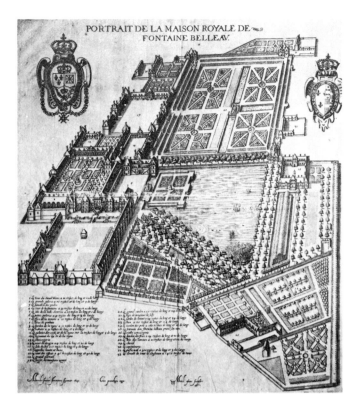

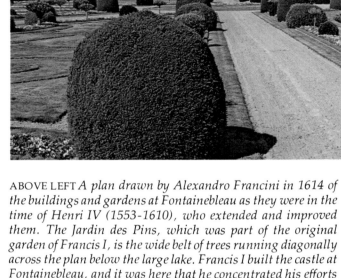

giants, and inside were fountains and effigies of sea-beasts. The flower-garden, which was cut up into four squares, was on the north side of the castle, between the canal and the buildings, the central point of this garden being the statue of 'Diana' later transferred to Versailles. Again there was no sort of order in the arrangement of the various gardens in relation to one another, or any overall unity; even the pergola was not in line with the axis of the garden or the facade.

Between 1524 and 1532 Anne of Montmorency, Constable of France, built a Renaissance castle at Chantilly, some twenty-five miles north of Paris, in the same style as Fontainebleau. Water in tanks or canals, mostly without ornamentation, was everywhere in this garden. Such use of water was a feature of French gardens, which hung on to the moat long after it was needed for defence, and much longer than did other countries, a characteristic that affected garden design. The ground plan was still quite irregular and all the garden components separate as though scattered by chance. This was not the case, however, at Bury, near Blois, where, for the first time, a Renaissance unity between house and garden began to appear. The small castle here was built by Florimont Robert in a square shape with a wide moat, the garden being divided into four parts. The gate led into a grassy court behind which was the kitchen courtyard. The third part was furnished with eight beds with fine geometrical patterns and a central double-shelled fountain in an octagonal basin. The last part was a vegetable garden with a pergola on the wall. Other smaller castles which were now built, of which Dampierre, near Boissy on the Seine, erected in Francis I's time, was the first, were not planned in this way. These were based like Fontainebleau on a large pond and canals, but had also

sets of geometrical beds and orchards, these being separate gardens with their own walls and canals, only crudely linked by paths. One unusual garden was that of Chenonceaux on the river Cher made by Thomas Bohier; it passed from his family to Francis I, then to Henri II, who gave it to his mistress Diane de Poitiers, from whom it was taken by Catherine de Medici. The castle was built partly on piles in the river, and because

of this site the garden had no real unity with the buildings. The parterres were separated by canals both from the castle and the park, and there was another large garden beyond the river which has disappeared.

One of the finest gardens of the day was that of Anet near Dreux built by Philibert de l'Orme for Henri II. Here the house and garden was designed as a whole in a way that rivalled Italian practice. The moat was relegated to the role of an ornament and on either side of the portal were thickets, a subtle compliment to Diane de Poitiers, for whom Anet was made. In compliment to her, too, as Diana the Huntress, were the effigies of a stag with dogs on top of the gate. The central front court was flanked by two others, each with a beautiful central fountain. The garden behind extended the whole width of the three courts, having a rustic gallery on three sides. The two fountains were orientated to the wings of the castle, the central court having a U-shaped front, giving the garden a double centre. There were two 'parks' behind the gardens, separate from one another, in one of which was a semi-circular grotto. As well as providing facilities for falconry and hunting, such parks contained what were virtually gardens where there were avenues with little canals between them, meadows, shrubberies and orchards, as well as warrens and fishponds. Two other gardens, that of Verneuil above the valley of the Oise, and Charleval, between Paris and Rouen, were very similar in style to Anet but both have vanished. All these gardens were basically water-gardens in the mediaeval castle style but had lost most of their sternness, and almost reached the point where the change to the Renaissance garden was complete.

Montargis, about forty miles east of Orleans, became in 1560 the home of Renée d'Este, daughter of Charles XII. She found it mediaeval, a great way behind what she had seen in Italy, and brought in Jacques Androuet du Cerceau to up-date it. On the steep mountainside he set out gardens on two concentric terraces around semi-circular walks and moats. The first terrace was a flower-garden with clipped box ornaments and clumps of trees at the side, the paths being trellised. The second terrace, which was a vegetable and fruit-garden, he bordered with fine wooden pavilions and arched ways. Although definitely Italian in feeling, the garden still had a French air.

After the middle of the sixteenth century French garden plans were always regular, but the shape could, within limits, be varied. There was, for example, a triangular formation at Azay-le-Rideau, a pentagon at Maune, and Rabelais invented a hexagonal plan for his fictional Abbey of Thelemites. It also became necessary for any garden with fashionable pretensions to have a grotto. The great expert on grottoes was Bernard Palissy, the potter and hand craftsman, who constructed many of them. They were made in a variety of situations and designs, the only common characteristic being the grotesque ornamentation. Sometimes they stood separately, in other cases they were in ground-floor rooms, and sometimes they were under terraces or otherwise below ground level. Palissy's *chef d'oeuvre* was made for Catherine de Medici at the Tuileries in Paris. The gardens here were on the flat,

separate from the building and bearing no relation to it. The lack of use of water in this garden made it less interesting than it might have been. Palissy's grotto, which was approached by enamelled bridges, was, however, a masterpiece. Another grotto which became famous was that at Meudon, near Paris, but this was not made by Palissy.

Hermitages were also in fashion. Du Cerceau describes one which Cardinal Bourbon made at Gaillon in the 1560s:

'If you walk from the upper garden through the park partly by terraces, partly by avenues of trees, always keeping your eyes on the lovely valley, you come to a little chapel and house and hermit's rock in the middle of water enclosed in a square basin, and all round it are narrow paths where you can stroll for pleasure. To get there you cross a swing-bridge. Close by you find a little garden, and in it are statues three to four feet in height, standing on a great plinth, depicting all sorts of allegorical subjects, and also several *berceaux* covered with greenery.'

Parterres were growing in complexity. Oliver de Serres, who wrote on agriculture in Henri IV's time, describes in one section of his book the plants which were used in them. The edges were made of 'sweet-scented low bushes' like lavender, thyme, mint, marjoram and others, but box became more popular than these because it was evergreen. The middle of the

ABOVE *An aerial view of the splendid restoration of the sixteenth-century garden at Villandry, on the Loire. The restoration re-creates today the authentic atmosphere of a grand French garden of four centuries ago. The French nation may be justifiably proud of this fine achievement.*

RIGHT *A close-up view of part of the restored sixteenth-century parterres at Villandry.*

parterre was filled with low-growing plants, violets, wallflowers, pinks, heartsease and lilies-of-the-valley. There were higher plants in groups at the edge of the footpaths, cypresses at the corners, and clipped box bushes of many designs. It was essential that the colours and shapes of all the plants harmonized and that there should be a fine view across the beds. In addition to the plants there could be statues, obelisks and pyramids of marble, jasper and porphyry. Claud Mollet, member of a famous gardening family, whose father worked for the French king and whose sons served foreign princes, was also an expert in making parterres, although his ideas differed a little from those of de Serres. He preferred box to cypress, which would not survive the French climate, and grew more tall flowers among the shrubs and round the edges. Du Cerceau's parterres were divided into small squares of geometrical pattern but when the architect du Perac returned to France from a long period of study in Italy he introduced ideas different from all of these. The notions he brought back originated, it is claimed, in

Italy but did not spread there because they were less suitable for the many terrace gardens in that country than they were for the flatter lands of France, where they entirely displaced the older styles.

In the new arrangement all parts of the parterre were included in an overall pattern made up of *comparti – ments de broderie,* a fine example of which was created at the gardens of the Luxembourg in Paris, made for Maria de Medici. Here she tried to have the Boboli garden reproduced, but with only moderate success; the parterre itself, although greatly admired, was quite unlike that at Boboli. In these *compartiments de broderie* there was a sequence of repeated plots all enclosed to form a limited design which suited admirably the wavy lines of the arabesque which was now adopted, replacing entirely the geometrical approach. The patterns were so popular that similar embroidery began to be made for dresses and upholstery, the craft of making these going hand in hand with that of parterre making, often being combined in the same person. Pierre Vallet, who described himself as embroiderer to the king, was one such. He was employed in the royal gardens and compiled a book entitled *Le Jardin du très Chrestien Henry IV,* a beautiful work containing many portraits of flowers. An added boost was given to the fashion by

the influx of plants from the newly discovered lands, which enabled new patterns to be made. The steady inflow of these new plants also stimulated the establishment of botanical collections in gardens, at first mostly in private gardens which later, particularly in the northern countries, developed into botanic gardens.

As France moved into the seventeenth century the parterre came into its own, the great artist in parterre making in this period being Jacques Boyceau, who set out his matured views on the subject in his *Traité de Jardinage* published in 1638. He discarded the idea of several separate gardens in favour of two only, one a kitchen garden and the other a flower-garden. He emphasized that the heights of trees and hedges must be proportional to the rest as must also be the lengths and breadths of paths. He insisted that parterres must have a raised surround, either a gallery, terrace or *berceau* (arched trelliswork forming a covered walk); although symmetry was essential, there must also be variety. Following these precepts he laid out magnificent parterres at the Tuileries. Henri IV also improved Fontainebleau, which he enjoyed as much as its creator, Francis I, had done a hundred years before. He had the parterre enlarged and enclosed with galleries, providing an aviary at one end and furnishing it with choice

139

statues in the Italian style. On the other side of the pond he made a new large square parterre with fountains arranged in pairs at the corners. A broad canal cut through the square and in the middle there was a colossal figure of Father Tiber reposing on a rock.

Henry IV's greatest effort, however, was probably that at Ste. Germain-en-Laye near Paris, where he improved the castle and provided it with perhaps the most complete Renaissance garden made in France, now, unfortunately, completely vanished. There was a descent from the castle to the river by great steps, set in a perfect line, through six terraces. The parterre on the lowest terrace by the river was geometrical in its main dimensions but the beds themselves, among the surrounding hedges, basins and fountains, showed designs of armorial bearings. Gianvittoria Soderini, author of an agricultural treatise, had commented with approval in the sixteenth century on the then new fashion of planting parterres in the form of coats of arms, clocks and human figures so that this practice was not new, but copied from Italian originals. The terraces were furnished with many clipped shrubs cut into figures and there were long rows of grotto rooms with water games. Orpheus was there, with trees and beasts moving about to his lyre, and there were dragon fountains and singing birds. *Giardini segreti* were made near the castle, which commanded a grand view from the upper terrace.

Cardinal Richelieu had a fine garden at his country house at Rueil, with a parterre and fountains in front of the house and avenues, clipped shrubberies, fields, meadows and vineyards elsewhere. One fountain in this garden was shaped like a basilisk; it sent water up to sixty feet and twisted so quickly that the unwary onlooker who ventured too close was sure to be drenched. Next to it was a *citron* garden containing a false Arch of Constantine so realistically painted that birds tried to fly through it. There was a very popular grotto with fine shell work within which water fell like rain and two musketeers (should it not have been three?) fired a water salvo at retreating visitors. A great cascade fell into several basins, each with a fountain and marble steps, and in the last basin a gigantic shell of lead. This cascade was not, however, central, as it would have been in an Italian garden, and the components of the garden were not part of any unified plan.

Gardens in Spain in the earlier part of the sixteenth

century were still heavily influenced by Moorish ideas, the final defeat of the Moors having been accomplished little more than thirty years before. The first building to show a change resulting from Charles V's sight of the Renaissance gardens of Italy was a palace that he built on the Alhambra hill. This was designed by Pedro de Machuca as early as 1526, its design being such that it may have been influenced by the Villa Madama. When he was planning to retire, as he did in 1556, to the monastery of San Jeronimo at San Yuste, Charles made a pleasant terraced garden around his dwelling.

About this time the Duke of Alva was commissioning the making of statues with which, in true Renaissance style, he filled his garden at Alva de Tormes and the garden of Lagunilla not far from Plasencia. Much of the latter garden has been preserved. He had a similar garden at Abadia on the borders of Estremadura which was described in verse by Lope de Vega, the famous dramatist and poet. The Duke of Alcala, in imitation of the Medicis, turned his house into a centre for Platonic discussion. His dependants, the Ribera family, surpassed the efforts of the Duke of Alva in what is now called the Pilatus House. In the double-pillared court of this house were placed four mighty antique goddesses. Above them the busts of twenty-four emperors looked down on the Janus fountain that occupied the centre of the court. Behind on one side of the house was the garden, two sides of which were closed in by buildings, the other two sides being high walls covered with tablets, inscriptions and old carvings. The bordered beds were adorned with baths and fountains and there was a grotto telling the story of Susannah.

ABOVE *An impression by the French nineteenth-century artist D. Lancelot of the parterres of the garden of the Tuileries, Paris, in the time of Henri IV (1553-1610): from* Histoire des Jardins *(Tours, 1883).*

RIGHT *Parterres of the gardens of the Tuileries, Paris, as they are today.*

Charles V asked in his will for a worthy tomb to be provided for him. In pursuance of these wishes, and to render thanksgiving for the victory of St Quentin on August 10th, 1557, Philip II built the Escorial in the foothills of the Guaderrama mountains, about thirty miles north of Madrid, on a slope protected from the north winds. The building, erection of which was commenced in 1563, is a monastery, royal palace and tomb all in one, built in an immense square, and contains a very large court, the Patio de los Evangelistas, in the centre of which is an octagonal temple in which the evangelists look out from their niches over four square basins. A wide esplanade, the Lonja, runs along the northern and western side and there are magnificient views from the terraces. The gardens are full of statues and fountains, many imported from Italy; the whole is completely Renaissance in feeling and execution.

Philip II began to rebuild the Alcazar in Madrid, providing it with an imposing front in the Italian style and using in the garden some half-length figures of Roman emperors presented to him in 1561. He also created a garden, the Casa del Campo, on the other side of the river Manzanares which had many statues and a fine shell fountain. Charles V had made Flemish gardens on the island of Aranjuez in Madrid and these Philip improved, altering them in 1562 into the Renaissance style, providing new avenues, fruit trees, fountains and statues. He also improved the other gardens at Aranjuez, but little of his work remains. In 1628 further work was done on the island garden at Aranjuez. Philip IV invited from Florence Cosimo Lotti, who had been employed on the Boboli gardens and brought with him two gardeners from those gardens. He turned the island garden into a grove richly supplied with fountains and ornaments, and the water-tricks so fashionable in Italian gardens. Lotti also worked at an old shooting box on the Manzanares called El Pardo, applying the latest ideas from Rome, and similar work was done to shooting boxes elsewhere.

The Alcazar in Madrid having become too cramped, Philip IV's minister Olivares built for the king a palace on a site in Madrid which was called Buen Retiro, to which the court transferred. This now functions as the principal public park in Madrid. Cosimo Lotti designed the gardens for this palace, but engravings show that Moorish influences were still at work as separate courts were built and there was no overall unity in the design. Under the influence of the monks of San Jeronimo, the first hermitages were established in these gardens, symbolizing in the Spanish mind the union of religious and secular affairs. The making of hermitages became part of garden practice, but, as we have seen in France, outside Spain, they degenerated into garden features with very little religious significance. The creation of

Buen Retiro marks the end of Italian influence in Spanish gardens. It had given rise to no particular style, and much that was done has been destroyed by later work, the relics being fragmentary.

Renaissance ideas spread to Portugal and some beautiful gardens were developed in that country. The first Portuguese garden to show Italian influence was that of Bacalhao, the owner of which travelled in Italy in 1521. The house was approached through a court flanked by pavilions and included an *alegrete*, the Portuguese equivalent of the *giardino segreto* of the Italian gardens, at the corner of a very large terrace. At the opposite corner there was a large sunken basin more than thirty yards long, shut in by walls, against one of which stood a hall constructed of three pavilions,

the rest of it being covered with tiles and terracotta busts. At the other corners were two little pavilions and below a second terrace of the same size. There was a surprising absence of fountains, but this garden was in any case unusual, there being nothing like it previously in Spain or Italy.

Large basins, generally by the side of high walls, were characteristic of Portuguese gardens. At Bemfica, in the valley of Alcantara, the basin lying at the side of the terrace wall occupied almost the whole length of the garden, which was otherwise furnished with fountains, statues and geometrically formed parterres in the customary Renaissance style. A development peculiar to Portugal was the conversion into water staircases within an avenue of trees of monastery 'Stations of the

A diagram from La Vie de Campagne: Quatre Siècles de Jardin à la Française *(1910) showing the various parts of a design for a seventeenth-century parterre.*

Cross' (uphill climbs simulating the way of Christ on Calvary, with prayers at various points). Such staircases were made at Bussaco, Braga and Lamego.

The spread of Italian ideas in gardening to northern Europe, particularly England, is usually attributed to Francis I, who came back from captivity in 1527. Evidence seems to point, however, to influences at work in England earlier than this. Henry VII's new palace at Richmond, built at the turn of the century, had gardens far more complex than anything hitherto known in that country. An account dated 1503 says in reference to Richmond Palace that there were 'under the King's wyndowes, Quene's and other Estats, most faire and pleasant gardens with ryall knots aleyed and herbid; many marvellous beasts as lyons, dragons, and such others of dyvers kynde, properly fachyoned and carved in the grounde right well sandid, and compasid with lede with many vynys sedis and straunge fruit, right goodly beset, kept and noryshid with much labor and diligens. In the lougher end of this gardeyn beth pleasunt gallerys and houses of pleasure to disporte

in . . .' This description is very reminiscent of Gaillon in Cardinal Amboise's time, with which it is contemporary.

The gardens at Richmond are believed to have been the inspiration for gardens at Thornbury Castle in Gloucestershire, not far from the Severn estuary, which Edward Stafford, third Duke of Buckingham, began to build in 1511. The gardens were not finished when Buckingham was beheaded in 1521, but there was a delightful courtyard garden overlooked by an elegant oriel window which may still be seen. It was Cardinal Wolsey's establishment at Hampton Court, however, which had the first really great garden in England, comprised of several separate gardens. These gardens, after they had passed into the King's hands, consisted of the Mount garden, the 'King's Newe Garden' (now called the Privy Garden) with gravel paths, raised mounds, sundials and railed beds, and the Pond Yard or Garden. Effigies of the 'King's Beasts' were raised aloft on green and white poles in the 'Newe Garden'; the enclosing rails were painted white and green and sometimes red; emblems were engraved on shields; stone effigies of kings and queens lined the walls bordered with box and rosemary; bronze sundials were treated in various decorative ways and figures and curious shapes were carved in topiary work. In a drawing by Antonius Wynngarde in the Bodleian Library the heraldic beasts are the most conspicuous feature, bristling over the whole garden.

When, in 1529, Wolsey's pageantry was summarily ended, his role was replaced for a time by that of Sir Thomas More, whose views were surprisingly modern. In his *Utopia* the inhabitants

'. . . sett great stoor be theyr gardeins. In them they haue vyneyardes, all manner of frute, herbes and flowres so pleisaunte, so well furnished, and so fynely kepte, that I neuer sawe thinge more frutefull nor better trimmed in any place. Their studye and delygence herin cumeth not only of pleasure, but also of a certeyne stryffe and contentyon that is between strete and strete, concernynge the trymmynge, husbanding and fur-nyshyng of theyr gardeyns, every man for his own part. And verily you shall not lyghtly fynde in all the citye annye thynge that is more commodyous. other for the proffytte of the citizins, or for pleasure.'

More's own garden was well-known in his own time. He bought a piece of land at Chelsea in 1620, overlooking the Thames, built himself a house and garden and turned the rest into a farm. It was described as 'a place of marvellous beauty', something of which can be seen in a contemporary painting which shows a simple geometrical pattern of flowers-beds going down to the Thames. Many others in the next few years built mansions and created gardens in England. The estates of the religious houses were taken over to become the seats of the *nouveaux riches,* who became the new 'noblemen and gentlemen' to replace the old families killed in the Wars of the Roses. Henry VIII followed up his work at Hampton Court by the commencement in 1538 of the building of the Palace of Nonsuch, in which some Continental influence began to be apparent. It

ABOVE *These beautiful parterres at the Château of Brecy, a few miles south of Bayeux, Normandy, were made in the seventeenth century.*

RIGHT *Detail of the parterre of the Castle of Angers seen from the ramparts, illustrating the similarity of parterre patterns with those used for furnishing and other materials.*

contained marble pillars, fountains with birds spouting water and other water-tricks. Ideas still continued, however, to be predominently mediaeval. Even in 1554 Stephen Hawes described such a garden in *The history of Grand Amour and La Bell Pucell.*

> Then in we went to the garden glorious,
> Like to a place of pleasure most solacious,
> With Flora painted and wrought curiously,
> In divers knots of marvelous greatness,

TOP *Clipped hedges and shrubs in the present-day Jardin de la Isla, Aranjuez, Madrid.*

LEFT *A water-tank with overhanging trees seen through an arch at the Casa de Pilatos.*

ABOVE *A court of the Casa de Pilatos.*

TOP *An area beside the pool in the seventeenth-century garden at Bemfica: Quinta of the Marquez de Fronteira, devoted to parterres, geometrical in design, with clipped shrubs and statuary.*

ABOVE *Box-edged beds and a rose pergola in El Retiro, Madrid, which is now a public park.*

Rampant lions stood up wonderfully,
Made all of herbs of dulcet sweetness,
With many dragons of marvellous likeness
Of divers flowers made full craftily,
By Flora coloured with colours sundry.
Amidst the garden so much delectable,
There was an arbour, fair and quadrant,
To Paradise right well comparable,
Set all about with flowers fragrant,
And in the middle there was resplendishant,
A dulcet spring and marvellous fountain,
Of gold and azure, made all certain.

By 1575 there had still been little change. The Earl of Leicester's garden at Kenilworth contained 'obelisks on the terrace at even distances . . . and white heraldic beasts, all made of stone and perched on artistic posts', much being made of such simple objects as that in the middle of each of the four sections of the parterre, which was 'a post shaped like a cube, two feet high; on that, a pyramid, accurately made, symmetrically carved, fifteen feet high; and on the summit, a ball ten inches in diameter', each being cut from a solid block of porphyry.

In the year Elizabeth came to the throne (1558) the first book on gardening in English appeared. This was Thomas Hill's *A Most Brief and Pleasant Treatise Teaching How to Dress, Sow and Set a Garden*, which, although only Continental material translated, went into seven editions. It was literary rather than practical, its significance arising from the fact that it indicates that

147

there was a public ready to buy gardening books. Its illustrations are valuable for their detail of the small Elizabethan garden and those of a later work by the same author, *The Gardener's Labyrinth*, for illustrations of people working in their gardens. Elizabethan gardens were usually divided into several enclosures, the flower-garden being on the south side of the house. As in Leicester's garden, the design was usually that of the four-plot arrangement brought back by the Crusaders. Statues, fountains, vases of lead or stone, sundials, obelisks, turfed seats, carved wooden figures and works of topiary were placed everywhere as fancy dictated, together with shady alleys, walks being regarded as very important. There were many arbours or resting places. The gardener still needed an impenetrable outer enclosure: the proximity of woodland in a land still largely unenclosed meant that there were many enemies to be kept out. The main entrance was generally a wrought-iron gate, set in the larger gardens between piers or arches, lesser internal openings usually having wooden doors. The mount of

ABOVE *The Pond Garden at Hampton Court Palace made in the time of Henry VIII (1491-1547). The use of modern garden varieties of flowers in the planting makes the garden more colourful now.*

RIGHT ABOVE *The garden of Hatfield House, Hertfordshire, made early in the seventeenth century: the vista, unlike those made later in the century in France, does not carry the eye into the distance, but terminates as the trees converge.*

RIGHT *Plan of an English Tudor garden from a seventeenth-century book showing the garden on the north side of the house split up into several separate compartments.*

FAR RIGHT *This relief carving on a newel post at Hatfield House, Hertfordshire, is thought to be a portrait of John Tradescant, senior, the famous gardener and plant collector, who worked for Robert Cecil there. His collection of curios eventually became the proerty of Elias Ashmole and was afterwards the foundation collection of the Ashmolean Museum at Oxford.*

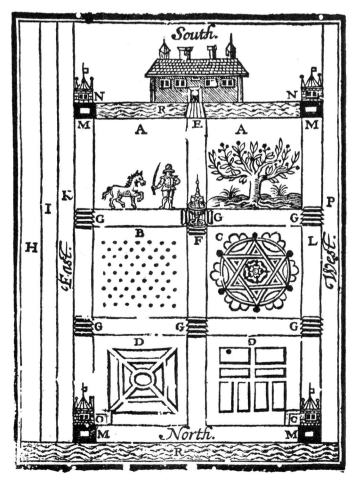

monastic and castle gardens, provided so that those inside could look over the wall without unlocking the outer doors, continued in the later gardens as a decorative feature, often being surmounted with an ornamental building.

Towards the end of the century larger gardens began to be made. The most notable were those made for Lord Burleigh at Theobalds in Hertfordshire, which had a white marble fountain and a summerhouse containing marble figures of twelve Roman emperors, and for James I at Hatfield in the same county, where a Neptune fountain was erected by Saloman de Caus, who had worked in Italy and was an expert in water devices, some of which he installed in the garden of Richmond Palace. Moor Park, with terraces carried on arches and a middle staircase embracing a grotto, had two fountains and eight statues in the parterre and thus reflected Italian ideas. The only garden made in England, however, that seems to have had any real pretension to rank with Continental Renaissance gardens was that constructed at Wilton in Wiltshire for Lord Pembroke by Isaac de Caus, Saloman's son. This was about 1,350 yards long by 350 broad and comprised three sections, cut by broad paths. The first contained parterres, viewed from a terrace at the end. Next there were two large thickets intersected by the River Nadder, in the centre of the woodland being statues of Flora and Bacchus, with covered walks each side. The road crossed the river with a fine bridge and at the end of the thickets were two water-tanks with middle columns and *jets d'eau*. Walks among grass bordered by cherry trees occupied the first part of the third

ABOVE *A view of the garden of the Mirabelschloss in Salzburg, which was laid out for Bishop Sittich in 1613-19, just before the start of the Thirty Years War, which greatly curtailed gardening activity in Germany.*

RIGHT *An engraving of the castle at Heidelberg, the garden of which was made by Saloman de Caus for Elizabeth, daughter of James I of England, who married Frederick V of the Palatinate. De Caus coped very successfully with the difficult site, which was not easily susceptible to the application of Renaissance principles, the slope being at right-angles to the axial line of the castle.*

section and then, in the centre, was the statue of the 'Borghese Gladiator', with more covered walks each side and pavilions at the crossings. The garden ended with a terrace and balustraded wall containing an arch giving access to a grotto with marble statues, niches and pillars, probably from designs by Inigo Jones. There were stairs up both sides with sea monsters on the balustrades squirting water up on to the terrace. Above the grotto was a large basin with a well. None of this garden remains. In spite of attempts by English garden historians to present as favourable an assessment as possible of English sixteenth- and early seventeenth-century gardens, they afford a picture of a scene still half-mediaeval with no more than limited use of Italian ideas, helped by the expertise of Continental practitioners such as the de Caus father and son in a few scattered gardens.

The Renaissance was felt in Germany first through

town gardens because of close trade links with Italy. The great Fuggers of Augsburg, money-lenders to the princes of Europe, had a garden full of water-tricks and devices and there were others in Augsburg as well as Breslau, Nuremburg, Frankfurt and Ulm. That of Johannes Schwindt of Frankfurt may be taken as representative. It comprised an enclosure of green lattice-work with pillars, windows and gates. There were pots of flowers in the windows and the pillars were crowned with small obelisks and busts. The parterre was geometrical in pattern, marked out by box with little trees at the corners, and there was a surrounding hedge with benches and flowers in pots. A wide middle path led into the flower-garden beyond, introduced by two huge statues, Hercules and Hermes. Two obelisks at the far end led into another parterre, the second and third sections being surrounded by alleys covered with green lattice and foliage.

Of larger gardens, those of the castle of Ambras in the Tyrol, made about 1566, showed Italian influence, as did those of Maximilian II's fortress-like Neugebäude at Vienna made a year or so later. The first purely Renaissance garden, however, was probably that of Rudolf II, at the Belvedere at Hradschin, the finest Renaissance building north of the Alps. Here was a level garden oriented with the castle, the main axis being the line of the fountains. German gardens reached their peak in the early years of the seventeenth century. Mirabelschloss in Salzburg, which was laid out for Bishop Sittich in 1613-19, was Renaissance in style but the garden had no unity with the castle, being

separated from it by high walls, while the beds were encircled with balustrades which also cut them off from the general scene. Hellbrunn garden, near Salzburg gates, was also created for the bishop. Grottoes were a great feature of this garden, a number being actually in the castle. They included a 'rain' grotto, a 'mirror' grotto and another with a dragon coming out of a hole in the rock, drinking from a fountain and vanishing again. There were also 'birds' singing and a 'vault of ruins' threatening to fall. An abundance of statues, water-tricks, automata and similar attractions made this very like an Italian garden. Other gardens, with varying faithfulness to Italian styles and practices, were made elsewhere in Germany. Duke William of Bavaria had two Carthusian monks actually living in a hermitage in his garden at Maxburg.

There were fine gardens at Haimhausen castle and Stuttgart castle, one of the best being that of Elizabeth, daughter of James I of England, who had married Frederick V of the Palatinate. She imported Saloman de Caus, who had been her tutor as a girl at Richmond Palace, to lay out her garden at Heidelberg, near Stuttgart, which he did with considerable success although the site, partly on a mountainside and not orientated with the buildings, did not favour the application of Renaissance principles. With the outbreak of the Thirty Years War in 1618 garden development was brought to a halt in Germany and the other northern countries involved in hostilites. Elsewhere, however, events moved on; the curtain rose on the next act to reveal a new and even grander setting for the garden scene, and new actors on the stage.

11
Long Vistas

So twice five miles of fertile ground
With walls and towers were girded round . . .

Coleridge

In 1665 René Rapin, the Jesuit poet, summarized the requirements of the Renaissance garden in France in his *Hortorum libri quattuor* but, as he did so, that style was already being replaced. There was no real interruption in garden design but at that moment Germany was recovering from the devastation of the Thirty Years War and England from Cromwell's rebellion, so that France under Louis XIV acquired political power with which went a high culture equalling that of the Italians, and unprecedented expansion.

The change began with Cardinal Mazarin's Minister of Finance Nicolas Fouquet who, at the beginning of 1650, bought three villages at Vaux-le-Vicomte near Melun and pulled them down to make a new estate. He seems to have had unlimited financial resources and employed at times as many as 18,000 labourers on the work, which cost 16 million *livres*. A fine building was made with pavilions around it encircled by a wide moat. In front there was a broad entrance court, the *cour d'honneur*, cut off by a handsome semi-circular balustrade and fine trellis barriers. The main broad carriage roads of the park led to this court. André le Brun, who was responsible for the decoration of the house, introduced a young man, André le Nôtre, whose father was superintendent of the Tuileries gardens, to plan the garden. He could not have made a better choice. Le Nôtre was a man ideally fitted to provide for a monarch able to spend lavishly, and he did.

At Vaux, however, he was working for Fouquet. Mme de Scudery described the garden at Vaux in *Clélie*. To her 'the most wonderful thing' was how it lay between two shrubberies, 'which agreeably break the view'. On both sides of the castle there were parterres decked with fountains which were comparatively simple in design in contrast with the complex *parterres de broderie* that lay below the house, which were very fine. To the right and left there were flower-gardens, again with many fountains, including *la fontaine de la couronne*, a round fountain with a crown of jets at the end of the parterre, which was completed by two small

PREVIOUS PAGE *The long view from the château at Vaux-le-Vicomte, looking between the two belts of shrubs and trees which Madame de Scudery thought was a 'most wonderful' situation for a garden. The picture also shows the parterres of highly complex pattern that she saw 'below the house', with the fountains, pools and terrace.*

LEFT *A view at Versailles showing Latona revenging herself on the peasants by turning them into frogs in the Basin of Latona in the foreground, and looking along the Tapis Vert to the Basin of Apollo, beyond which the Grand Canal stretches into the distance and the vista shades off into infinity.*

ABOVE *An engraving of a portrait by Carlo Maratta of André le Nôtre, master of garden-design for nearly a century.*

narrow canals. From this the main path went down
through lawns edged with fountains and furnished
with flowers until the water found its way into a great
square basin. The garden ended with the canal and a
natural hill behind.

This hill was marked out and ornamented with grotto
work and there were fountains, including a cascade and
water beasts, all the way to the top, where stood a large
figure of Hercules, and a great column of water rose in
the air. On each side of this garden on the hill there
were shrubberies. To the left of the castle more rising
ground provided a terrace with a fine set of steps and
another cascade as an approach to it. On the other side
were more shrubberies with trellises bordering the
walks, lawns, flower-gardens, paths with fountains
and a water theatre. Finally, leaving the castle terrace
and going down through the water road to the terrace of
the grand canal, there was another cascade to be seen at
the dividing wall of the castle and the canal. Le Nôtre
showed in this first effort that he had realized the need
for a scene no less magnificent than the castle: a scene
that could be viewed as a whole from the house and
formed a fitting setting for it. It was clear that he had
also understood that there must be variety among the
components in order to avoid monotony. He used the
shrubberies to frame the picture he had made.

Fouquet's lavish expenditure aroused the suspicion
of the king and he was disgraced for embezzlement in
1661, but although he had excited the king's envy he
was also his teacher because Louis XIV took over those
who had been working on Vaux, including Le Nôtre,
and set them to work at Versailles. Here there was a
small house with a pleasant garden that had been
designed by Jacques Boyceau, set in a large stretch of
marshy ground. A new garden was planned in 1662-3
and work commenced on it, the plan being changed
many times as the years went on. The stories told about
the creation of the magnificent palace and grounds are

LEFT ABOVE *A painting made at the beginning of the eighteenth century by Jean Rigaud of the Bosquet de l'Arc de Triomphe at Versailles showing the exuberant fancy with which Le Nôtre decorated these woodland scenes.*

LEFT *An impression by a nineteenth-century French artist, D. Lancelot, of the principal fountain in the Bosquet de l'Arc de Triomphe, made for* Histoire des Jardins *by Arthur Mangin (Tours, 1883).*

TOP *An engraving by Adam Pérelle (1640-95) of the Basin of Latona at Versailles.*

ABOVE *The Fountain of Bacchus, or Autumn, by Gaspard Marsy, in the pool of the Bosquet of the Girandole at Versailles, one of the four Fountains of the Seasons in the Allée Royale.*

hard to believe. The levelling of the ground for the garden and park, the making of a road to Paris and the erection of the Aqueduc de Maintenon to bring water from the Eure, are said alone to have occupied 36,000 men and 6,000 horses for years. As Le Vau went ahead with re-shaping the house, Le Nôtre began on the gardens. Almost the first thing that he did was to cut out vast basins in the lower levels framing them in stone. and decorating them with gilded lead figures. He brought down horseshoe paths from the upper terrace and laid down a second parterre, following this with a wide avenue which passed through thick park-like shrubberies to the great basin, beyond which a cross-road marked the end of the garden.

At this stage of the garden, a wide *parterre de broderie* lay under the stone-balustraded terrace by the house; this contained four great square beds filled with arabesque patterns in box and other dwarf evergreens and was intersected by sanded paths. The extreme edges of the parterre were bordered with dwarf shrubs in square boxes, the corners being marked by tall clipped cypresses. To the south of the house was the railed 'King's garden' or *parterre d'amour,* where masses of flowers surrounded a Cupid fountain, a small orangery being built below this parterre in 1664. On the north wide steps led down from the main parterre to the Parterre du Nord which led in its turn to the long alley running down through bosquets to the Bassin du Grand Jet. To the west the main *parterre de broderie* ended in a semi-circle with a flight of steps, above which lay a round basin, the steps themselves leading down to a new parterre, the Jardin-bas, which had a central oval basin. The new wide avenue, the Allée

157

TOP *One of the two large sheets of water called the 'mirrors' that lie on the west side of the Palace at Versailles.*

LEFT *The pool and retaining wall of the Basin of Neptune at Versailles showing the groups of statuary protraying sea myths.*

ABOVE *A magnificent sculptured group made by Jean-Baptiste Tubi about 1670 of the sun-god Apollo driving his four spirited horses up out of the water of the Basin of Apollo while four giant tritons, riding dolphins, announce his rising through conch-shells. The sculptor, in spite of the fact that the sun appears to travel from East to West, has made Apollo drive towards the East.*

The Orangery at Versailles showing the orange trees and palms standing outside in the warmth of the summer sun. The orange trees used to be put outside during the summer to flower and then their fruits would be gathered and they would be brought indoors in the winter.

Royale, ran west to the Bassin des Cygnes, being bordered on either side by high palisades of greenery, and continued on to the canal. Halfway down the canal widened slightly at one point, aligning with the menagerie buildings, octagonal in shape, in the south-west of the gardens, which were of some splendour. Contemporary with the menagerie was the magnificent Grotto of Thetis, designed by Claud Perrault and placed in a corner of the main parterre to the north of the palace. This was furnished with three splendid groups of statues, a reclining Apollo being greeted by Thetis and her nymphs, while to right and left the horses of the sun-god were being watered by tritons.

Almost all that has been described so far was no more than the first phase of the development of Versailles. In 1668 Louis XIV decided to enlarge the palace and the gardens, most of what already existed being swept away. One of the earliest effects to be completed which may still be seen is the long line of fountains in the Parterre du Nord and the Allée d'Eau. On the higher level is the Fountain of the Pyramid, comprising five tiers of leadwork, the theme of which is oceans and

their mythology, and which is one of the finest pieces of its kind in the gardens. There are two other fountains, those of the Sirens, in the Parterre du Nord. At the head of the Allée d'Eau is a cascade, the Bassin des Nymphes de Diane, in which the water slides over a shallow wall into the pool. The Allée d'Eau itself is a long shaded walk containing two lines of eleven fountains, all varied but each consisting of a group of three children clustering round the centre plinth holding up the shallow fountain basin.

At its lower end the Allée d'Eau emerges into the clearing of the Bassin du Dragon, formerly the Bassin du Grand Jet, but renamed because of the installation in it of a dragon group. This fountain had a novel feature: lead vases containing clipped shrubs were placed round its edge. On either side of the Allée d'Eau were the Bosquet de l'Arc de Triomphe and that of the Trois Fontaines. Of the ornaments that embellished these glades only a group representing 'France Triumphant' survives. Other *bosquets* (groves of trees) were the settings for the Théâtre d'Eau, now replaced by the wide grassy Rond Vert which is separated from the Avenue des Trois Fontaines by the bosquet of that name, and the Marais, now replaced by the Bosquet des Bains d'Appollon. Both the Théâtre d'Eau and the Marais were water-works of great complexity. The former was a *chef d'oeuvre*, a vast cloud of bubbles arising from one corner of the glade while innumerable small jets covered the delicate ironwork with streaming silver. The latter was an iron tree, exuding water from every branch and leaf while reeds sprayed round in jets.

159

Le Nôtre provided the garden with a labyrinth that was quite unique. It lay in the south woods to the side of and below the Orangery. It contained thirty-nine fountains decorated with coloured stones and shells, representing fables from Aesop, and was populated with animals of lead, painted in natural colours, set in elaborate niches against a background of lattice and smoothly cut hedges. It was described as a 'veritable garden of enchantment'. It has disappeared, the site now being occupied by the Bosquet de la Reine, which gets its name from later associations with a trumped-up scandal concerning the tragic Marie Antoinette.

Some notable new fountain groups were added to the garden in the early 1670s. Symmetrically placed on each side of the long axial line of the Allée Royale, in the Bosquet de la Girandole on the south and of the Dauphin on the north, were the four Fountains of the Seasons, portrayed as reclining leaden figures each with the attributes of its particular time of the year. The great oval basin in the Jardin-bas now received the tremendous group of the revengeful Latona surrounded by frightened peasants being turned into frogs at her behest, and has since been known as the Fountain of Latona. Two smaller round basins continuing the theme at the lower end of the parterre surrounded by flower-beds go by the name of the Bassins des Lézards. The long sanded Allée Royale, now the grass Tapis Vert, continues westward from Latona to the former Bassin des Cygnes, renamed from the splended group of Apollo with his chariot and horses that was now placed in it. Driving his horses to the east towards Latona, Apollo's basin is the most outlying of the fountains.

After 1675 two more famous bosquets, those of Enceladus and Renommée, were provided with

ABOVE *This long vista in the garden of Marly is almost the only thing now left of Louis XIV's retreat, which was very famous and much admired in its day.*

BELOW *A painting by Jean Rigaud at the beginning of the eighteenth century of the great lake at Fontainebleau as altered by Le Nôtre.*

ABOVE *The lake at Fontainebleau as it is today.*

BELOW *The Ile d'Amour and figure of Eros in a pool backed by a* bosquet *at Chantilly, one of the ancient gardens altered by Le Nôtre.*

decorative fountains. That of Enceladus is a most powerful work. Enceladus, punished by Zeus, lies writhing under the crumpled volcanic rock of Etna, his great hands (he is four times natural size) clutching at the debris as he sinks, while water simulating fire pours from his contorted face and open jaws. Circular basins that formerly surrounded the main body of water with jets forming a moving transparent screen for Enceladus have disappeared. The Renommée, now called the Bosquet des Dômes, from domed pavilions which have gone, consists of a hexagonal basin surrounded by a fine double marble balustrade, set among clipped trees. This is one of the most charming *bosquets* in Versailles. A single graceful jet drops water into the basin which flows out through the balustrade, while eight statues against the hedge look on. To the north of the Enceladus, from which it is separated by the Allée de Flore, there is another *bosquet* which was originally called the Salle du Conseil, or des Festins, from the retired nature of the island in the vast tank which was formerly situated there, but which is now called Obélisque from a later fountain on the site.

The Great Canal was lengthened in the years before 1680 to become slightly more than a mile long, being for the most part 400 feet wide. About midway transverse arms extend at right angles, one to the menagerie on the south, the other to the Grand Trianon to the north. With this, the second phase of the development of Versailles was completed, but there was a third to come. The first step in this was the transformation of the parterre lying under the facade of the palace on the west side, which was not developed into the immense Parterre d'Eau that it is today. The principal features of the new parterre were two vast and lovely sheets of water called 'mirrors'. Around each of these was placed

twelve beautiful bronze groups representing rivers, nymphs and children. This change, if any single change can be said to have done it, made Versailles what it is, probably the grandest garden ever made. The Parterre d'Eau carries with it a sense of infinite space. Looking out from the palace, with which it is in perfect harmony, the eye is carried by it beyond the Mirrors to the gardens and avenue dwindling to a far horizon. Of the long vistas that were characteristic of Le Nôtre's style, this is the greatest. After this, nothing could be added. It was perfection of its kind.

At the far end of the Parterre d'Eau were 'water cabinets'. These flanked the steps of Latona, where beautiful and highly praised bronzes of animals were set in rectangular marble tanks, water from the mouths of the groups flowing over the side into the trough in front. After a visit by Le Nôtre to Italy in 1679, from which he brought back much material for garden decoration, Salle des Antiques was established in the south woods. This is now called the Salle des Marroniers. In the wood between the Salle des Antiques and the Allée Royale was built the Colonnade,

LEFT *The great cascade in the garden of the Duke of Devonshire at Chatsworth, Derbyshire, one of the few gardens in England showing the influence of Le Nôtre.*

ABOVE *Detail of the parterre at Herrenhausen, Hanover. This was the garden of the palace of the Kings of Hanover, who were also Kings of England from 1714 until Victoria succeeded to the throne in 1837, when the Salic Law, which forbade descent through a woman, required the crown of Hanover to pass to Victoria's uncle, the Duke of Cumberland.*

a magnificent circular arcade of thirty-two columns, in the centre of which was placed a beautiful group of the Rape of Persephone.

An enormous new south wing added to the palace obliterated the old Parterre d'Amour and a very large new parterre was formed which looked down upon the Orangery which was built below it, beyond which had been dug out the stretch of water named the Pièce d'Eau des Suisses. This new south parterre was elegantly designed around two circular ornamental basins lying to the sides of the central walk and harmonizing perfectly with the designs in which they were set. On the north side of the palace, beyond the Dragon fountain, was established another large stretch of water, the Fountain of Neptune; along the retaining wall were groups of statuary based on sea myths.

Knowledge of Chinese buildings and customs was beginning to percolate to western Europe through the letters of the Jesuits who had managed to obtain entrance to China and gain the emperor's confidence. In 1670 Louis XIV commissioned the building at Versailles of the Trianon de Porcelaine in imitation of the Porcelain Tower of Nanking. Lacking porcelain, faience was used in the Dutch manner. The main building was small, no more than a tea-house, and side pavilions were erected around a court, setting a fashion which was copied elsewhere. Colourful flowers in the parterre set off the blue and white motif of the building, which was carried through to the garden seats and flower boxes, and there were spectacular fountains. At a higher level than the parterre was another colourful garden with a timber house that enclosed a winter garden stocked with oranges, lemons and flowers, and surrounded with myrtle and jessamine. The delicious scents were so strong in this garden that some found them overpowering.

The Trianon de Porcelaine was so popular that its name and style were imitated everywhere, eventually being caught up and becoming synonymous with the hermitage which was also found in every large garden. This did not, however, prevent Louis XIV from demolishing it a few years after it was made and replacing it with a marble house for Madame de Maintenon. The new garden was less elaborate than that of Versailles and in some respects resembled that of Clagny, next door to Versailles, which Louis had built between 1674 and 1680 for his earlier mistress, Madame de Montespan, which was also somewhat simpler than that of Versailles.

163

LEFT *A pavilion in a clipped* bosquet *garden at Herrenhausen.*

LEFT BELOW *The beautiful pool, fountain and parterres at the Palace of Queluz in Portugal, where house and garden combine in perfect harmony to form one of the most attractive seventeenth-century royal estates in Europe.*

RIGHT ABOVE *A pavilion in a* bosquet *beside the canal at Herrenhausen in Hanover.*

RIGHT BELOW *The cascade in the garden at Nymphenburg on a branch of the River Würm in Bavaria, showing the river gods Danube and Isar.*

terraces, one of clipped yew, another of globular leafy trees, while the third was a portico of greenery. Behind the wide show garden were more pavilions and secluded groves, all furnished with much statuary. There is nothing left now but an avenue or so through the trees to catch the eye in the old way and carry it into the distance.

Le Nôtre dealt with the king's other estates as well as those in the neighbourhood of Versailles. At Fontainebleau he consolidated the smaller parts into an up-to-date design but the broad plan remained as Henri IV had left it. At Ste Germain-en-Laye he enlarged the parterres and made the main terrace which extended in front of the upper garden as a walk across the river. At St Cloud, belonging to the king's brother, the Duke of Orleans, which already had fine gardens, he made enlargements and brought together all the smaller parts into a unified design as he had done at Fontainebleau. The cascade he transformed into an imposing triple waterfall flowing over steps into a huge semi-circular basin. This cascade was supreme in its time, being surpassed only later by that made at Marly. Le Nôtre laid out the gardens at Meudon, where the famous grotto and parterre still remained, for Louis' minister Louvois, extending the castle terrace into a large flower-garden with a splendid view over the Seine and Paris. The terraces descended to the Orangery but rose again, marked out by fountains and basins, to a woody hill above. The great Condé borrowed Le Nôtre to remake Chantilly. Here he collected the water into a broad band of canal which cut off the garden crosswise as at Vaux-le-Vicomte. He made a great stairway as conclusion to the parterre southward on the castle terrace. In the centre the canal cut across the parterre, spreading on the other side into a semi-circular bay, with meadows and avenues adjoining. The parterre was, in fact, a water parterre, the open flat spaces being laid out with groups of five round ponds surrounded by grass, box and strips of flower-bed. It was bordered on one side by a fine colonnade, and on the other side, east of the lake, there was a second parterre with wonderful flower arrangements behind which were many groves, one containing a great cascade.

The fame of Versailles spread throughout the world and Le Nôtre's style was copied everywhere. England's Charles II lacked funds and could not do much, although he imported the Mollets to help him make St James' Park in London. The attitude of the average English country gentleman at this time was expressed

The Trianon de Porcelaine did not, in fact, satisfy Louis for long; he craved for somewhere away from Versailles where he could lead a less formal life when he felt like doing so. He finally fixed on another site not far from Versailles to develop as a retreat. It was 'a narrow valley behind Louveciennes, unapproachable because of its marshes, shut in by hills on every side, and very narrow, with a miserable village on one slope, which is called Marly'. He built the palace halfway up the hill and framed the garden, as at Versailles, around a water axis. The buildings were designed like the Trianon de Porcelaine in separate pavilions round a court on a terrace. Behind the castle a grand cascade passed down through the park towards the palace ending in a half-moon-shaped pond from which there was a descent by the southern castle terrace. Wide steps took one from terrace to terrace in front of the buildings, each terrace having a pond and many fountains. On both sides of the palace there were originally four basins adorned with faience but these were later replaced by *cabinets de verdure* used as outdoor rooms by the ladies. Twelve little pavilions attached to the buildings were interconnected by *berceaux* which formed a semi-circle round the palace as far as the foot of the cascade. Three avenues separated these from the open

by Sir Thomas Hanmer in his *Garden Book* of 1659 (not published until 1931) which shows that French influence had already affected English gardens although it was, of course, written before Le Nôtre created Versailles. Hanmer comments on the changes since Elizabethan times:

'. . . in these days the borders are not hedged about with privet, rosemary or other such herbs which hide the view and prospect, and nourish hurtful worms and insects [here speaks the practical gardener], nor are standard fruit trees suffered to grow so high and thick as to shadow and cumber the soyle, but all is now commonly near the house laid open and exposed to the sight of the rooms and chambers, and the knots and borders are upheld only with very low coloured boards or stone, or tile.'

It is clear from this that the rather claustrophobic crowding of the old-style gardens had been somewhat eased, at least near the house. He goes on to say that 'if the ground be spacious, the next adjacent quarters or *parterres*, as the French call them, are often of fine turf, but as low as any green to bowl on; cut out curiously into embroidery of flowers and shapes of arabesques, animals or birds or *feuillages*, and the small alleys or intervals filled with several coloured sands and dust with much art, with but few flowers in such knots, and those only such as grow very low, lest they spoil the beauty of the embroidery.' Passing on from these parterres near the house he comments, with regard to those further away, that:

LEFT ABOVE *The great cascade (the water was not flowing on the day the photograph was taken) at Wilhelmshöhe on the Weissenstein near Cassel in Germany, where the stream plunges down until in a great rush it sweeps over Neptune's Grotto at the bottom and into the basin.*

LEFT *A cage of birds spouting water: one of the water-devices in the garden of Charles Theodore of Bavaria at Schwetzingen.*

TOP *An impression by a nineteenth-century French artist, Anastasi, of the garden of Frederick the Great at Sans Souci near Berlin: from* Histoire des Jardins *by Arthur Mangin (Tours, 1883).*

ABOVE *The parterre in the garden of the archbishop of Cologne at Brühl, Germany, seen from the castle.*

'. . . those remote from habitation are *compartments*, as they call them, which are knots also, and borders destined for flowers, yet sometimes intermixed with grass-work, and on the outside beautified with vases on pedestals, or dwarf cypresses, firs and other greens [evergreens] which will endure our winters, set uniformly, at reasonable distances from each other, and in these great grounds beyond are either labyrinths with hedges cut to a man's height, or thickets for birds cut through with gravelly walks, or you have a variety of alleys set with elms, limes, abeles, firs and pines, with fountains, cascades and statues. These large grounds are commonly a third part longer than broad . . .'

The last part of this description gives the impression that Hanmer is talking of a large estate but he says, in fact, that 'it suffices most gentlemen to have only a square or oblong piece of ground of three score or eighty yards, with handsome gravel walks . . .' so that his idea of a garden is very modest and not at all on the Le Nôtre scale. One strange trait in English gardening at this time was an apparent indifference to flowers, gardens being mainly lawns and gravel walks, which did not go without hostile comment from contemporary garden writers like John Rea and John Worlidge. Hanmer's account is a case in point, as it forbids any but those 'such as grow very low' near the house and provides for flowers only in the remoter parts of the garden. This lack of flowers is strange in a country so interested in the plants from the newly-discovered lands.

In the later years of the century the influence of Le Nôtre began to make some changes in England. Hampton Court on the Thames up-river from London, a favourite place of William III and much altered by him, was provided with fountains, avenues and an extended canal in the French mode. The establishment of such avenues, often radiating in a star-like way from a centre, *a patte d'oie, rondpoint* or something similar was, indeed, the main idea the English took from the French. Although other gardens such as Badminton in Gloucestershire, Bramham Park in Yorkshire, and Melbourne and Chatsworth in Derbyshire showed French influence, none could really compare with the French originals and England was the country least affected by the seventeenth-century gardens of France.

Germany, recovering from the Thirty Years War, had to start again almost from scratch, but towards the end of the century, when Le Nôtre's ideas began to spread, several of the princely rulers, both secular and ecclesiastical, began to make beautiful gardens. Duke Ernest Johann Friedrich of Hanover made a garden at Herrenhausen under French guidance which was very like the first stage of Versailles. Duke Max Emanuel of Bavaria was exiled to Paris at the beginning of the eighteenth century. When he returned in 1715 he had gardens laid out at Nymphenburg and Schleissheim in the French style. Those of Nymphenburg were of considerable grandeur, this garden being the first one in Germany where French ideas were fully carried out on a level site. It contained many fountains, some of them very attractive, and an imitation of the Trianon de Porcelaine. Schleissheim had an individual flavour because a small building meant to be a Trianon assumed an importance of its own as a focal point for the view

LEFT *A fountain and pool, with radiating* allées *between the* bosquets, *at the greatest of all Austrian gardens, Schönbrunn in Vienna, rival of Versailles in grandeur and execution.*

ABOVE *A design for a garden by Johann David Fülck, head gardener for the Schönborn family, who played a prominent part in the development of garden design in Germany in the seventeenth and eighteenth centuries.*

from the castle, a situation which would not have been allowed to occur in the long vistas of a French garden. At Durlach, a hunting lodge of the Margrave Charles William of Baden-Durlach, the idea of the *patte d'oie* expanded into fantasy: there were no less than thirty-two paths radiating from the vicinity of the hunting tower. Duke Eberhard, Ludwig IV of Würtemburg, made a fine French-style garden at Ludwigsburg near Stuttgart.

Among the ecclesiastical princes who made gardens in the French style was Clement Augustus, Archbishop of Cologne, whose garden at Brühl used water rather in the way of the older French gardens, the chief feature being a great canal in the form of a cross in the arm of which leading to the palace was an island. This garden contained a Chinese-style building. The Schönborn family who filled a number of ecclesiastical posts made

several fine gardens, all of which have vanished. Among them were the Marquardsburg and Pommersfelden at Bamberg; the Favorite at Mainz, which was called 'the little Marly'; Gaibach, which still had a Renassance flavour; the residence at Brüchasal, which also had a Chinese-style pavilion; Kieslau, a few miles away from Brüchasal; Waghäusel Hermitage, a few miles further still, which foreshadowed the fashion for ruins; the gardens at Würzburg and Mannheim, which fitted in with the fortifications at these places; and Veithochsheim, a bishop's pleasure castle.

In Leipzig, the brothers Bose made gardens of marvellous beauty, a particular feature of which was a sunken orange parterre with beds radiating in a great semi-circle. The garden of the Apel family also had, behind the house, avenues radiating fanwise and coming to an end in a circumference richly furnished with statues and thickets. Saxony had a number of water castles which were up-dated in the French style. At Dresden Augustus the Strong made a giant court in

TOP *An eighteenth-century engraving of the upper cascade in the garden of the Prince Schwarzenberg in Vienna.*

ABOVE *Ornate treillage (trellis-work) in the style of this pavilion in the garden of Count von Althann in Vienna was a feature of European gardens of the seventeenth and eighteenth centuries.*

Zwinger gardens which was really a gigantic parterre with buildings. Count von Flemming built a palace nearby which the king bought in 1717 and joined the two with parterres along the Elbe on gently sloping terraces. On the other side of Dresden the Great Garden of Johann Georg II was laid out in accordance with French principles but had a flavour of its own. The garden of Gross-Sedlitz was also imposing, having two rows of terraces beside one another. Pillnitz on the Elbe reflected the growing passion for games, having 44 little plots for playing games and places for shooting, billiards and wrestling, which were cleverly incorporated in the garden without detracting from its dignity. Dresden was noted for the beauty and variety of its fountains of which the Neptune fountain in the Marcolini garden was a fine example. There was also a fine French-style garden attached to Falkenhurst castle at Moritzburg.

Frederick, first King of Prussia, had gardens at Oranienburg and Charlottenburg which, although

RIGHT ABOVE *An engraving dated 1715 of the garden of the Baron von Hildenberg, the envoy of George I of England, which had been made over a period of six years under the baron's personal direction at Weidlingsau, near Vienna.*

RIGHT BELOW *An eighteenth-century engraving of a bosquet with a fountain and pyramidal clipped shrubs in the garden of Adam von Liechtenstein in Vienna. This part of the garden was used as a standing-out ground for orange trees in the summer. Some are already in position and others are being moved there on a trolley.*

plain in design, were entirely French. The latter was remarkable for its unusual supply of water, the River Spree running the whole length of the garden. He also had a small pleasure house and garden that he called Marly Garden without, it seems, much justification. His wife had a house on the Spree near Berlin with a pretty garden like that of the Trianon which was called, suburban-style, Mon Bijou. Their son, Frederick the Great, built the palace of Sans Souci opposite his father's Marly Garden, the estate being designed round a vineyard on a south-facing terrace. There was a magnificent parterre on the lowest terrace with a large basin and gilded group in the centre. The garden was furnished with much statuary and a number of buildings, including a colonnade in imitation of the colonnade at Versailles, a Belvedere, pseudo-Roman ruins, and an imitation Chinese pagoda and tea-house, which was rather amateurish in design. Nevertheless, it was a large and splendid garden. Another garden of importance was the Hermitage set up by the Margrave George William at Bayreuth, below which was an arcaded orangery with spectacular fountains set in a parterre.

The Austrians were slow to make large gardens because of their preoccupation with the Turkish menace, but when this was finally defeated in 1683 Prinz Eugen of Savoy laid out the Belvedere on the hills outside Vienna, a fine formal garden on the grand scale. The estate next door, which passed into the hands of the Schwarzenburg family, was also very fine, as was the garden made by Adam von Liechtenstein on the north side of the town. The designs of all these gardens were coloured with Italian ideas of terrace gardens. The Italian style was also prominent in the terrace garden made by Prinz Eugen at Schloss Hof in the estuary between the March and the Danube, but there were in all these gardens parterres in the French style. The greatest garden of Austria was, however, that at Schönbrunn, which was meant to rival Versailles, and was, indeed, magnificent. Gardens of Hungary developed similarly to those of Austria, being mostly owned by the same nobles.

Queen Christina of Sweden imported André Mollet to lay out her gardens. There was no lack of water, which reduced the role of canals in designs for gardens made in that country. The garden of the principal estate, Jakobsdal, which was transformed into a Renaissance garden, stood on a terrace washed on three sides by the sea. Later Swedish gardens showed the influence of Le Nôtre, Drottningholm showing more of such influence than any other. The largest garden was

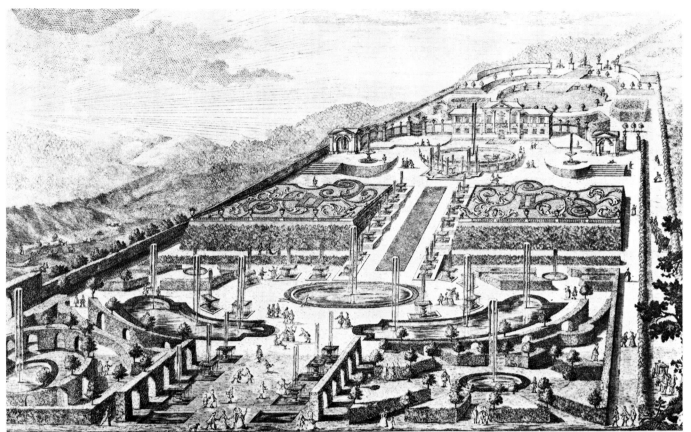

Maison de plaisance de Mr. le Baron de Huldenberg, Envoyé Extr.de S. M. le Roy George de la Gr.Bretagne, u. Electeur de Br.Lunebg. qu'il a fait bâtir à Perchtoldsdorf près de Vienne, en 1716. etc. ayant ordonné lui même le tout, achevé l'an 1715.

Prospect des Bosquet mit einer Parterre von Raasen, da im Sommer Orange-Bäume zu stehen kommen.

Veüe du Bosquet avec une Parterre gasoné ou l'on arrange le orangers en Été

171

172

LEFT ABOVE *The garden of Drottningholm in Sweden, the Swedish garden most influenced by the French style.*

FAR LEFT *A topiary garden in the French style on a beautiful site looking across the water at Sandemar, Sweden; the statues are made of wood.*

LEFT *A water-trick at Peterhof, Leningrad. Having trodden on a patch of rough stones, visitors are scrambling to escape the jets which have suddenly surprised them from below.*

ABOVE *The splendid canal and fountains between the bosquets at Peterhof near Leningrad made in the French style by the French architect Alexandre-Jean-Baptiste Le Blond for Peter the Great after he had visited western Europe at the end of the seventeenth century.*

that of Carlsberg, but it had less character than Drottningholm. Danish gardens were like those of Sweden, Fredericksborg and Hirschholm showing most traces of French influence. This influence spread to Russia after Peter the Great had visited western Europe. He first made a garden in the French style on an island in the river Neva which has disappeared, and then imported the French architect Le Blond to lay out Peterhof, built on a natural terrace nearly forty feet high. The advantages of the site enabled Le Blond to make a most beautiful garden but it was the only one of its kind made in Russia.

Although French gardens had little influence in most of Italy, they had some effect in the flatter lands of the north, particularly around Venice, the style suiting the terrain better there than it did the hillier country further

TOP *The grand cascade in the gardens of the Royal Palace at Caserta, Naples, which were conceived and made on the grand scale in the early eighteenth century in rivalry to Versailles.*

ABOVE *The garden of Fredericksborg Castle in Denmark, the design of which was influenced by the French style. Modern planting adds a bright note in the foreground.*

south. There was, however, one new and spectacular garden in the French style made in the south. When Charles III became King of Naples in 1734 he laid out a garden at Caserta which was deliberately designed, like Schönbrunn, to rival Versailles. The principal feature of this garden is the great cascade which falls fifty feet into a pond decked with groups in Carrara marble representing the story of Diana and Actaeon. The water then falls step by step through much statuary until it arrives in a great basin representing the seat of Neptune. Although the garden is splendid in conception, it is generally criticized for want of proportion and the absence of a unified scheme integrating the whole. In Spain the influence of French ideas was principally expressed by the melancholy Philip V at La Granja, the garden laid out on the western slopes of the Sierra de Guadarrama, again to rival Versailles. It is, in fact, more like Marly, having been built, like that garden, as a place for retreat from the world. It was furnished on a magnificent scale, outshining Marly because of the precipitous situation, of which full advantage was taken. In detail, perhaps, Le Nôtre would have made a nobler scheme, some parts of the garden being over-ornamented, but some things in it, such as the Neptune fountain, called the Carreras de Caballos, and the Andromeda fountain, are magnificent. Philip V also remade and enlarged Aranjuez but kept, in the main, the original style.

The gardens of Holland have been criticized by supporters of the picturesque, but the Dutch evolved a style of their own stemming from their geographical situation, the standard of which, within its own limits, was very high. There were some great gardens in the country which reflected French styles. Neuberg, near Ryswick, was one, and Het Loo another. The latter was meant by William III to compare with Versailles, but was more Renaissance in character. Other large gardens were at House Honselaersdyk, the Hague, and Heemstede, near Utrecht. Owing to the flat nature of the terrain, there was a lack of the cascades which were so prominent a feature of gardens elsewhere. The bulk of Dutch gardens were also small. Often made on land reclaimed by engineering, they tended to be divided regularly, which encouraged formality, many small gardens consisting of a simple parterre with a fountain in the middle, albeit clean and well-groomed like everything Dutch. Space being limited and the owners rich because of the great prosperity of the country, Dutch gardens tended sometimes to be overfilled with ornament. Bulbs were everwhere, but when their flowering time was over colour had to be derived from other sources. Other flowers were used but were supplemented by other things. Many coloured globes which mirrored the garden, little balls, coloured clays and coloured statues were some of the devices used. A vogue for naturalistic statuary developed into a taste for figures clipped from shrubs and topiary became a very marked feature of Dutch gardens.

The influence of the French style was not confined to Europe. On the other side of the world the Jesuits persuaded the emperor of China to make a western garden in the grounds of his summer palace at Yuen-ming-yuen. The first thing they constructed was

ABOVE *The marble cascade in the garden of La Granja, made for Philip V of Spain. The fountain of Amphitrite stands in the semi-circular pool at the foot of the cascade, the two-shelled Fountain of the Graces in front of the pavilion at the top, and statues and vases in the shade of the* bosquets *on either side.*

LEFT *A fountain and* allée *at La Granja with the snow-covered mountains as backcloth.*

a highly artistic cascade and to this they added *bosquets* and all the other trappings of the western garden at the end of the seventeenth century, finishing with a garden which was a fascinating mixture of Chinese ideas and western baroque at its most exuberant. The emperor was pleased and the water-tricks amused the Chinese, but that was as far as it went. Western garden ideas did not spread and after the emperor died the garden decayed. Not so with influence in the other direction. Chinese buildings were already being imitated in French and French-style gardens in the seventeenth century. These were the forerunners of a change in style in western gardening in the eighteenth century as dramatic as the change Le Nôtre had effected in the seventeenth. Once again the initiative shifted from one country to another. This time it was England that took up the baton.

12
Landscape Triumphant

So will I build my altar in the fields
And the blue sky my fretted dome shall be,
And the sweet fragrance that the wild flower yields
Shall be the incense I will yield to thee.

Coleridge

Gardens in England in Charles II's time were so formal and lacking in flowers that John Worlidge complained in his *Systema Horticulturae* that 'the new mode of Gravel walks and Grass-plots is fit only for such Houses, or Palaces, that are situated in Cities and great towns, although they have now become presidents [precedents] for many stately Country Residencies, where they have banished out of their Garden Flowers, the Miracles of Nature, and the best ornaments ever discovered to make a seat pleasant. But it's hoped that this new useless and unpleasant mode will, like many other vanities, grow out of Fashion.' Worlidge cannot have been pleased at the way things developed after he wrote this. Formality increased with the accession to the English throne in 1689 of William and Mary from Holland. According to Defoe, William 'was particularly delighted with the decoration of evergreens as the greatest addition to the beauty of a garden . . . With this particular judgement, all the gentlemen of England began to fall in, and in a few years fair gardens and fine houses began to grow up in every corner.'

Prominent at this time was William Bentinck, first Earl of Portland, a Dutch intimate of the King, who was appointed Superintendent of the Royal Gardens. Many of the choice plants growing at Hampton Court, which will always be associated with the names of William and Mary, were brought from Soestdyk, Bentinck's seat in Holland. Under Bentinck, George London became Master-Gardener and Deputy Superintendent of the Royal Gardens. London was the leading partner in the firm of London and Wise, which had been founded by London in 1681, Henry Wise joining in 1689. London had been in royal employment under Charles II and, recognized as being exceptionally talented, had been sent to France to study, working after his return in Fulham for Bishop Compton who was the most prominent grower of exotic plants of his day. London had been trained not only in the French style, but also in Dutch practices, so that he was well qualified. For the next twenty years, indeed, the firm of London and Wise

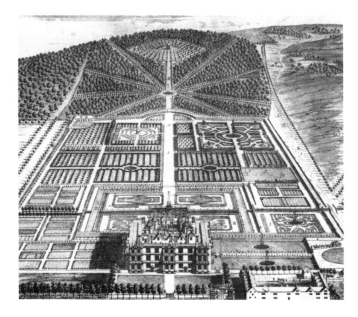

LEFT *The Turf Bridge, with the Pantheon visible in the distance across the lake, at Stourhead in Wiltshire, England. This garden was created by Henry Hoare about 1750 from a bare valley. Although it did not start a fashion, Stourhead has a claim to be regarded as the most beautiful garden ever made in England.*

ABOVE *A view of Longleat house and gardens in Wiltshire, England, drawn by Leonard Knyff and engraved by Johannes Kip for the series published in* Britannia Illustrata *(1709) and* Nouveau Théâtre de la Grande Bretagne *(1724).*

dominated garden design in England, not for any originality in design but because they equipped themselves so well to create the kind of garden that, following William III's predilections, the gentlemen of England now clamoured to have.

About the time that Queen Mary died (1694) and William began to rule alone Leonard Knyff began a

A painting by Leonard Knyff of Hampton Court west of London. It shows the palace and grounds as reconstructed for William III and Mary in the Dutch version of the French style. The tiny original Pond and Privy gardens of Henry VIII may be seen, with their fountains playing, between the palace and the river.

series of topographical drawings of the larger gardens of the time, which were engraved by Joannes Kip. They show a magnificence which in some cases is hard to believe and were no doubt designed to bolster the standing of the patrons. An essential of the Dutch version of the grand manner was level ground with an abundance of water, as at Hampton Court. The irregular hilly countryside of much of Britain did not lend itself readily to the style, but in some cases where it was adopted the results were very successful, as at Powis Castle near Welshpool and Dyrham in the Cotswolds. Celia Fiennes, who travelled through England in William and Mary's time, described many gardens and her account, together with Knyff and Kip's plates, provides a clear picture of the gardens of the period.

The vogue for evergreens, of which the best were tender and had to be overwintered under shelter, led to an improvement in greenhouses, then in their infancy. Evergreens suited formality because they could be clipped into shape and varied little throughout the season. Plants housed in this way were oranges and other members of the citrus family, myrtles, pomegranates, bays and cypress. Greenhouses at this time were still of the lean-to style facing south with solid back and

ABOVE *Topiary in the Dutch garden of Kasteel Twickel at Delden, Holland, of the kind that roused the scorn of Joseph Addison and Alexander Pope.*

RIGHT ABOVE *Clipped hedges at Kasteel Weldam at Goor in Holland, illustrating the Dutch fondness for topiary.*

RIGHT BELOW *Topiary in the seventeenth-century gardens of Levens Hall in Westmoreland, one of the few gardens in the Dutch style to survive in England.*

end walls and roof. Heat came from a fire behind the wall through a flue. London and Wise did a thriving trade in the supply of evergreens, their nursery at Brompton exceeding a hundred acres in extent.

A style adopted so uniformly was bound to provoke a reaction. While it was still at its height the first hint came of a possible change in an essay by Sir William Temple. Sir William was well acquainted with Dutch gardening at first hand as he had been ambassador to the States-General of the Netherlands from 1668-71 and again from 1674-8 and was a great lover of horticulture. He would also have been aware of the vogue on the Continent for Chinese buildings started by Louis XIV's Trianon de Porcelaine and the letters from the Jesuits in China describing Chinese gardens. In his essay, which was entitled *Of the Gardens of Epicurus*, he says that the Chinese scorn planting by rule and rote as favoured by the West, regarding this as fit only for children, and preferring something much more subtle. 'Their greatest reach of imagination', he says, 'is employed in contriving Figures, where the Beauty shall be great, and

strike the Eye, but without any order or disposition of parts, that shall be commonly or easily observed.' Although it was to be some time yet before the full effect was felt, this passage is generally held to be the forerunner of the introduction of Chinese influence into British gardening. Other influences were also at work.

There were some who, like the third Earl of Shaftesbury, were perceptive enough to realize that the whole of garden design had got off on the wrong foot with the Renaissance attempt to recreate the Roman scene; that all the gardening since that time had put the buildings and the garden architecture first and the plants second, whereas the true instincts of man urged him always towards the natural scene, the paradise of the Garden of Eden to which in his primitive state he had been so long accustomed. Shaftesbury, one of the principal Deist writers, who exercised a wide influence, particularly on the Continent, set out his view in a work published in 1711. 'I shall no longer', he wrote, 'resist the passion for things of a natural kind: where neither Art, nor the Conceit or Caprice of Man has spoiled their genuine order by breaking in upon the Primitive State. Even the rude Rocks, the mossy Caverns, the irregular unwrought grottos and broken falls of Waters, with all the horrid graces of the Wilderness itself, as representing Nature more, will be the more engaging, and appear with a magnificence beyond the mockery of princely gardens.'

Powerful allies reinforced the attack. On June 25th, 1712, Addison wrote in the *Spectator* that 'if the natural Embroidery of the Meadows were helpt and improved by some small Additions of Art and the several Rows of Hedges set off by Trees and Flowers, that the Soil was capable of receiving, a Man might make a pretty landskip of his own Possessions' but 'our British Gardeners . . . instead of honouring Nature, love to deviate from it as much as possible. Our trees rise in Cones, Globes and Pyramids. We see the Marks of the Scissars upon every Plant and Bush . . . for my own part, I would rather look upon a Tree in all its Luxuriancy and Diffusion of Boughs and Branches, than when it is thus cut and Trimmed into a Mathematical Figure . . .' Pope reiterated and reinforced this view in a passage in the *Guardian* and added to it a mock catalogue of examples of topiary for sale:

Adam and Eve in yew; Adam a little shattered by the fall of the tree of knowledge in the great storm: Eve and the Serpent very flourishing.

The tower of Babel, not yet finished.

St. George in box; his arm scarce long enough, but will be in condition to stick the dragon by next April.

A pair of giants, stunted, to be sold cheap.

Divers eminent modern poets in bays, somewhat blighted, to be disposed of, a pennyworth.

A quickset hog, shot up into a porcupine, by its being forgot one week in rainy weather.

Noah's ark in holly, standing on the mount; the ribs a little damaged for want of water.

In the face of this ridicule, and its own extravagancies, which could not endure against the strong promptings of instinct, the vogue for extreme formality and the excessive use of clipped evergreens subsided and the pendulum began to swing in the other direction. There had been isolated moves already towards more irregularity but it was the two professional gardeners Stephen Switzer and Charles Bridgeman who first introduced somewhat freer practices into their designs.

Switzer was a product of the firm of London and Wise, being taken in as a partner when London died in 1713. In 1715 he published the *Nobleman's Gentleman's and Gardener's Recreation*, republished three years later, greatly amplified, under the title of *Ichnographia Rustica*. This showed some concessions to irregularity and dispensed with the ornate parterre, so that the break with the past had undoubtedly commenced, although it had not gone very far. Bridgeman succeeded Wise in charge of the royal gardens. Horace Walpole said of him that although he 'still adhered much to strait walks with high clipt hedges, they were his only great lines; the rest he diversified by wilderness, and with loose groves of oak, though still within surrounding hedges . . . . As his reformation gained footing, he ventured farther, and in the Royal Gardens at Richmond dared to introduce cultivated fields, and even morsels of forest appearance.' Walpole considered that the first step toward the revolution in gardening was the introduction of the sunk fence or 'ha-ha', which he attributed to Bridgeman, although the generally received opinion now is that, although Bridgeman took it up and used it, he did not himself invent it. The introduction of the ha-ha achieved, as the Japanese achieved in their gardens, integration of the garden with the landscape beyond it, by removing any artificial barrier to the vision.

In 1719 Lord Burlington, whose skill and patronage founded Palladian architecture in England, brought back William Kent with him when he returned from Italy and installed him at Burlington House in Chiswick. Although Kent designed few gardens, and did not enter the field of garden designing until 1730, it was he who gave direction to the movement away from regularity in design. The pictures of Claud Gelée of Lorrain, Gaspard Poussin and Salvator Rosa, in which Roman ruins, temples and other objects are depicted against a background of nature, greatly impressed him and seemed to him to capture the feeling that Shaftesbury had expressed. Kent tried to reproduce the essence of these painting in the English landscape. In so doing, says Horace Walpole, 'he leaped the fence, and saw that all nature was a garden.' If he had truly seen this, in its simplest sense, he would have turned to the Garden of Eden for inspiration. What he really saw was expressed more aptly by the German poet Schiller, who felt that Kent and his followers sought not for what nature unadorned could show, but for something in their own minds that was 'Nature excelled by Art'.

One only of the gardens designed by William Kent remains as he left it, the garden of General Dormer at Rousham in Oxfordshire. Bridgeman had been called in to work on this garden as early as 1725 but what he did was caught up in Kent's design when the latter took over. Bridgeman thereafter worked under Kent carrying out his plans. The house at Rousham stands on level ground looking out over a lawn between woodlands to an artificial ruin on the other side of the river Cherwell, which glides by in two sharp turns at the foot of a sloping bank. In the woods to the right was

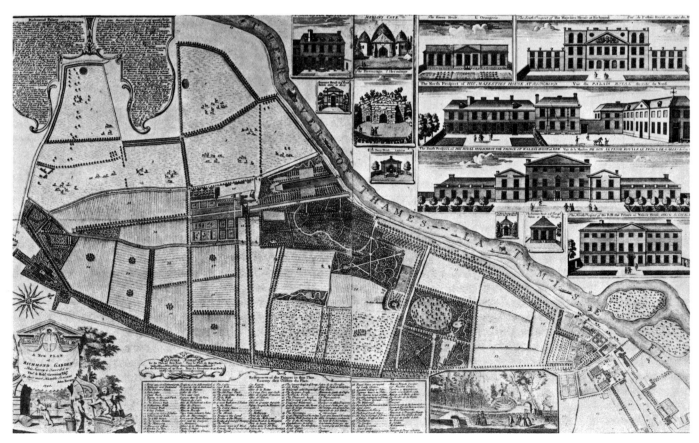

a house with a pyramid roof, the main part of the garden being in the woods to the left. A path which begins at the further end of the lawn from the house passes through woods on the river side which were balanced by a more open grove on the other side. At the end of this path the statue of the Dying Gladiator appears to the right between two Terms (busts on pedestals). The eye is carried from these over a balustrade across the sharp bend that the river makes at this point to the land on the other side of the river, a pleasant agricultural scene. Turning half left there is also a view over the balustrade through an alley in the trees to a giant statue of Apollo silhouetted against a tree clump with his back to the viewer.

Continuing along the balustrade the path leads into the Vale of Venus opposite the largest of three ponds. Up the vale to the left is the first of the ponds and the upper cascade surmounted by Venus, with Pan and a faun peeping from the undergrowth. The light and shade of the trees was carefully chosen by Kent, who lopped the lower branches in some cases, to give precisely the mixture of mystery and beauty the scene demanded of which, even today, some of the effect may be felt. Below the largest pond is the lower cascade beyond which the vale leads into the alley previously mentioned. Looking to the right at this point there is a delightful view of the arcade that supports the balustrade to which, when it was first built, the name Praeneste was immediately applied, and which may be seen at its best at an angle as from this place. A path leading back into the woods on the left takes the viewer to a dark octagonal woodland pool called the Cold Bath behind which is a small arched cavern-like building.

BELOW LEFT *A plan made by John Roque in 1748 of the gardens of George II at Richmond, Surrey, the northern part of which (the right-hand part in the picture) is included in present-day Kew Gardens. The winding lines of Charles Bridgeman's paths, and the 'cultivated fields' and 'morsels of forest appearance' mentioned by Horace Walpole may be seen in the centre of the plan. Two garden buildings of the kind fashionable on the Continent, Merlin's Cave and the Hermitage, are also illustrated.*

ABOVE *Radiating* allées *giving a view of the Doric Column and Deer House respectively at Chiswick House, Middlesex.*

BELOW *An exedra (a semi-circular area at the end of a garden bounded on the curved side by a hedge) at Chiswick House.*

The artificial rill that drains the ponds is self-consciously serpentine, and one of the first examples of this fashion, which became the badge of the new style. A walk down the alley to the giant Apollo reveals another fine view beyond the clump of trees near it to the ancient Heyford Bridge across the river.

There are two straight lines only in Kent's plan for Rousham, the path from the lawn down into the woods and that of the alley leading to the Apollo. The rest is wholly irregular and the views carefully calculated to produce a picturesque effect. The conception at the time was revolutionary and the design the antithesis of gardens made at the beginning of the century. With it the new era was inaugurated. Alexander Pope put the new doctrine into words in his poem 'Epistle to Richard Boyle, Earl of Burlington', published in 1731, at almost the same time as Kent ventured into garden design. The two were friends and influenced one another. Here is Pope's poetic guide to the principles on which the garden designer should proceed:

> To build, to plant, whatever you intend,
> To rear the Column, or the Arch to bend,
> To swell the Terrace, or to sing the Grot;
> In all, let Nature never be forgot.
> But treat the Goddess like a modest fair,
> Nor over-dress, nor leave her wholly bare;
> Let not each beauty ev'rywhere be spy'd,
> Where half the skill is decently to hide.

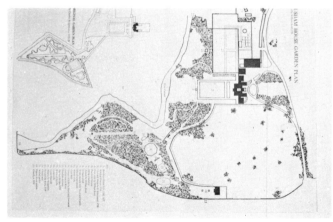

TOP *An engraving of a landscape by Claude Gellée of Lorraine (1600-82), who inspired William Kent to try to reproduce the scenes of Claude's landscape paintings in the English countryside. The effect is softer and altogether more poetic than the starkness and severity of the picture by Bril.*

ABOVE *Plan of the garden at Rousham House, Oxfordshire, England, showing William Kent's plan for the garden and, as an inset, Bridgeman's original layout which Kent altered.*

TOP *The upper cascade in the Vale of Venus at Rousham House, showing the statue of Venus with cupids.*

ABOVE *The cascades and pools in the Vale of Venus in the garden of Rousham House, Oxfordshire.*

He gains all points, who pleasingly confounds,
Surprises, varies, and conceals the Bounds.
Consult the Genius of the Place in all;
That tells the Waters or to rise, or fall;
Or helps th'ambitious Hill the heav'ns to scale,
Or scoops in circling theatres the Vale;
Calls in the Country, catches op'ning glades,
Joins willing woods, and varies shades from shades;
Now breaks, or now directs, th'intending Lines;
Paints as you plant, and, as you work, designs.

Pope had a garden of his own at Twickenham. As it was small, about 100 by 200 yards, scope for applying his ideas was limited, but the garden did become famous. His house faced east with a lawn sloping to the Thames, being separated at the back by the Hampton Road from the five acres extending westward which formed the main garden. He had a tunnel built under the road for access and turned this into a grotto with rough rocks, shells and bits of glass to reflect the light of lamps, using also a natural spring.

With all respect to Pope, however, it was a poor thing compared with the magnificent grottoes of the great gardens of the Continent. Coming out of the grotto the

NEXT PAGE *Sir John Vanbrugh's massive bridge at Blenheim Palace, Oxfordshire, is matched by the extensive lake which was created by 'Capability' Brown to set off its majestic proportions.*

eye was first attracted by a temple decorated with shells in the shadow of a mount. Along the south edge of the main garden was a strip of kitchen garden with a vineyard and pineapple stove cut off from the rest by a screen of trees. The rest of the garden was composed of three sections. From the mount in the eastern piece a short alley led between open plantations into the bowling green which was about 40 yards long and had curved sides. Beyond it, loosely framed by trees, was a vista about 60 yards in length not quite aligned with the axis of the garden. This vista rose slightly and narrowed towards the terminal obelisk, which commemorated Pope's mother and was set amid cypress trees. Each section was different from the next but merged into it via urns or statues or some greenery. The shrubberies at the sides were penetrated by walks mostly straight but irregular in direction, meeting and diverging at various focal points and coming here and there out into the glade comprising the vista. Horace Walpole thought highly of this garden. 'The passing through the gloom', he wrote, 'from the grotto to opening day: the retiring and again assembling shades: the dusky groves, the larger lawn, and the solemnity of the termination of the cypresses that led up to his mother's tomb, are managed with exquisite judgement.'

The new interest in nature, the beginning of the movement that was to culminate in Romanticism, spread through arts other than garden-making. James Thomson was at this time writing and subsequently revising 'The Seasons', a poem of immense influence in

LEFT *A landscape painted by Paolo Bril (1554-1626), whose work had a considerable influence upon Agostini Tassi, who taught the painter Claude Lorraine, from whose paintings William Kent drew his inspiration for the kind of landscape he tried to create in the English countryside. The family relationship between the ruin portrayed in the middle ground of Bril's picture and William Kent's 'eyecatcher' at Rousham is striking.*

ABOVE *The 'eyecatcher' at Rousham House, Oxfordshire, is sited to create the illusion of a landscape with ruins in the distance. The views in this garden, of the countryside and of particular objects, were carefully calculated to give a picturesque effect.*

its day throughout Europe. In contrast to the classicism of Pope, nature, in Thomson's work, while being treated romantically, is dealt with in a truthful and unaffected manner. Hogarth, too, was developing the ideas that led him to draw a serpentine line on his palette and claim that this was the 'Line of Beauty', thus eschewing the regularity of the straight line. Surging up through the artificiality that had held sway for so long was the craving for parkland, water and trees released from the slavery to architecture, the craving for the Paradise in which all but the last fraction of the early years of the human species had been passed. So fundamental an urge could never be fully satisfied in a country where the population was large enough to require extensive areas of land to be devoted to food

production but, once released, it was a powerful factor for change.

The efforts of Kent and Pope still contained many elements of artificiality and even at the time they were first giving solid form to their notions of the new style it was already changing into something different. Philip Southcote, scion of an old Catholic recusant family, married the dowager Duchess of Cleveland in 1734 and, with her money, being almost penniless himself, bought Wooburn Farm a mile or two west of Weybridge in Surrey. Here, over the next few years, he developed the first *ferme ornée,* incorporating in it several ideas of his own. Southcote moved in circles which would have fully acquainted him with the ideas of the day and in designing his estate he made full use of these, providing ornamental buildings and beautiful if artifically created effects. He saw at once, however, that the confining of these to one area, as at Rousham, left the rest of the estate to agricultural purposes which, although possessing their own rough beauty, could with some attention be made as beautiful as the rest of

the estate, so that it formed one harmonious whole enveloping the house like the setting round a jewel. He therefore took borders of trees, shrubs and flowers out among his fields, so that there was colour and variegated verdure to set off the grass or the crops. He paid great attention to heights, shades of colour and shapes of what he used and worked according to certain rules, though he still looked upon what he was doing as 'painting' the landscape. Round the whole he made a peripheral walk backed on the outside by a screening tree and shrub border so that he could see every part of his farm in a brisk walk round within half an hour. Miles Hadfield has very aptly said in *Gardening in Britain* that 'Kent strove to create an Elysium: a classical Paradise seen through the eyes of a Claude. Southcote's ambition was an Arcady: the ideal countryside. The Roman gods themselves dwelt within the first; mortal Strephons and Uranias, Phillidas and Corydons, slip in and out of the second.'

Southcote's garden became very popular, many coming to see this new and beautiful conception, including a number of landowners who were so impressed that they went back to their own estates determined to reproduce what they had seen. Chief among these was William Shenstone the poet, who at Leasowes, a small farm near Birmingham, created his own version of Southcote's ideas. Shenstone was the publicist of the *ferme ornée* and is remembered, unjustly enough, in literature far more than Southcote, who was the true originator of the fashion. Three or four miles south-east of Wooburn Farm, on the other side of St

TOP *The stream running down through the woods in a serpentine channel at Rousham House. Although traces of earlier serpentine streams exist, notably at nearby Heythrop in Oxfordshire, the channel at Rousham is the first architecturally constructed channel to survive: it set the fashion and ousted the straight line altogether.*

ABOVE *Wooburn Farm at Weybridge, Surrey, as shown in an eighteenth-century engraving; here, in the 1730s, Philip Southcote created the first* ferme ornée *(literally, 'a decorated farm'). The long shrub and flower border by which the pasture land in the foreground is divided from the serpentine stream may be seen stretching across the picture following the curve of the water.*

TOP *A Chinese bridge at Pain's Hill, near Cobham, Surrey; the garden, created by Charles Hamilton in valleys running down to the River Mole, was described by Horace Walpole as a 'savage' garden in contrast to the quiet agricultural domesticity of Wooburn Farm, Southcote's ferme ornée nearby.*

ABOVE *The still and gloomy pool known as the Cold Bath and the serpentine stream and shelter under the trees in the garden of Rousham House, Oxfordshire.*

George's Hill, another garden development was taking place at this time on a site rather different from that of Wooburn Farm. At Pain's Hill near Cobham in Surrey, the Hon. Charles Hamilton was forming an ornamental park on a site where valleys ran steeply down the hill to the River Mole. He made a thirty-acre lake and erected a number of ornamental buildings, including many of the stock items such as a hermitage and a grotto under a bridge, but the charm of the garden lay in the clever use of the site to produce a number of fine views and the way it was embellished with a large number of the exotic trees and shrubs that were now becoming available. The scenery was much wilder than the mild farmland and gentle hill of Wooburn farm, which caused Horace Walpole to distinguish Pain's Hill as a 'savage' garden distinct in type from the *ferme ornée*.

Also near Wooburn Farm, about three miles to the south, was the village of Byfleet, which in 1748 became the home of Joseph Spence, a clergyman and friend of Pope who, in his *Anecdotes (Observations and Characters of Books and Men)*, acted as a kind of Boswell to him and is thus a figure of some importance in the literary world. He was also much in demand as an amateur garden designer and left among his papers a set of rules for garden design which are the distilled essence of what he learnt from Kent, Pope and Southcote. They are too long to set out in full but emphasized two points very strongly: nature must be the first guide and anything that savoured of geometrical design must be avoided, and variety in every aspect is vital. There was everything to be said for helping nature, e.g. in

providing water where none existed, but art must not appear in whatever is done; if the ground is flat, it must be made irregular; disagreeable objects must be concealed and agreeable ones brought out; there must be a unity drawing the parts together not only with themselves but with the surrounding countryside; the useful and ornamental could be mixed, as in the *ferme ornée*; objects near should be made to appear far off and vice versa as circumstances demanded; in choosing plants the greatest regard should be paid to harmonizing colour and shape at all times of the year; and that, with regard to light and shade, preference should always be given to the former as more cheerful. Spence had the greatest admiration for Southcote's *ferme ornée*, remarking after a visit to Wooburn Farm, 'Where the old place of Paradise was I know not, but where the present is, I know full well.'

One of the great estates under almost continuous development in the first half of the eighteenth century

ABOVE *This Gothic garden house on the estate of Lord Cobham at Stowe, Buckinghamshire, a garden worked on by Bridgeman, Kent and 'Capability' Brown, illustrates the eclectic taste for different architectural styles in garden buildings which developed during the eighteenth century. Later on the taste for so-called 'Gothic' novels developed and the vogue swelled into the Gothic architectural revival of the nineteenth century.*

RIGHT ABOVE *This attractive water-parterre on the terraces of Blenheim Palace, Sir John Vanbrugh's grand creation in Oxfordshire, in the early years of the eighteenth century, is the rival of anything of its kind to be seen in France, or, indeed, in the rest of Europe.*

RIGHT BELOW *The Eleven-Acre Lake at Stowe, Buckinghamshire, seen through the arch of the Hermitage on the south side of the lake.*

was that of Lord Cobham at Stowe in Buckinghamshire. Employed there in the 1740s carrying out works first under Bridgeman and then under Kent was a young northerner named Lancelot Brown. When the two older men dropped out Brown continued, sometimes being lent to neighbouring estates. By 1751 he felt confident enough to launch out on his own as a garden designer and moved to Hammersmith. There was every encouragement to take this step. In 1739 a writer in the *World* had commented, 'Every man now, be his fortune what it will, is to be doing something at his place, as the fashionable phrase is, and you hardly meet with anybody who, after the first compliments, does not inform you that he is in Mortar and moving of Earth, the modest terms for building and gardening. One large Room, a Serpentine River and a Wood are become the absolute Necessities of Life, without which a gentleman of the smallest fortune thinks he makes no figure in the country.' There were a number of factors contributing

RIGHT *This frontispiece, drawn by Samuel Wale and engraved by Isaac Taylor for William Hanbury's* A Complete Body of Planting and Gardening, *was published in 1773. Hanbury's work was one of a procession of books on gardening that were disseminating knowledge of the art of garden design and of the new plants becoming available at that time and the picture is a fair specimen of the type of illustration with which they were provided. The goddess Cybele is in the centre of the picture, crowned and seated against a tree, with a basket of fruit and flowers in her lap and Zephyrus on the left. On the right the gardener leans on his spade while the putti in the foreground are ready with the tools, bucket and roller.*

to this ferment. Common land was being enclosed, new methods of reclamation and husbandry were coming in, better roads were being made and many new species of trees and shrubs were becoming available. Kent had worked on a small scale only: he had not had to deal with the large areas that were now confronting Brown. A new approach was needed and Brown was equal to the challenge. Although trained by Kent, he did not, as Kent did, see each landscape as a picture conceived by Claude or Salvator Rosa. He did not, indeed, see the landscape pictorially at all. He had in his mind's eye pleasant natural forms which could be fitted or adapted into each landscape in turn. To his quick eye, each stretch of countryside was capable of being transformed into a scene which seemed to be a product of nature but in which many of the pleasant effects were artificially produced. His talent lay in seeing what he called the 'capabilities' of any stretch of farmland, rough hillside or natural water, and translating his vision into actuality.

Later in his life, in a letter sent in 1775 to someone who wanted to advise a friend in France about making an English garden he wrote:

'To produce these effects there wants a good plan, good execution, a perfect knowledge of the country and the objects in it, whether natural or artificial, and infinite delicacy in the planting, etc., so much Beauty depending in the size of the trees and the colour of the leaves to produce the effect of light and shade so very essential to the perfecting a good plan; as also hideing what is disagreeable and showing what is beautiful; getting shade from the large trees and sweets from the smaller sorts of shrubbs, etc.'

This is not so very different from Spence's list of Kent's rules. Brown had, in fact, absorbed all that had been said about the 'natural' style and Hogarth's 'Line of Beauty' and had been influenced, too, by Edmund Burke's essay 'On the Sublime and Beautiful'. Indeed, what he produced on each estate was exactly what Burke had in mind, a gentle smooth serenity in the landscape which he achieved by a sweep of lines, owing little to colour, texture or contrast.

When analysed, Brown's ideal landscape resolves itself into some simple basic elements. From Southcote he had taken the idea of the encircling belt of woodland. Horace Walpole comments rather disparagingly in a letter sent in 1751 that a particular estate had been 'well

ABOVE *The 'Pavillion' in this eighteenth-century engraving of the 'Menagerie and Pavillion' in the garden of Princess Augusta of Wales at Kew, Richmond, Surrey, was made by the architect Sir William Chambers in 1760, and said by him to be a copy of a 'Chinese open T'ing'. It is one of the earliest examples of the eighteenth-century vogue for Chinoiserie in gardens.*

RIGHT *This elegant Palladian bridge over the River Nadder at Wilton House in Wiltshire was one of the early fruits of the Palladian revival. It was made for Henry Herbert, ninth Earl of Pembroke, in 1735-7. The design was successfully copied on several other estates.*

laid out by one Brown who has set up on a few ideas of Kent and Mr. Southcote'. The belt was interrupted for any fine distant view or object of pictorial interest. Whenever possible, there was water in the middle distance. If it had to be made artificially then the ends must be concealed by a hidden dam, bridge or other device, as, for example at Blenheim, where he most successfully enlarged the water to cope with Vanbrugh's majestic bridge. River banks were left unplanted so that the sight of the green turf against the water could be enjoyed. Ha-has were used so that no intrusive barrier interrupted the sweeping view. Groves or isolated trees were planted or retained as the needs of the scene dictated. The flower and kitchen gardens were tucked discreetly away behind walls near the house.

By 1764 Brown was famous enough to attract royal attention and in that year was appointed Master Gardener to George III and given a residence at Hampton Court. One of his early tasks was to landscape the grounds of the king's country residence at Richmond, which included both the Old Deer Park and the part of modern Kew Gardens near the Thames. Queen Caroline, wife of George II, had had both Kent and Bridgeman working here. Included in the garden were two well-known buildings, the Hermitage and Merlin's Cave, as well as some other edifices from Queen Caroline's time. Brown swept all this away, planted his groves and single trees, got the Staffordshire Militia, in attendance on the King, to dig out the Laurel Vale, now the Rhododendron Dell, and produced, as far as he could on the absolutely flat site, his usual landscape, but without any great water, which seems strange with the Thames bordering one side: perhaps that was felt to be sufficient. There was in any case a two and a half acre lake on the estate next door, the relic of which is the present Palm House Pond of modern Kew. This estate, the eastern half of the Kew Gardens of today, belonged to Princess Augusta of Wales, George

ABOVE *Marie Antoinette's Hameau in the Petit Trianon in Versailles was made in the tradition of the* ferme ornée.

RIGHT *The ancient château of Chantilly, about twenty miles north of Paris, seen from its English garden, made in the eighteenth century.*

III's mother. She had employed Sir William Chambers to lay out and embellish her gardens.

Chambers had served with the Swedish East India Company and had been to China. Although Sir William Temple had drawn attention to Chinese views on garden design little was known in detail of these in the West until the letter of the Jesuit missionary Jean-Denis Attiret about them was published in 1747 in *Lettres édifiants écrites des Missions.* This was translated into English by Joseph Spence in 1749 and published in London under the pseudonym of Sir Harry Beaumont. The Chinese gardeners, the translation said:

' . . . go from one of the valleys to another, not by formal straight walks as in Europe; but by various

turnings and windings, adorned on the sides with little pavilions and charming grottos; and each of these valleys is diversified from all the rest, both by their manner of laying out the ground, and in the structure and disposition of its buildings. All the risings and hills are sprinkled with trees; and particularly with flowering trees, which are here very common. The sides of the canals, or lesser streams, are not faced (as they are with us) with smooth stone, and in a straight line, but look rude and rustic, with different pieces of rock, some of which jut out, and others recede inwards; and are placed with so much art, that you would take it to be the work of nature. In some parts the water is wide, in others narrow: here it is serpentine, and there spreads away, as if it was really pushed off by the hills and rocks. The banks are sprinkled with flowers, which rise up through the hollows in the rock work, as if they had been produced there naturally. They have a great variety of them for every season of the year.'

The publication of this letter not only gave a kind of *imprimatur* to the 'natural' style in England, it set off a new vogue in the country for Chinese buildings.

Chambers' layout for Princess Augusta's garden at Kew divided the grounds into three parts with a peripheral belt. The area to the north of the lake contained the White House where Augusta lived, a beautiful orangery in the classical style which Chambers built next to the house, the nine acres of the embryo botanic garden, a flower-garden and the menagerie; there were also several classical temples among the trees. South of the lake were two irregular meadows each surrounded by a ha-ha. Sheep and cattle grazed in these meadows, there being more buildings in the surrounding groves. The southernmost area contained the more exotic buildings. The whole formed a kind of Kentian version of the *ferme ornée*.

Altogether, Chambers built or restored eighteen buildings in Augusta's estate in the period 1756-63. He inherited a 'House of Confucius', which he moved, a 'Gothic cathedral' designed by Muntz, and probably also the menagerie, providing in addition to these ten small temples or similar constructions in the classical style and eight other buildings, including a Roman ruined arch, a Mosque and an Alhambra, as well as a 'Chinese open T'ing' in the menagerie, and the famous Pagoda, still a landmark today. The crowding of all this into Augusta's less than one hundred perfectly flat acres invited criticism and, indeed, received it. Chambers finished his work as Brown began his task on the next-door estate for George III and the contrast between the two soon became obvious. Brown was too sure of himself to be perturbed. It was Chambers who was put out and in his *Dissertation of Oriental Gardening*, published in 1772, attacked Brown. In this work Chambers, who was in reality a very good architect with a fine talent for the classical style, advocates some fanciful and even silly things and was heavily attacked by the Rev. William Mason in *An Heroic Epistle to Sir William Chambers*, published in 1774.

A page of designs for garden buildings, 'Chinese or otherwise', of the kind now called eighteenth-century 'follies', from Grotesque Architecture or Rural Ornament *by William Wright (1790).*

195

ABOVE AND RIGHT *Water-colour drawings from Humphry Repton's Red Book for Sherringham Park in Norfolk, showing in the first picture the scene before any work had been done on it and in the second the overlay scene revealed when the flap is placed over the picture to show the effect of changes proposed. Part of the curved line where the edge of the overlay falls may be seen in the first picture where the clouds not covered by it have darkened more than those under the overlay making a sharp division visible when the overlay is lifted.*

RIGHT *Humphry Repton who, in the closing years of the eighteenth century, filled the gap in the landscape gardening world left by the death of 'Capability' Brown and developed ideas of his own.*

There was some resentment by the architects of Brown's self-taught ability to design a comfortable and attractive house and Chambers was not the only one who attacked him, but the real quarrel was between those who preferred the Kentian landscape with its ruins, waterfalls and savage rocks and caverns and those who liked the smooth serenity of Brown. He did not vary his style, which satisfied his clients, but continued as he had always done until he died in 1783, making plans in his lifetime for some 211 estates, on many of which he also put the plans into effect. It is difficult now to appreciate fully the change he brought about, so much of the English countryside still bears the shape he gave it: the typical parkland gently sloping down to a stretch of water, a glimpse of a house or church through clumps of ancient trees, the whole set in the cup of the surrounding hills. His best epitaph is perhaps that of Horace Walpole, who said that 'so closely did he follow nature his works will be mistaken' for it.

Brown scrapped many fine gardens in the older styles that would have been worth preserving and has been blamed for this but blame, if any, should be laid on the owners. Although the England he created excited interest and admiration it was, in fact, the Kentian or 'picturesque' garden that was imitated abroad and was called, because the fashion was stimulated by Père Attiret's letter, *le jardin Anglo-chinois*. Most of the so-called English gardens on the Continent were, however, so poorly conceived that they were travesties of English landscaping ideas, consisting often of a stretch of shrubbery, perhaps half an acre or so in extent, penetrated by winding paths and furnished with a miscellaneous collection of hermitages, grottoes, temples and bridges. Among those still remembered are Ermenonville, the Parc Monceau south of Paris, the Little Trianon of Marie Antoinette at Versailles and Chantilly, but the German contemporary writer

Hirschfeld indicates that there were many such gardens laid out in or near Paris. It was Hirschfeld who stimulated the fashion for the English garden in Germany, prominent gardens in this style being made at Wörlitz, Schönau and Weimar. The garden of Charles Augustus at Schwetzingen outstripped even Kew in its mixture of architectural styles, and is condemned by Hirschfeld for it, but the most bizarre was that of Count Hoditz at Rosswald near Troppau in Silesia. Everything was put into this that could be entertained. There was a Chinese garden and temple, a Holy Grove, a Christian hermitage, Indian pagodas, a picturesque hill, a town for dwarves (enough of these could not be found, so children were substituted), Druid caves with altars, and an antique mausoleum. Other gardens had similar contents, the scope of which was widened when the craze for knightly chivalry swept Germany at the end of the century. There was a vogue for buildings masquerading as something that they were not, e.g. a servant's lodging disguised as a pile of logs. This even spread back to England, there being a hay-wagon at Windsor with a room inside it. The *jardin anglais* spread over the Continent from Drottningholm in Sweden to Potsdam in Germany and Queluz in Portugal. Even splendid Renaissance gardens in Italy were defaced to conform to the fashion, which was as widespread in influence in the eighteenth century as Le Nôtre's influence had been in the seventeenth century.

For a few years after Brown's death no real successor emerged but in 1788 Humphry Repton took up the vacant place. Born at Bury St Edmunds in 1752, he owned for a time a small estate at Sustead near Norwich, making several unsuccessful ventures which reduced his fortune before he lighted on his true vocation. Repton was a man of intelligence and education. He subscribed to most of the ideas of Brown but was more flexible in some respects, using features such as a terrace from older styles and even

incorporating 'monastic' or 'Tudor' flower-beds in his designs. His gift for drawing was a great help to him. For each estate he drew up a set of notes which was accompanied by a coloured sketch of the existing landscape. Over this he superimposed a transparent sheet with a sketch of the estate as he suggested it should be. He bound his proposals in red (sometimes brown) morocco leather and in that handsome form presented them to his clients. Many of Repton's 'Red Books', as they are known, of which he produced over four hundred in his career, have survived. Repton's schemes were seldom of such great extent as Brown's had been and often fitted into parks originally laid out by Brown. They included work at such famous estates as Welbeck, Woburn in Bedfordshire, Uppark, Harewood, Holkham, Sherringham and Stanage.

Repton had not been practising long before a storm blew up. William Gilpin, the chief advocate of the 'picturesque' style, that is, nature in its most savage and romantic moods, published *Observations Relative to Picturesque Beauty* in 1789. The subject was taken up by two Herefordshire landowners, Uvedale Price of Foxley and Richard Payne Knight of Downton Castle. The former published an *Essay on the Picturesque* in 1794 and the latter a didactic poem in support. Price's book attacked Brown and Repton felt bound to defend him in a book of his own published shortly afterwards. He rejected the 'picturesque' approach as too limited, taking the sensible view that 'in whatever relates to man, propriety and convenience are not less objects of good taste than picturesque effect.' He did not agree with the view that landscape gardening was a form of painting; he pointed out that the situation for the painter was a self-chosen static view, while the gardener saw the scene changing as he moved, over a much greater field of vision, and in many changing lights. Repton died in 1816; in his later years many changes were taking place that were soon to produce an entirely different gardening scene.

13
The Coming of the Flowers

See how the flowers, as at parade,
Under their colours stand displayed . . .

Andrew Marvel

Humphry Repton died in the year after Waterloo and it might almost be said that with him died the art of landscape gardening. While the English landscape style continued to influence the making of gardens in other countries for many years after this, the heart had gone out of the movement in the home country. Conversation on 'improvements', formerly a topic of perennial interest, suddenly lost its savour in the world of the Industrial Revolution, and ceased almost overnight. It was as if Brown and Repton had said the last word on garden design and nothing remained to be done. The truth is, of course, that interest had not ceased, but that pressure of new developments had brought about a change in direction.

The seeds of the change had been sown in the previous century. Even while Brown was firmly establishing his style, John Bartram was sending quantities of American plants over to Peter Collinson at Mill Hill and others were coming in from all over the world. These were grown mainly at first by Philip Miller at the Chelsea Physic Garden and then after 1760 at the Royal Botanic Gardens at Kew, but there were also a number of private collections. Among the new plants were many that were more colourful than any that had hitherto been at the disposal of the gardener and the accumulated weight of these accessions gradually tilted the scale away from Brown's idea of trees, lawns and water, with the flowers, such as they were, tucked away inconspicuously in a walled garden. The desire grew to show off these handsome plants and to plant them where they could be seen. The first step was the making of shrubberies of American plants, as these could be grown outside all the year round in the English climate, but they formed only a small proportion of the whole. The less hardy plants had to be grown in glasshouses and the number available began to be an embarrassment.

The new plants filling the glasshouses included the South African heaths, mainly introduced by Francis Masson, the first Kew plant collector, who was working

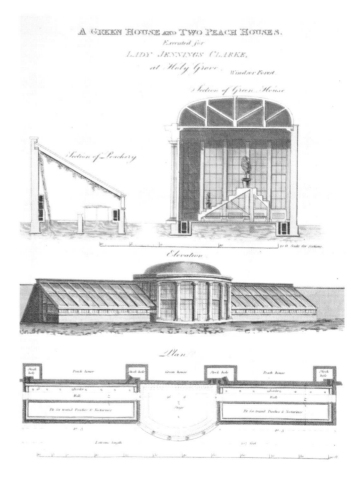

LEFT *Herbaceous border by the Orangery and Theatre Tower at Chatsworth.*

ABOVE *An illustration from* Plans of Hothouses, Greenhouses, etc., *(London, 1812) of one of the many new glasshouses built in the early years of the nineteenth century. In this case the designer has economically combined a greenhouse for taller plants with two peach houses.*

in the 1770s. Some 250 species were still available from nurserymen in 1830 and there had been many more. From South Africa, too, came the pelargoniums. Sir James Edward Smith wrote in *Rees Cyclopaedia* of 1819 that 'the writer . . . well recollects the pleasure which the novel sight of an African geranium *(Pelargonium)* in Yorkshire and Norfolk, gave him about forty years ago. Now every garret and cottage window is filled with numerous species of that beautiful tribe, and every greenhouse glows with the innumerable bulbous plants and splendid heaths of the Cape. For all these we are primarily indebted to Mr. Masson, besides a multitude of rarities, more difficult of preservation or propagation, confined to the more curious collections.' The first fuchsia came into Kew in 1789 and a specimen obtained by James Lee, of the nursery firm of Lee and Kennedy, was promptly propagated very profitably, the firm being reputed to have made £300 from plants raised from it. Lady Bute received dahlias from Mexico in the same year but the stock was lost and these were not reintroduced until imported by Lady Holland in 1804. Twenty years later there was hardly a plant more popular.

The making of shrubberies of American plants and the hardier species from elsewhere was soon followed by the making of beds for flowers which would survive outdoors. As it happened, once the idea was launched that the green expanse of lawn around the house, hitherto inviolate, could be breached, it was not difficult to fit the new beds into the landscape garden. Marie Elizabeth Jackson wrote in the *Florists' Manual* in 1816 that 'A flower garden is now become the appendage of every fashionable residence,' and complained that, because it had become an accepted thing, novice owners frequently left it to their gardeners to fill and wasted their money:

'It is more frequently left to the direction of a gardener than arranged by the guidance of genuine taste in the owner, and the fashionable novice, who has stored her borders from the catalogue of some celebrated name with a variety of rare species, who has procured innumerable rose trees, chiefly consisting of old and common sorts, brought into notice by new nomenclature, who has set aside a portion of ground for American plants, and duly placed them in bog soil [peat], with their names printed on large-headed pegs, becomes disappointed when, instead of the brilliant glow of her neighbour's *parterre,* she finds her own distinguished only by paucity of colour and fruitless expenditure.'

Maria Jackson envisaged the new flower-garden as set 'in the midst of pleasure grounds, surrounded by shrubs'. Beds she illustrates were 25 feet long, of tadpole shape and 4 feet across at the widest part; they were twisted in the grass in irregular ways, there being 5 or 6 feet of grass between the beds. There were also 'baskets' at various points. These were circular beds, surrounded by cast-iron made to resemble the open edges of a basket and painted dark green. The ironwork (basket willow edging was also used) was sometimes put round all the beds. One form of 'basket' consisted of

a series of diminishing circles of rustic woodwork raised to a height of several feet, the lowest ring being 12 or 15 feet in diameter, each tier being planted with rows of geraniums or other brightly coloured flowers in the summer.

It was a small step only from this type of bedding to the next phase: in 1825 Richard Harris advocated for the first time in his 'Essay on Landscape Gardening' the practice of 'bedding out' half-hardy subjects. 'The beauty of the flower-garden in the summer season', he said, 'may be heightened by planting in the beds some of the most free-flowering young and healthy greenhouse plants. Where there is an extent of greenhouse, a sufficient quantity of plants should be grown annually for this purpose, and should be sunk in

TOP LEFT *A nineteenth-century view of Dytchley House, showing a conservatory of attractive curved design looking out over carpet bedding.*

ABOVE LEFT *A very early example of the then new art of photography, showing the great Palm House at Kew Gardens under construction in the mid-1840s. This large glasshouse, built to allow the housing of palm trees until they grew to maturity, was designed by Decimus Burton and erected by Richard Turner, ironmaster of Dublin, who greatly influenced the design. Its erection parallels the building of the 'Great Eastern', the largest iron ship yet made, which was constructed at almost the same time.*

TOP RIGHT *A row of glasshouses built down the slope of the hill at Chatsworth, Derbyshire, by Sir Joseph Paxton to which he gave the name of the 'Conservative Wall', 'conservative' being used in the sense of 'conservatory' and not with a political meaning.*

ABOVE *A mid-Victorian engraving of the Palm House at Kew Gardens, Surrey, showing beds filled with a mixture of flowers, shrubs and trees resembling the sub-tropical bedding of later in the eighteenth century. Kew being a botanic garden devoted to growing exotic plants, the bedding depicted may not, however, be typical of the time.*

ABOVE *A mid-nineteenth century artist's impression from* Der Wintergarten in der Kaiserlichen Königlichen Hofburg zu Wien *painted by Franz Antoine (Vienna, 1852) of a winter garden under cover. The great number of attractive new plants which were almost hardy and could be grown in such gardens encouraged many to make them. One of the most popular plants in winter gardens was the camellia, with bright showy flowers and a long flowering period.*

LEFT *John Claudius Loudon (1783-1843), whose voluminous writings in the first half of the nineteenth century had an immense influence over the whole field of horticulture, including garden design.*

the beds about the middle or end of May.' Plants were thought to look better in masses and beds were filled with different flowers according to the time of the year, mixed with plants with coloured leaves. Plants recommended were *Anagallis grandiflora, Anagallis monelli, Heliotropum grandiflorum, Fuchsia coccinea, Lobelia erinus, Alstroemeria pelegrina, Bouvardia triphylla, Lychnis coronaria, Linum trigyna* and geraniums of all sorts. Thus was founded the practice of 'carpet bedding', which flourished and remained practically unchallenged from this time until 1880. The invention by Budding in the early 1830s of the

ABOVE *A mid-Victorian artist's painting from* The Gardens of England *by E. Adveno Brooke (1857) of the Earl of Harrington's garden at Elvaston Hall, near Derby, England, showing a formal garden ('Mon Plaisir') with an enclave surrounded by a thick serpentine clipped hedge. The central object of this enclave is one of the new conifers introduced by David Douglas from America, planted in a star of carpet bedding. A number of other conifers are scattered throughout the garden, showing their popularity.*

lawn-mower, which enabled the neatness of the beds to be much enhanced by a closely shorn frame of grass.

While these changes were taking place, the range of attractive plants of all kinds was steadily increasing. Roses originating in China which were imported in the 1790s formed the foundation stock from which modern roses have been developed and it soon became the practice to make a separate rosery in a sheltered spot among the shrubberies. The roses, both dwarf and standard, were arranged in neat little beds with wire arches between them. The new hybrids, such as were hardy enough to grow outdoors, were grown alongside the older roses, the damasks, the York and Lancaster rose, the moss rose and others of the old shrub roses. Other kinds of shrubs were rapidly increasing in number. Shrubberies containing American plants, which were still being made as separate creations in 1830, contained magnolias, rhododendrons (including azaleas), *Andromeda, Kalmia* and *Vaccinium* species and allspice. Collectors sent out by the Horticultural Society (now the Royal Horticultural Society) which had been formed in 1804, by Kew Gardens and by some of the great nursery firms, speeded up the acquisition of more material. By 1840 the gardener had a range from

which to choose, among them being deutzias, diervillas (*Weigela*), *Pyrus japonica*, spiraeas, veronicas, and *Berberis*.

Glasshouse populations continued to be augmented at a rapid rate. The introductions from South Africa had already caused such pressure that separate accommodation had to be provided by those who grew them in quantity. In the 1790s plants began to come in from Australia and soon acacias, eucalyptus, *Melaleuca, Metrosideros, Boronia, Banksia* and others were competing for space and repeating the problem. After the Napoleonic wars cacti from the New World and aloes, mesembryanthemums and crassulas from the Old were grown. It was not long, indeed, before succulents, particularly cacti, became the objects of wealthy collectors. Specimens of choice shrubs such as magnolias had for a long time commanded high prices and now rare cacti joined the high price range, some fetching a very high figure indeed.

Orchids had proved difficult to grow and although some had flowered in cultivation, the number was few. They began to come in at a greater rate after 1815 but for a time there was still little success in growing them because of lack of information about their natural habitat. John Smith, at the time a young foreman at Kew Gardens, had many under his care that had been sent in by Kew plant collectors. When, in the 1820s, one of his Kew colleagues, David Lockhart, sent him orchids from Trinidad still growing epiphytically (i.e. perched on the support but not rooted in it) on the tree branches where they had been found, he was able to adopt methods which achieved greater success. Their beauty soon caused new orchids to be much sought after and for them, too, very high prices were paid by

203

TOP *Stones designed as carpet bedding in an eighteenth-century parterre at Tsarskoye, Leningrad.*

ABOVE *An engraving from the* Suburban Gardener and Villa Companion *(London, 1838) by John Claudius Loudon of the flower-garden at Wimbledon House, Surrey, showing a fussy arrangement of beds, shrubs and trees typical of the first half of the nineteenth century. This is the style that Loudon called 'gardenesque', in which for the first time interest in particular plants took precedence over design. It was the first step towards the collector's gardens that later came into being.*

collectors. So lucrative was the orchid trade that as the century progressed many commerical collectors were sent abroad, competition leading even to the felling of trees over large areas and the denudation of whole districts of orchids, a sorry chapter in garden history.

John Smith was also concerned in the rise in interest in ferns. He grew many from spores taken from ferns sent in by plant collectors, even using those from dried herbarium specimens, and built up a very large collection at Kew. J. C. Loudon continually urged in his publications that the beauty and ease of cultivation of ferns made them very desirable plants. Some were

found to be very good house plants and when Dr Nathaniel Ward invented the Wardian case in the 1830s, which was a kind of small portable glasshouse, it was soon adapted for use for growing ferns in the house, and the fern case became an indispensable article of decoration in the Victorian home. Later in the century many outdoor ferneries were made in gardens using the hardier species.

Up to the end of the eighteenth century glasshouses were heated by hot air led in through flues, but the greatly increased demand for heated glasshouses stimulated experiments to find better methods of heating. Attempts were made to use steam but it was soon realized that hot water was much more easily managed and many systems were devised to use it, so that a degree of reasonable facility in its use was soon developed. In the 1830s a very large glasshouse was built at Chatsworth by Sir Joseph Paxton for the Duke of Devonshire. A few years later, between 1844 and 1848, the greatest glasshouse of all was built, the Palm House at Kew Gardens, of sufficient height (62 feet) to house forest trees, so that palms could be seen for the first time in something like their full growth. Such large glasshouses were for the very wealthy or the state to build, but sizeable and ornate iron glasshouses and conservatories on a smaller scale were built in many gardens. The conservatory, indeed, played an essential part in upper-class Victorian social life.

The plant collector who stimulated the greatest change in the outdoor garden in the first half of the century was David Douglas, who travelled in North America for the Royal Horticultural Society between 1824 and 1834, when he was accidentally killed. He sent over many species of conifer, in which the flora of America is rich. A number of these took kindly to the British climate and were so widely planted that in a few years they had made a considerable change in the garden scene. Collections were formed, the pinetum at Dropmore formed in the 1830s probably being the first; the Kew pinetum was planted in 1843.

Reference has already been made to J. C. Loudon, the most remarkable and prolific writer on gardening in the first half of the nineteenth century. It is often said that Loudon subscribed to Repton's views on landscaping, but this is not true of his earlier days: he criticized Loudon subscribed to Repton's views on landscaping, that the gardening world was changing and that other gardens existed besides those of the wealthy on their large estates. Firstly he commented on the larger gardens, in which he distinguishes between the picturesque garden formerly made and the 'gardenesque' garden that had come into being, in which the quality of the 'picture' is subordinated to the display of the individual beauty of the trees, shrubs and herbaceous plants; later, in 1838, he added his observations on smaller gardens in *The Suburban Gardener and Villa Companion.* Careful to observe the social divisions so important in his day, he begins with 'fourth-rate gardens . . . of houses in a connected row or street', then the 'gardens of double detached houses, that is, of houses built in pairs and forming part of a row', then the 'gardens of houses which are detached on every side, but which still form part of a line', the last

This Chinese temple in the garden of James Bateman, made between 1842 and 1856 at Biddulph Grange in north Staffordshire, is part of an imitation Chinese garden containing also 'the ruined wall of China itself' with a watch tower, 'Chinese waters' over which this temple projects, 'a joss house, a gigantic frog, a red gravel dragon parterre, and moutans [tree paeonies] in an irregular bed.'

being 'first-rate gardens which can scarcely be less than from 50 to 100 acres'.

Loudon was responsible also for a new phenomenon in the gardening world, the production of a practical journal for gardeners, the *Gardener's Magazine* which he began in 1826 and maintained until his death in 1843. There were already publications devoted to illustrating plants, directed mainly towards those who were botanically inclined, *Curtis's Botanical Magazine,* founded in 1787, being the first, but Loudon's new periodical dealt with all aspects of gardening. Others followed, the *Gardener's Chronicle,* the paper for the professional gardener, being started in 1841 with the horticultural section edited by John Lindley of the Royal Horticultural Society. Both the *Botanical Magazine* and the *Gardener's Chronicle* are still published today.

The practice of making beds for flowers not having been laid down according to the rules of a gardening style but evolved from interest in the display of new plants, they had never been formally arranged into a standard pattern, but placed according to the gardener's whim. Round and square beds alternately, or diamond and octagon, or more fantastic shapes, were sited anywhere in the grass, or in a circle or fan in front of the house windows, on either side of the gravel walks and ribbon borders, with twist and cable patterns. A writer in the seventh edition of the *Encyclopaedia Britannica* published in 1838 stated that

The Pagoda Fountain at Alton Towers, Staffordshire, a late example of Chinoiserie in the English garden. This remarkable garden, made in the period 1815-27 by the Earl of Shrewsbury, was full of almost every exuberant conceit that ever found place in a garden and is eighteenth rather than nineteenth century in spirit.

mondii, Erysimum perofskianum, Gilia tricolor and *Lupinus nanus*. All except the *Convolvulus* had been introduced since 1826. The rather tender *Plumbago larpentae* was also used. *Ageratum mexicanum* was much in demand for planting in masses in the summer and was regarded as 'a capital thing for bouquets'. These were made for most of the century of flowers pressed closely together and arranged so as to present a flat surface of circular shape, geraniums, calcolarias and a rosebud or two being added. It was not until towards the end of the century that the loose bunch of flowers came into vogue.

The comatose state into which garden design on the grand scale in Britain had apparently fallen after the death of Repton was lifted to some extent in the period 1840-60. Not that activity had entirely ceased. The remarkable Alton Towers in Staffordshire was made in the period 1815-27 by the fifteenth Earl of Shrewsbury. This garden was full of almost every exuberant conceit that has ever found its place in a garden, but it was exceptional and relates rather to the age of the eighteenth century than to its own time. Some of the Earl's fancies may still be seen, including a graceful pagoda. Now, however, development took a different turn. Under the influence of the architect Sir Charles Barry and the landscape designer William Andrews Nesfield, the great landowners began to make what were called 'Italian' gardens around their houses. A piece was taken from the lawn close to the house but usually on one side of it and laid out as a sunken parterre, filled in season with bedding plants. The corners of the beds were marked with dwarf trees, tall trees being kept out of the garden. If the site permitted, the garden was laid out in terraces with Italian balustrades. There were sometimes a few statues and open summerhouses, but there was no real attempt to re-create the magnificence of the Italian Renaissance garden, the colour effects of the carpet bedding being more important than the design.

These gardens were all very similar, though there were some individual differences, Italian gardens in Scotland, for example, being almost always terraced. Typical English specimens were made at Harewood House, Holland House, Longford Castle in Wiltshire, Woburn Park, Worsley, Trentham and Castle Howard. One of the earliest, which was thought to be especially effective, was the garden made by Barry and Nesfield for Lord de Saumarez at Shrubland Park near Ipswich. An elegant flight of steps ran between an upper and

'respecting the situation of a flower garden, no very precise directions can be given'. It should not, he said, be at any great distance from the house unless location in that vicinity would spoil a good view. It could be of any shape, and might lead on into a shrubbery gradually becoming woodland. Individual beds could also be of any shape, kidney shape being perhaps too frequently used. The garden could include flowers in pots but, if it did, the pots must suit one another and the situation. There should be a good space between figures otherwise there was a danger of 'spottiness' (we should perhaps have called it 'fussiness'). A gravel walk was necessary on one side for access in winter and wet weather. Where beds were not made in turf they needed to be larger, narrow borders and concentric curves being taboo in all cases. The centres of figures should be marked with a tall shrub or evergreen (yew or holly) and a sundial, a few seats and arbours, with an urn or two, improved the scene.

The range of plants available for bedding had increased greatly as the century progressed. Lists made in 1847 included different varieties of *Verbena, Salvia, Lobelia, Oenothera, Veronica speciosa*, antirrhinums and *Mimulus*. There were many annuals, cockscombs and balsams being much favoured. One list of the twelve best annuals in 1847 included *Bartonia aurea, Clarkia pulchella, Clarkia elegans, Clintonia pulchella, Collinsonia grandiflora, Convolvulus tricolor, Nemophila insignis, Ursinia speciosa, Phlox drum-*

lower parterre at the head of five steep terraces, all of which were bordered by balustrades and emphasized at top and bottom by an open Italian summerhouse. Taste had by now become quite eclectic, and there was no objection any more to the mixing of styles. The Duke of Westminster set up statues of knights and ladies at the neo-Gothic Eaton Hall in Cheshire instead of Renaissance-style statuary. At Newstead Abbey, home of the Byrons for several hundred years, the ancient fishpond of the monks was flanked by Italian, French and Spanish parterres set side by side, but it was hard to distinguish between them.

At Chatsworth, where the Duke of Devonshire made everything bigger and better than elsewhere, as if largeness were in itself a virtue, the main paths of the old formal style were retained and Italian and French parterres made in that style. In front of the Orangery Paxton placed a *parterre de broderie,* adding statues on small pillars at the end of it, which gave a distinctly French flavour to the scene. Paxton improved the old cascade and restored other water-works. There was also a main axial line after the European fashion from the south front of the house to the canal-like pond at the end, but these features could not overcome the effect of the gravel walks and lawns which gave the whole an English air. The general effect was something like the gardens made in England after the Restoration, shown in the engravings of Knyff and Kip. There was, however, much in the planting that was different, Paxton being a 'plantsman', interested in plants for

their own sake.

At the other end of the scale the Industrial Revolution had begun to create in the towns an artisan class, skilled workers better off than the great mass of the exploited poor, whose lot, either in town or country, was a very hard one. There had always been a few with an interest in what used to be called 'florist's flowers', such as the tulip, auricula, carnation, pink, anemone, ranunculus, hyacinth and polyanthus; now in the industrial towns among the 'manufacturing class' more attention was paid to these and they were brought to new standards of perfection, their cultivation becoming an absorbing pursuit that brightened up the drab surroundings. Particular flowers were associated with particular areas, pinks with Paisley, and auriculas with Cheshire, Lancashire and parts of Scotland. Dean Hole, the great Victorian rose-grower, wrote enthusiastically in his *A Book about Roses* of the artisan rose-growers of Nottingham. Many specialist societies were set up which formulated standards for their particular plant. Although there was no question of garden design being influenced, the flowers that might be grown were greatly improved by these efforts. An anonymous writer comments that 'the auricula is to be found in the highest perfection in the gardens of the manufacturing class, who bestow much time and attention on this and a few other flowers, as the tulip and the pink. A fine stage of these plants is scarcely ever to be seen in the gardens of the nobility and gentry, who depend upon the exertions of hired servants . . . 'Even among these

LEFT *An idealized view from the upper terrace walk of the fountain, parterre and loggia in the Italian garden, at Shrubland Park, Coddenham, near Ipswich, taken from* The Gardens of England *by E. Adveno Brooke (1857).*

ABOVE *Mid-Victorian flower-filled parterres in the Italian garden at Eaton Hall, Cheshire, as portrayed in* The Gardens of England *by E. Adveno Brooke (1857).*

RIGHT *An idealized painting of the young Joseph Hooker (afterwards Sir Joseph Hooker) collecting Asiatic rhododendrons in the Sikkim-Himalaya in 1848-52. Before this collecting journey there were 33 species of rhododendron in cultivation. To these he added 28 new ones, almost all with showy flowers. Hybridized in Britain to produce hardy varieties, they were planted so freely that they changed the look of the British countryside.*

comparatively poor people, not much above the poverty line, the urge to surround themselves with the beauties of nature and blot out their ugly man-made environment could not be repressed.

At mid-century the appearance of the British landscape was once again radically changed by the discoveries of an individual plant-collector. Just as Douglas's conifers from North America brought a new element into the country scene with their new and striking silhouettes, patterns of foliage and shades of green, so did the Asiatic rhododendrons discovered by

Dr Joseph Hooker (later Sir Joseph Hooker, Director of the Royal Botanic Gardens, Kew, and President of the Royal Society) in the Sikkim Himalayas. These he found on an expedition made in the period 1848-52; their introduction altered the look not only of the great estates but, as the years went on, many lesser gardens also, down, eventually, to Loudon's 'fourth-rate' gardens, where perhaps, a single specimen of their descendants has been planted. The species that Hooker introduced were barely hardy, growing satisfactorily only in the mildest districts of the south-west and in gardens on the western seaboards and islands of England, Scotland and Ireland, but they were extensively planted and easily hybridized, many of the offspring being reasonably hardy. These large-leaved

evergreen plants, often reaching a substantial size, growing down the valley sides in the wilder parts of the garden, on the edge of and within the woodland, and singly or in island clumps in many other places on the estates, greatly thickened up the thin winter countryside and brought a new brightness in the spring and early summer, enlivening the landscapes of Brown and Repton, now coming into full maturity, with unexpected patches of colour, bold enough to compete with the carpet bedding of the parterres near the house and, as it were, to echo it in the distance.

The situation in France in the early nineteenth century was somewhat different from that of England. The French Revolution swept away all the old gardens as if they had never been and there was every incentive,

therefore, to make something new. One or two gardens, such as that of Chandon de Briailles at Epernay, were kept up in the traditional formal style, but, in the main, gardens were landscaped on the English model. Carpet bedding very quickly caught on, and by the time of the Second Empire (the third quarter of the nineteenth century) there was the same fashion for formal flower parterres in France as there was in England. French gardens of this kind were renowned, being known under the name of *jardins fleuristes*. In Germany, Prince Pückler emerged in the earlier part of the century as the greatest apostle in that country of the English style. On his estate at Muskau he created what at the time was thought to be a masterpiece, changing the vast Neisse valley into a great park so impressive

that it long survived unchanged. Around the house, however, he fell for the new fashion and created an extensive area of carpet bedding. Interest in landscaping had dropped as much in Germany as it had in England, prompting Goethe to remark that 'park sites, once the ambition of all Germany . . . are now quite out of fashion . . . and it looks as though the fine gardens we have will soon be broken up to make potato patches.'

Activity had not wholly ceased: in the time of Frederick William IV of Prussia in mid-century there was much being done, Sans Souci being the most important of a series of princely gardens around Potsdam. The movement for the making of Italian gardens reached its peak here. The chief new feature

LEFT *Woodland at Bowood House, Wiltshire, showing the way that the rhododendron hybrids bred from those introduced by Joseph Hooker in the 1850s have thickened up the undergrowth and brightened the British countryside in flowering time.*

BELOW *Formal cascades disappeared from gardens when the English landscape style became popular, but where it was possible to incorporate a waterfall, as here at Bowood House, the pleasant sound of falling water continued to be heard in gardens.*

ABOVE *A rustic 'Belvedere' (a shelter from which to view the scenery) built out from the shore in a lake with access for a boat from the lower level, taken from Victor Petit's* Parcs et Jardins des Environs de Paris. *Such buildings would be found in the larger gardens where the water was extensive enough to permit the use of a boat.*

LEFT *A painting of a design for a grotto with a pavilion above it from the same work. These gardens were in the style of* le jardin Anglo-Chinois, *a French version of the English landscape garden often on a small scale and unrecognizable as English in origin.*

was an Orangery in which there were towers pierced and furnished with loggias that connected by corridors on pillar supports. Three terraces, the highest of which carried a flower-parterre, descended to the main road. Ludwig I of Bavaria, the great patron of the arts, made a winter garden of note at the Residence in Munich in the earlier part of the century and his grandson Ludwig II was responsible for several bizarre efforts in the period 1860-80. He tried to combine the flora of India in his palace with the architecture of the Moors but the lake he put on the roof of the building caused difficulty, and soon after his death it was abandoned. At Linderhof his ideas were more sensible. He made a great terrace garden in the baroque style, the castle being on the lowest level with a cascade behind it. On one side there were three imposing terraces with flower-beds mounting up by steps to a temple, with *giardini segreti*

ABOVE *Statuary in the gardens of the Schloss Herrenchiem-see, Bavaria, which were made by the unbalanced Ludwig II of Bavaria in imitation of Versailles on a most unsuitable site on the island of Herrenworth in the centre of Lake Chiemsee.*

RIGHT *A drawing by the French artist Anastasi from* Histoire des Jardins *(Tours, 1883), showing the garden of A. M. Furtado at Rocquencourt in France, with a rustic climber-covered building in the foreground.*

at the sides of the house. The project was never finished. His most extraordinary effort was an attempt to create a Versailles in the Bavarian mountains on a most unsuitable island site in the Herrenchiemsee.

Side by side with these royal aberrations, the final fantasies of German petty princedom, a more democratic change was taking place. Great gardens in many countries had always been open to the general public at the whim of their aristocratic owners. Now the feeling had grown that, with the rapid extension of towns into cities, some part of the land within the cities should be set aside for public use both to beautify the city and afford a place of recreation for the people. This movement was not confined to one country, nor instigated by one particular country, although it was basically the English landscape garden that provided the model. In London Kensington Gardens, Hyde Park, the Green Park, St James's Park and Regent's Park were all made available, providing 1,200 acres of green open land within the expansion of the urban area. A standard arrangement developed naturally to combine relaxation with amenities for more strenuous recreation.

The large picturesque lake of the landscape garden was essential for this second purpose and on it boats were provided for hire. The shady walks led into wide meadow grounds which could be used for gatherings or

games. Around the buildings, along the edges of the paths and in areas specially set aside for the purpose carpet bedding found, towards the end of the century, what was probably its most congenial home, where it still survives, in spite of much vituperation directed against it over the years. The rose-garden, too, came into its own, as did also the herbaceous border. Refreshment houses were provided, but hidden by trees so as not to intrude on the scene. Smaller towns echoed this pattern throughout Britain. The movement was not unaccompanied by small-town pettiness. Many parks did not permit visitors to walk on the grass in case they damaged it. There may have been some reason for this on certain soils but in the main it was a fatuous restriction still prevalent, the necessity for

LEFT *The Schloss Linderhof made by Ludwig II of Bavaria in the period 1860-80, showing the garden in the baroque style.*

BELOW *An elegant Moorish pavilion erected c.1867 in a superb setting against the mountains at the castle of Linderhof.*

NEXT PAGE *This aerial bridge between rocky heights creates an impression of grandeur in the park of Buttes-Chaumont in Paris, one of the parks made in the mid-nineteenth century.*

which is disproved by the enlightened policy of Kew Gardens, whose visitors, totalling well over a million each year, far more than any provincial park, have always been allowed free access to practically all the grass, with no more than minimal damage. The idea that the landscape is a picture to be looked at, rather than physically enjoyed, dies very hard.

In 1852 the Paris municipal authority took over the Bois de Boulogne from the crown. Several monarchs had erected buildings and made other changes in the area of the Bois, but its final design was that of a landscape garden on the model of Hyde Park. Buttes-Chaumont, formerly a squalid rubbish dump, was converted into a fine landscape park in the 1860s. Montsouris was added and the Bois de Vincennes restored. Paris also had the Tuileries, the Champs Elysées, the Palais Royal and the Parc Monceau on the right bank of the Seine and Jardin des Plantes and the Luxembourg on the left bank. In Germany, Magdeburg was first, the making of the park being commissioned in 1824. Berlin was next; Friedrichshaim was modernized and laid out a little later. Other towns followed this lead. There were scarcely any flowers in the earliest parks, even in England, where Hyde Park has retained this early form which followed, of course, the flowerlessness of the Brownian landscape. Hilly sites were preferred, as they were more easily converted to the English style. In Leipzig a movement started by a Dr

Schreiber, who left money to provide citizens with small garden plots, 200 square meters in area, gave a rather different twist to developments. Adjoining plots added together formed a basis for park-like areas to which a gynasium or hall could be added and a playground made in the middle.

As the park system developed in France, a taste arose for the use of 'stove plants', that is, plants which require a somewhat higher ambient temperature in the glasshouse than do the ordinary half-hardy bedding plants. Groves of rubber plants, caladiums, palms, cannas and begonias were made. The vogue for these and their use as 'sub-tropical' bedding spread rapidly elsewhere during the last quarter of the nineteenth century. It was first tried in England as early as 1864 by

John Gibson, Superintendent of Battersea Park Gardens. He used the hardier kinds of palms and ferns together with bamboos that were found to be hardy and such things as *Berberis, Aralia, Gunnera scabra, Aristolochia, Heracleum, Arundo donax, Rhus, Spiraea, Polygonum cuspidatum,* Solomon's Seal, *Bocconia cordata, Acanthus, Ailanthus glandulosa* and Japanese maples, grouped with smaller ferns and grasses. Those who could not afford the hothouse plants made 'floral rugs' on their lawns with sempervivums and sedums used in quantity.

In 1853 J. Dominy of Veitch and Sons began hybridizing orchids, greatly stimulating the craze for these plants, so that many others followed his lead. Paxton flowered the *Victoria amazonica*, the giant

LEFT *Cycads (primitive, palm-like, cone-bearing plants) at La Mortola, Italy, part of the collection of exotic plants begun by Daniel Hanbury in 1867.*

ABOVE *Carpet bedding at Dives-sur-Mer, Calvados, Normandy.*

water-lily of South America, in a specially built hothouse at Chatsworth in the 1840s. Some aquatic plants were being grown outside at this time; as the article in the seventh edition of the *Encyclopaedia Britannica* of 1838 previously quoted mentions, small pieces of water were set aside for growing such plants. The aquatic garden did not, however, come fully into its own until the French nurseryman Marliac-Latour produced greatly improved varieties of water-lily in the 1880s.

The article in the *Encyclopaedia Britannica* also reveals that rock-gardens of a kind were being made at the time it was written. Such a garden had been created at the Chelsea Physic Garden in the eighteenth century from rocks from Iceland provided by Sir Joseph Banks,

stones from repairs to the Tower of London, flints, chalk and broken brick, but rock-gardens had not yet become a prominent feature of the average garden. The article says, however, that 'among the accompaniments of the flower garden may be mentioned the rockwork. This consists of variously grouped masses of large stones, generally such as are remarkable for being figured by water wearing or for containing petrifactions or impressions, and into the cavities between the stones, filled with earth, alpine or trailing plants are inserted.' Helianthemums, gentians, penstemons, primulas, *Campanula carpatica*, *C. pumila* and *C. nitida*, *Saponaria ocymoides* and *Adonis vernalis* are the plants stated in the article to have been used. It is usually said, however, that 'rockwork' of this kind with no attempt to imitate natural rocks cannot really be considered a rock-garden in the modern sense and that, although the firm of Backhouse of York made a fine rock-garden with alpines in 1859, this was an isolated example and the true rock-garden did not develop until George Carling Joad of Wimbledon gave his collection of alpines to Kew and the Kew rock-garden was constructed in 1882. Once the idea caught on, the rock-garden found its way into every garden, and even the smallest grew a few plants among stones.

A reaction against carpet bedding and 'sub-tropical' bedding began to set in during the 1860s. A feeling had been growing and was expressed by horticultural writers such as Shirley Hibberd and William Robinson that gardeners were spending a disproportionate time on bedding and excluding many beautiful plants from the garden to make room for it. Another difficulty with bedding, too, was that it provided colour for half the

ABOVE *A stone wall and pergola in the garden of La Mortola, a formal touch in this collector's garden.*

LEFT *A cool water-scene with an elegant statue at La Mortola, one of the most charming spots in this lovely garden.*

year only. Nothing had yet been developed that would make a reasonable show in the beds in winter while waiting for spring bulbs to appear. William Robinson started a magazine in 1871 called *The Garden* which was dedicated to combating the bedding system. There were many who agreed with him and a number of herbaceous plants that had dropped out of use were restored to the garden, often in new and improved varieties. Carnations and roses were more used and masses of colour and contrasts were obtained by, for example, groups of tall scarlet lobelia surrounded by *Centaurea ragusina*. Similar combinations were made with violas or 'tufted pansies', pentstemons and antirrhinums. Paeonies were grown with daffodils between the clumps, so that the yellow should appear against the deep red spring growth, with *Lilium auratum* coming up later to contrast with the green foliage. In many gardens more permanent flowers were placed in beds that had for fifty years been given over to geraniums.

William Robinson proposed to replace the bedding system, an entirely artificial way of displaying plants, with something which was almost the exact opposite. This came to be called, from the book he published about it in 1881, the *Wild Garden*. He advocated the naturalizing of plants in shrubberies, on banks and in wild places, and grouping them to produce apparently natural striking effects. His ideas were almost diametrically opposed to those of Brown and Repton. Robinson used hardy plants to extend the flower-garden into the surrounding country and was thus much nearer in his views to Philip Southcote and his *ferme ornée*, although Southcote's flowers were not naturalized but grown in borders around the farmland. Among the suggestions made by Robinson were the growing of iris, meadowsweet, monkshood, *Trollius* and day-lilies along the margins of lakes, which he thought were much better suited to the waterside than dahlias and geraniums. He suggested that instead of growing climbers such as roses, wistaria, clematis and Virginia creeper on pergolas, ironwork or up walls, they should be allowed to grow up trees.

Shrubberies, Robinson was certain, could be greatly improved by growing in between the shrubs groups of trilliums, funkias, Solomon's Seal, lily-of-the-valley, daffodils, snowflakes and meadow saffron. Other possible subjects were *Gentiana asclepiadea*, hypericums and lilies. Walls he would decorate with stonecrop, houseleeks, Cheddar pinks, *Corydalis lutea* and similar plants. Finally, he advocated allowing the lawns to go for hay and enjoying the wild-flowers in them, the wheel thus coming full circle, back to the 'flowery mede' of mediaeval times, although Robinson would up-date it by planting spring bulbs, narcissi, daffodils, anemones, tulips, Star of Bethlehem and others in the grass. Among the first to establish 'wild gardens' were Longleat, Crowsley in Oxfordshire, Tew Park and the garden of a Mr Hewitson at Weybridge. Robinson published his best-selling book, the *English Flower Garden* in 1883. This went through a number of editions and converted many to his ideas.

One of the great virtues of the 'wild garden' was its use of bulbs, which were now planted in masses, as recommended by William Robinson, instead of being formally bedded out. Naturalized in grass, in glades and on the edges of lawns, *Chionodoxa luciliae, Scilla sibirica, Tulipa sylvestris* and others brought a new brilliance to the spring garden, equalling that of the summer flowers to come. So successfully was this done at Belvoir that the spring garden there set a fashion. Not only were the beds filled with forget-me-nots, *Iris reticulata* and *I. sibirica*, silenes, violas, wallflowers, *Heuchera sanguinea*, aubrieta, *Cerastium tomentosum* and the like but many primulas, anemones, gentians, cyclamens and various alpines were naturalized.

Robinson's doctrines were not accepted by everybody. Architects such as T. James in 1839 had raised their voices in favour of the more formal approach, and some gardens of this kind had continued to be made during the nineteenth century, notably Penshurst in Kent, Arley in Cheshire, Blickling in Norfolk and Montacute in Somerset. William Morris expressed the view at the end of the 1870s that a garden should be shut off from the world and should on no account imitate nature. J. D. Sedding in *Garden Craft* in 1891 supported the formal approach and the feeling for the older styles erupted in 1892 in *The Formal Garden in England* by

TOP *An engraving of an architectural terrace garden from* Garden Architecture and Landscape Gardening *(London, 1866) by John Arthur Hughes, a book which illustrated the formal approach just as the reaction against formality was about to begin.*

ABOVE *An engraving from William Robinson's book* Garden Design and Architect's Gardens *(London, 1892) of the garden at Thrumpton Hall; the informal planting around the lake near the house met with his approval, demonstrating that formal architecture and clipping of trees and shrubs was not necessary to achieve a fine effect.*

Reginald Blomfield and F. Inigo Thomas. Both Robinson and his opponents were adept at vituperation and invective and hot words flew on both sides. Blomfield and Thomas contended against Robinson that natural landscape gardens were no more natural than formal gardens, that the landscapers had lost the Renaissance idea of unity between the house and the garden and that plants were quite wrongly the only thing now regarded as of importance. The degeneration of landscape design added point to these objections and rallied support to the view of the advocates of the formal garden. Amid the clamour of controversy, albeit temporarily stilled by the Boer War, the nineteenth century slid into the twentieth when new trends, already beginning to emerge, were to bring further changes.

14
Armigers and Artisans

Thy gardens and thy gallant walks
Continually are green;
There grow such sweet and pleasant flowers
As nowhere else are seen.

There was more support for the advocates of a return to the formal garden than might have been expected, but Blomfield and Thomas, although they did not know it, were writing for a world which was about to vanish. The hey-day of private garden-making on the grand scale had passed with the eighteenth century; the great estates and rich landowners continued to exist, but with a considerable admixture of *nouveaux riches* from the Industrial Revolution. These might have provided a framework for the work of a new Brown or Repton, had such arisen, to bring together into a new style efforts which during the nineteenth century had still produced some fine gardens. But the writing was already on the wall for the great private estate, in the hands of a single individual or family. Death duties were introduced into England in 1894, two years after Blomfield and Thomas's book was issued. England had remained the leader in garden-making, gardens in the English style still being made in Germany after the turn of the century, but in England this tax began the process which in the subsequent eighty years, reinforced by other circumstances, has broken up many of the great estates and dissolved the world of private patronage and cheap labour that in the past supported the great garden designers.

Although the process of breaking up the large estates was beginning, there had been for some time, lower down in the social scale, a move in the other direction. The prosperity brought about by the Industrial Revolution had produced a class of people of substantial means well able to buy an old manor house, a Tudor wool-merchant's house, the home of a Georgian professional man or some similar residence which had slid down the scale into a farmhouse and had probably been neglected because of the depression that afflicted farming after the repeal of the Corn Laws. These new owners not only wanted the house reconditioned, they wanted a garden made for it also. In many cases, a suitable old house was not available and many new houses were also built, with the same

LEFT *Borders and flagstone paths in Gertrude Jekyll's style at Christopher Lloyd's garden at Great Dixter, Northiam, Sussex.*

ABOVE *A scene in the garden of Munstead Wood, the house in Surrey designed and built for Gertrude Jekyll in 1896 by Sir Edwin Lutyens.*

requirement. It so happened that there were gifted architects available for the purpose and also a garden-maker of superlative quality. Edwin Landseer Lutyens and Harold Ainsworth Peto, both later knighted, were the architects; Miss Gertrude Jekyll the gardener.

For a few years at the beginning of the century the world of great estates and great landowners continued

to exist in spite of the cracks even then beginning to spread through the fabric, but, nevertheless, Gertrude Jekyll did not have the opportunity to work on the scale of the great masters of the past; she yielded nothing to them, however, in the subtlety of her effects. She was born in 1843 into a family of what used to be called 'gentlefolk' and, accustomed to an interest in the arts and sciences as a normal part of life, decided eventually to become a professional artist. Her childhood at Bramley in Surrey gave her a deep knowledge and lasting love of plants which, although she travelled widely, she never lost. In 1875 she met William Robinson, with whose views on gardening she agreed and was therefore, at this stage, firmly on the 'wild garden' side of the controversy rather than in the 'formal garden' camp, although it seems likely that she was never as rigid in her views as was Robinson himself.

Under Robinson's influence Miss Jekyll laid out a garden for her widowed mother in Surrey and began to write articles for Robinson. This brought her in the 1880s commissions to design gardens and she began to establish a reputation. In 1896 she built herself a house at Munstead Wood in Surrey, the architect being Lutyens, who had much in common with her in his outlook on country life and buildings. The partnership they formed brought out the best in both of them. They worked together on a number of estates, mainly in Surrey, and a group loosely formed around them, of which William Robinson was the titular head, called the

TOP *Part of the garden made by Sir Edwin Lutyens and Gertrude Jekyll at Hestercombe, Somerset, showing a rill with water plants, a long border and a pergola, with a sunken garden to the left.*

ABOVE *The pool and hexagon framework which terminates the rill at the Deanery, Sonning, shown before the plantings made by Miss Jekyll had fully developed. Later roses smothered the framework and irises and lilies had spread and were flowering profusely.*

RIGHT *The sunken rose garden and pool, overlooked from a clipped yew alcove sheltered by hedges, in the garden designed and planted by Gertrude Jekyll and Sir Edwin Lutyens at Folly Farm, Sulhampstead.*

'Surrey School'; it included such people as Christopher Lloyd, who made a wonderful garden at Great Dixter in Sussex, and George Fergusson Wilson, whose garden at Heatherbank eventually became the Royal Horticultural Society's Wisley garden in Surrey.

Miss Jekyll, Lutyens and Peto all had a profound respect for and knowledge of traditional country craftsmanship, and the use they made of this is the hallmark of their work. In the partnership Lutyens was responsible for the general form of the gardens, carrying the geometry of the house outwards to conform with the functions of the various parts of the gardens. He had great skill in siting both house and garden and his main axiom echoes the Renaissance. 'Every garden scheme', he said, 'should have a backbone, a central idea beautifully phrased. Every wall, path, stone and flower should have its relationship to the central idea.' Miss Jekyll's great gift was her sense of the appropriate in choosing, from the multitude of plants available and new ones coming in from plant collectors, those most apt for her purpose both in form and colour. The selection and display of hardy plants, individually interesting or beautiful, yet harmonized by careful association to make colour schemes both of flower and foliage, and laid out with deceptive simplicity, was her strong point. Her sensitivity in this respect has probably never been equalled.

Miss Jekyll's work stood out in contrast both to William Robinson's extreme naturalism, which led him into some absurdities on his own estate at Gravetye in Sussex, where he moved earth to make a 'natural' scene before planting it 'naturally', and the strict formalism of Blomfield and Thomas. The strength of the formal school may be judged from *Gardens Old and New* published in several volumes by Country Life, which dealt with the larger gardens. Almost all the illustrations in this work show the formal areas of the gardens, as if the wilder parts, extensive in many cases, did not exist. The work of the Surrey school did, in fact, reshape the ideas of the protagonists of the wild garden, who were reconciled by Miss Jekyll's work to some formality in the garden and admitted the role of architects. The architectural slant came out very clearly in her book *Gardens for Small Country Houses,* written in conjunction with Sir Laurence Weaver, first published in 1912, where again almost all the illustrations are architectural in setting, and she even admits and praises the work of Blomfield, Robinson's principal antagonist.

Miss Jekyll was a clear and competent expounder of her own views. *Gardens for Small Country Houses* went through several editions. The two books she wrote about her house and garden at Munstead Wood are gardening classics and her *Colour Schemes for the Flower Garden* was also very influential. Of the gardens she worked on with Lutyens, Orchards, Godalming, Surrey; Marsh Court, Hampshire; Hestercombe, Somerset; Gledstone Hall, Yorkshire and Tyringham, Buckinghamshire may be mentioned. One of the

TOP *The Japanese garden at Fanham's Hall, Ware, designed by a Japanese gardener. This is one of the best of the Japanese gardens made in Britain in the period when they were fashionable before the First World War.*

ABOVE *The Japanese garden at Compton Acres, Poole, one of the gardens in various styles made on this estate in the period around the first World War.*

earliest which did much to enhance her reputation was the Deanery Garden at Sonning in Berkshire, made in 1899. In this garden 'an archway made in the old wall', providing access from the road, says *Country Life*, 'and fitted with a wrought-iron grille, gives direct entrance . . . into a cloister, vaulted in brickbanded chalk, and opening into a courtyard, in the middle of which the Pompeian boy pours water from his wineskin into a little pool at his feet. The sun plays delightedly in this engaging trap for varied light and shadow and the plash of the water . . . refreshes the visitor. ' It is necessary to turn to the left and out through a wide arch to reach the main garden square, which is 'bounded on the west side by the house and on the east and north by the old enclosing wall, so that it occupies the full width of the upper flat before it falls southward to the orchard . . . There is some diversity of level which admits of the flights of steps pleasantly breaking and relieving the long run of the broad flagged way.'

The account continues: 'This portion of the garden swings round so as to occupy, on its main level, an area of grass and flagstone in front of the eastern end of the main or south elevation of the house . . . The platform we are now on', decorated by a sundial, 'dominates towards the south and west two lower-lying garden sections of wholly different character. The great segmental stairway to the south (followed by other circles, flagged and stepped, breaking the stretches of sward) leads down to green alleys and to the orchard, sprinkled and starred by daffodils, tulips and anemones.' Here, perhaps, may be seen in operation the unerring instinct of Miss Jekyll for the right plant in the right place, for the *Country Life* reporter is enchanted. 'Never did we see', he says, 'plants of *Anemone fulgens* more vigorous and full-stemmed, more proudly and prosperously opening their great flowers to the radiant sun, than rose out of the luscious orchard grass on the gay morning of early May, when we enjoyed this scene of happy growth, these clusters and colonies of bulbs rioting in the strength which the excellent soil gave them, with the added help of clever setting and good nurture.'

Going back to the upper level, the western part of the garden could be seen, a narrower garden lying in front of the hall and other rooms of the house and extending beyond it to the boundary. 'Standing against the balustrade and over a depressed arch, under which lurks one-half of a circular pool, the other half lying out in the sun', one could see 'the surface rippled by the jet of water which spouts from the mouth of the satyr that forms the keystone of the arch. Opposite to this, the pool has a break in its edge,' admitting the water to a flagged and formal rill which 'runs down the centre of a long grass plat [a small plot], and widens into a square basin in the centre of its course and into a circular one at the end. It is tenanted by the flowering rush and many another vigorous water plant . . .'

Country Life (Gardens Old and New, Vol. 3, pp. 324-5) gave two pictures to illustrate that the western or circular end of this little water garden was perhaps the most striking. They were taken on different dates and displayed the 'curved sweep of easy steps' that closed that end of the garden and led to a 'rose-clad hexagon and the end seat'. The first picture showed the scene in the early days of the garden and the second how it appeared 'when rose and iris and lily had been given their chance and seized it', exhibiting 'a wealth of foliage and of flower'. We are 'at once struck by the thoughtful and clever planting of the garden,' concludes the writer, adding that 'complete success has been gained by the sympathetic partnership of Miss Gertrude Jekyll and Mr Lutyens.'

Similar accounts could be given of other gardens

ABOVE *The Italian garden at Compton Acres, a modern reali-zation of an ancient inspiration.*

RIGHT *The Italian garden created by Sir Harold Ainsworth Peto at Ilnacullin, Garinish Island, Eire, one of the most beautiful and effective of the Italian gardens made in Britain.*

created by Lutyens and Miss Jekyll. Folly Farm, Sulhamstead, near Reading in Berkshire, has some-times been claimed as their masterpiece. Here was a bulb-filled orchard, a fine sunken rose-garden, a lime-tree walk and yew hedges sheltering herbaceous borders edged with broad paving stones where a vista taking in Miss Jekyll's beloved grey foliage plants could be seen through the archway. Great Dixter, Northiam, Sussex, already mentioned, although restored by Lutyens, was not actually planted by Miss Jekyll but by Christopher Lloyd. This garden also had a long hedge-backed border, a bulb-filled orchard, yew hedges, topiary and a sunken garden. The influence of Miss Jekyll was discernible everywhere in the planting and arrangement. Her advice was given to many people whose gardens she did not actually design and it has been estimated that she helped with more than 300 all told. It is unfashionable to criticize Miss Jekyll, the centre of a chorus of universal praise, and it is perhaps captious to point out that her delicate use of colour in herbaceous plants was not new; Sir Henry Wotton records, however, at the beginning of the seventeenth century that Sir Henry Fanshawe, at his seat at Ware

Park 'did so precisely examine the tinctures and seasons of his flowers, that, in their setting, the inwardest of those which were to come up at the same time should always be a little darker than the outmost, and to sow them for a kind of gentle shadow, like a piece, not of nature, but of art.'

At the same time as Miss Jekyll was working another influence was affecting English gardens. In the 1860s Japan had at last opened its doors to the West. It is all too apparent why the Japanese, when first brought into

ABOVE *Spring colour from rhododendrons with magnolias in flower in the distance in the garden at Trewithen.*

BELOW *The splendid blue poppy* (Meconopsis betonicifolia) *from south-east Asia, one of the many striking new plants introduced by the plant collectors.*

ABOVE RIGHT *A sub-tropical scene in the garden at Tresco in the Isles of Scilly, founded in Victorian times.*

contact with Europeans, recognized them at once as barbarians and tried to keep them out. The arrogant and ignorant attitude of which western visitors are capable is very well shown in a German book on Japanese industries published in 1889. The author says:

'The Japanese gardener tries to keep all bushes and trees constantly pruned and trimmed and in many ways to obstruct their natural development; now to produce symmetrical forms, after the fashion of old French gardening and again to prevent symmetry by fanciful creations, dwarf and deformed figures, and to work in a way utterly incomprehensible to us . . . Our gardeners help nature; the Japanese do her violence . . . They admire and collect also natural malformations of every kind. They admire a stone, e.g. through which water has worn a hole, or an old decaying tree-trunk with one or more plants growing out of a knot-hole where seeds have been accidentally lodged. This is due to the same intellectual laziness . . .'

The British were no better: Algernon Freeman-Mitford, afterwards Lord Redesdale, who was one of the first English diplomats to go to Japan in the 1860s, and later became an authority on bamboos, making a noted bamboo garden at his home, regarded the Japanese garden 'all spick and span' and 'intensely artifical', as 'a monument of misplaced zeal and wasted labour'. Even Reginal Farrer, the noted plant collector and authority on rock gardens, who spent a year in Japan in 1903,

thought that the Japanese 'brutalized' and 'harried' plants, torturing them to produce a perfect composition or symbolic effect, as if he had never heard of pruning or shaping by his own countrymen.

The bland assumption of western superiority revealed in these quotations and the superficial narrow mindedness justifies the Japanese attitude. As this book is being written the Japanese are beating the West at its own industrial game, the truth being that in their relationship with one another and ability to co-operate for a corporate end the Japanese are centuries ahead of the West. They have learnt from the West, but the West, because of its stupendous self-satisfaction, has not learnt from Japan. Until recently in America, this has been in no subject more true than in gardening.

Between 1880 and 1910 many so-called Japanese gardens were made in Britain. These were part and parcel of the vogue in the West for all Japanese things that followed the opening of that country, but this was no more than a superficial fashion for these things because they were different, often beautiful, and 'quaint', a word usually used to describe things not

understood. In some cases Japanese gardeners were imported to construct and even to care for these gardens. The Hon. Louis Greville, for example, imported a Japanese tea-house and workmen to make a water garden around it at Heale House in Wiltshire. Ella Christie at Cowden in Perthshire, at the foot of the Ochils, induced a lady Japanese gardener, Taki Honda, to make a Japanese garden on her estate and in 1925 brought a Japanese gardener, Matsuo, to make his home in this country to look after it. There was also a Japanese water-garden at Charleton, Kilconquhar, Fifeshire. Ireland possessed a notable Japanese garden at Tully, near Kildare, designed by the Japanese gardener Eida, in 1906. Another garden designed by a Japanese gardener is at Fanham's Hall, Ware, Hertfordshire. Such a garden existed at Wakehurst Place, near Ardingly in Sussex, the satellite establishment of the Royal Botanic Gardens, Kew, when that garden was acquired by the National Trust on Sir Henry Price's death in 1963, but it has since been altered. There were also others, but although some attractive effects were achieved in these gardens they were, in the main,

merely superficial attempts to capture the Japanese atmosphere created without any real understanding of the principles on which Japanese gardens were based.

Part of the vogue for Japanese things arose from the activities of the plant collector John Gould Veitch of the nursery firm Veitch and Son, who collected very successfully in Japan as soon as the country was opened. He was one of the succession of plant collectors that followed David Douglas and collected in many parts of the world in Victorian times. The plants these men discovered filled western gardens, helping to establish Loudon's 'gardenesque' garden and to foster the 'botanic' type of 'plantsman's' garden, in which the owner is primarily interested in the new plants rather than in garden styles. At the end of the nineteenth century this type of garden received a great fillip. Dried

LEFT *A spring scene in the garden of Leonardslee, Sussex, a 'plantsman's' garden, showing colourful rhododendrons en masse reflected in the still waters of the lake, contrasting with the sober green of the clipped shrubs and conifers among which they grow.*

BELOW *The lake in the garden at Sheffield Park, near Uckfield, Sussex. Sheffield Park is noted for the colour of its trees and shrubs in autumn and is a place of annual pilgrimage for many at that time. This picture, not taken in autumn, shows that the colours of the trees are beautiful at other times of the year.*

specimens from south-east Asia had shown how fruitful that area was likely to be in living plants which would tolerate the conditions in western gardens. In 1899 Veitch and Son sent Ernest Henry Wilson on his first journey to western China. Thus began the great succession of plant collectors, Wilson, George Forrest, William Purdom, Reginal Farrer, R. E. Cooper, Frank Kingdon-Ward, Frank Ludlow and George Sherriff (accompanied in later times by my former chief, Sir George Taylor, later distinguished Director of Kew Gardens) who harvested the wild plants of south-east Asia in the first half of the twentieth century and introduced into the West hundreds of new plants, many of them outstandingly good garden plants.

Almost the showiest of all was the 'Pocket Handkerchief Tree', *Davidia involucrata,* which was among the first that Wilson collected, having been specially commissioned to look for it. There were also many other trees. Of shrubs, the most important were the rhododendrons, which were introduced in great variety, camellias, *Hamamelis* (Chinese witch-hazel), *Berberis, Viburnum, Cotoneaster* and roses. They also introduced lilies, gentians, primulas and a great number of other herbaceous and alpine plants, including the famous blue poppy, *Meconopsis betonicifolia.* Collectors in other parts of the world were not idle and there was therefore every incentive for those botanically inclined and with suitable gardens to make or augment collections. The garden at Tresco in the Isles of Scilly, where many things will grow which will not tolerate mainland conditions, was founded in Victorian times and is still maintained today, being in many respects unique in the British Isles.

In the south-west of England there were other gardens in which fine collections were built up. Probably the most important in this area was the garden of John Charles Williams at Caerhays in Cornwall. J. C. Williams began growing rhododendrons in 1885 and increased his collection, mainly from George Forrest's discoveries, until in 1917 he was growing some 267

ABOVE *Rhododendrons strike a colourful note under tall trees in the Dell, part of the garden of Bodnant, North Wales.*

RIGHT *A superb view through the trees lining the stream in another 'plantsman's' garden at Mount Usher, Eire, framing the more distant garden in the centre of the picture as if it were some painted scene in a Roman* topia.

different kinds. He was the founder of the Rhododendron Society, which caters for those infected with what Miles Hadfield calls 'rhododendronomania', a disease which has smitten many in the past 70 years. He also grew camellias, developing a hybrid Camellia x williamsii by which he will always be remembered. Other gardens where fine collections were assembled and still exist in Cornwall were Penjerick near Budock, Tremeer at St Tudy, Trengwainton, near Penzance, which has mostly been planted since 1920, and Trewithen at Probus.

Other notable 'plantsman's' gardens in England are the group of gardens in Sussex which includes Nymans, Handcross; Borde Hill, Hayward's Heath; Leonardslee, Lower Beeding; Sheffield Park, Uckfield, and Wakehurst Place, Ardingly. Wales also has such collections, notably at Plas Newydd, Llandfairpwll, Anglesey: Dyffryn, Glamorgan and, probably the finest of all, Bodnant, Tal-y-Cafn, a vast garden which takes in as its view the sweep of Snowdonia, where the upper garden, comprised of various formal sections, each magnificent of its kind, lies above a deep wild valley in which grows a great collection of trees, rhododendrons, magnolias and camellias. The west coast and islands of Scotland provide ideal conditions for the making of gardens of this kind. Osgood Mackenzie began planting rhododendrons at Inverewe, Poolewe, as early as 1864. Further south are Achamore on the island of Gigha; Crarae Lodge, Minard, on Loch Fyne; the rhododendron section of the garden of Brodick Castle

231

on the Isle of Arran, begun in 1923; Kiloran on the Isle of Colonsay, begun in 1930; and, further east Dawyck, Stobo, Peebleshire. Ireland has similar notable collectors' gardens at Howth Castle; Mount Usher, Wicklow; and Rowallane, near Belfast. The Muckross estate at Killarney grows tender plants similar to those that flourish at Tresco. These lists of gardens are not exhaustive: there are many other collections scattered throughout the British Isles, formed under the impetus of the influx of new plants from the plant collectors of the nineteenth and twentieth centuries. Without exception these gardens, irrespective of the collections they contain, are woodland gardens of great beauty, often on magnificent sites. They are William Robinson's 'wild garden' brought to the pinnacle of perfection.

Four gardens whose formation was commenced in the first half of the twentieth century are of interest because of their originality. One of the greatest English gardeners of this period was Edward Augustus Bowles, who gardened at Myddleton House, Bull's Cross, near Enfield, making one of the most remarkable collections of plants in England: anemones, crocuses, snowdrops and cyclamens were among his favourites.

A gardener of similar stature was Sir Frederick Stern, who at Highdown on the Littlehampton Road, Goring-by-Sea, quashed for ever the notion that a chalk soil was a difficult medium on which to garden satisfactorily by creating the most wonderful garden at the foot of a chalk-pit, where he made rock- and

LEFT *A splendid view under noble trees in the gardens at Nymans, Sussex, one of the group of 'plantsman's' gardens to be found in that county.*

ABOVE *Considered by many to be the most beautiful garden in Britain, the terrace at Bodnant looks out across a magnificent view to the mountains of Snowdonia. A 'plantsman's' garden, made on a site that might have been chosen by one of the great garden designers of the Renaissance, the immense treasures of the plant collection are mostly in the Dell, the valley below, out of sight in this picture.*

water-gardens. Sir Frederick was also not satisfied with anything less than the best. He was an international authority on paeonies and snowdrops and a fine cultivator of lilies, iris and narcissus, as well as *Eremurus,* which he grew in mixed borders.

The third gardener of original turn of mind was Laurence Johnston. Soon after 1900 he made a garden at Hidcote Manor, Hidcote, in Gloucestershire, formal in pattern, but split up into compartments which with great ingenuity he devised so that the visitor is tempted on from one to another and there is always something fresh to see: here a long vista, springing from the basic formal design, there a 'garden room' with a sense of being cut off from the rest, and further on a stream with little waterfalls, and so on. There seems an almost

endless variety. Hidcote is, in fact, quite different from any other English garden since Elizabethan times, when separate compartments were the norm. A similar effect was obtained by the fourth gardener of note, Victoria Sackville-West, Lady Nicholson, at Sissinghurst Castle in Kent, but here there were existing divisions which she most charmingly and originally adapted to get effects of much the same kind as at Hidcote.

The world in which Gertrude Jekyll began her work changed greatly with the impact of the First World War. Although she continued her activities for a number of years after the war (she did not die until 1932), the atmosphere of developing prosperity in a powerful British Empire on which the sun never set had passed away. The world of the 1920s was an uneasy place, troubled first by the aftermath of the war, and then by the gathering clouds of economic disaster that broke in the storm of 1929. Influences were at work that were changing the gardening scene. E. H. M. Cox in the

ABOVE *A view of the garden at Rowallane, near Belfast, Northern Ireland, showing rhododendrons in pinks and reds contrasting with the bright orange of* Berberis linarifolia *in the foreground.*

LEFT *Rare plants in bloom in the fifty acres of the Savill Garden in the southern part of Windsor Great Park, created by Sir Eric Savill in 1932 and the years following for George VI and Queen Elizabeth the Queen Mother. These are probably the finest expression of the principal trend in twentieth-century gardening in Britain, that of semi-wild naturalistic planting of the wealth of attractive trees, shrubs and other plants which have been added to the stock available for gardens in this century.*

Modern English Garden, wrote in the introduction that 'gardening has never been so popular in the British Isles as it is at the present time,' but it was not gardening on the grand scale he was talking about, or even on Miss Jekyll's scale: her gardens, anyway, were already becoming a financial burden because they required so much labour. Cox wrote:

'Modern transport is one of the main factors in the growth of horticulture . . . At the start of the present century gardening knowledge was a closed book to the majority of city dwellers. If they worked in the city they lived in it: and few living in the country made the daily pilgrimage to town. So gardens were mainly divided into two groups only, the large, worked entirely by paid labour, and the cottage, where the worker, who gained

A beautiful and colourful semi-formal scene in the splendid gardens created at Mount Stewart, Newtownards on the east shore of Stranford Lough, Northern Ireland, by the Seventh Marchioness of Londonderry.

his livelihood from the soil, grew enough fruits, vegetables and flowers for his own needs. The consequence was that gardeners were divided into two classes, the professional . . . and the cottager, who was quite satisfied if he knew enough to raise sufficient potatoes, cabbages and apples for his pot and flowers to decorate the small plot in front of the cottage.'

I can add to this account, since I was born to life in a cottage in a Kentish village where, with cottages fronting directly on the road, as my home did, flowers were few. Books have been written of late years extolling old cottage gardens as if they had made a great contribution to gardening. It is true that in older small country gardens, almost forgotten varieties of garden plants have sometimes survived, but these have rarely been the gardens of genuine cottagers. Those who have written such books, read by the country-starved city public responding to their unconscious urge to return to the original home of their species, can know nothing of the lives of the country poor, and nearly all were poor, of former times. They must be unaware that, until after the First World War, the average country worker got to work at six o'clock in the morning and did not stop until the light failed, when he came home dead beat after a day of heavy physical labour. It is not surprising that he

had little inclination to grow more than vegetables, while his wife looked after a few chickens and rabbits, and possibly a pig on the allotment, if he had one. There was, it is true, a village flower show and village clubs, and there were some, better off than the rest, as told in the last chapter, who were able to pursue a love for flowers, for men will make what they can of what they have, but they were a small minority.

Flowers were, indeed, grown in cottage gardens, but much said about cottage gardens by recent writers is romantic myth. It is not surprising that Edward Hyams had to commence his account with the remark that 'the principal historians of the English garden have virtually nothing to say about the cottage garden' and to confess in the second paragraph that 'there are no, or very few, documents of any kind' about it. He had to admit, before the end of his book, that 'the ornamental cottage garden' was found only among 'the small number of middle-class cottagers in the country'.

It is regrettable to have to say it of a person who loved country things so much, but one of the principal creators of this myth was Gertrude Jekyll herself. 'I have learnt much from the little cottage gardens' she says, and often refers to the planting of good cottage gardens in her books, but the fact has to be faced that she was, unfortunately, a snob, dividing people into 'armigerous' (of knightly rank) and 'non-armigerous' and her cottage garden what a Marxist might call a bourgeois fantasy. She simply did not see the yard-cum-garden of the average cottage, with its chicken-house, rabbit-hutches and outdoor earth-

ABOVE *A pleasing combination at Hidcote Manor, Gloucestershire, of still water, green water-lilies and grey foliage plants, set off with a touch of pastel-pink in the foreground against red fuchsias and darker conifers behind.*

RIGHT *A flower-crowned gateway at Sissinghurst Castle, Kent, giving access to a claustrophobic* allée *of clipped hedges deliberately contrived to make each garden to which it leads an opening into light and colour.*

FAR RIGHT *The 'white' garden at Sissinghurst Castle, Kent, where a conception that would have delighted Gertrude Jekyll has been expertly realized.*

closet: her cottage garden was a reflection of *Cranford* and *Our Village,* delightful books, but creations of middle-class authors which had little to do with real cottagers who lived in the average village cottage.

E. H. M. Cox continues his introduction to *Modern English Garden* by saying: 'Modern transport has brought the city within easy reach of the country. Suburban areas now exist where were only fields and wood before. Each has its gardens. Bedding and formal gardening are now too costly . . . it has made us evolve a manner of gardening in which the garden is designed to suit the plant as well as the garden . . . No longer is the strictly formal at all popular, when the architect had as much to do with the laying out of the garden as the gardener.' Here, too, I can add my own experience. My family moved from the village into the town after World War I and, in 1926, a year before E. H. M. Cox wrote, into a newly-built estate of semi-detached houses at Luton in Bedfordshire. In the garden, about 30 by 90 feet, my father planted eight standard roses in a straight border about five feet wide. They were 'Daily Mail' 'Betty Uprichard', 'Frau Karl Druschki', 'Ophelia', 'Madame Butterfly' 'Caroline Testout', 'George Dickson' and 'Crimson Glory', growing between them herbaceous plants, mostly common varieties which he got from friends, and annuals.

On the sunny fence on the other side of the garden he planted espalier apples and pears, 'Laxton's Superb', 'Conference' and 'Louise Bonne of Jersey', and even

tried a peach, although this did not thrive. He was of an experimental turn of mind, because in the square bed at the end of the garden, where he grew a few vegetables and chrysanthemums for cutting, he grafted apple trees, putting four different scions on one stock, all of which succeeded, but after a few years the most vigorous took over. He also took *Amateur Gardening.* Perhaps a little more knowledgeable and skilled than the average, he represented the new class which E. H. M. Cox described, which not only included the commuter, but the working man, who no longer had to get to work at 6 a.m., but at 7.30 or 8 a.m., and probably finished somewhere between 5 and 6.30 p.m.; who had more leisure, more energy and, when he had a job (there were three million unemployed) more money than before the war, and had begun to read about gardening.

While this class was coming into being, the greater gardens were many of them running into difficulty. These gardens had always been the training grounds for the professional gardener. The training they provided was excellent. Those who went through it became an élite. They had the task of producing suitable flowers, fruit and vegetables for the great house without fail and in variable quantity, according to the number of guests, for every day of the year, much being required out of season and having to be forced. If they could not do it, their employer had a simple remedy: they went out of the gate and someone else took their place. Such a situation was like that of the man about to be hanged. It concentrated the mind wonderfully.

These gardeners were a highly skilled but poorly paid class, and were already beginning to diminish when the Second World War came, giving many of them opportunities to learn new and more highly paid skills; after the war there were many vacancies in the new trades which they could fill. This and other factors produced a new situation and a new gardening scene in Britain.

The influences that affected England and Scotland in the first half of the twentieth century produced similar effects in Ireland. Mention has been made of the Japanese gardens and the fine plant collections in that country, but the story would not be complete without a reference to what was one of the most effective productions of the Lutyens-Jekyll period. Sir Harold Peto created at Ilnacullin on Garinish Island, a mile out in Bantry Bay, in circumstances that allowed the use of sub-tropical plants, a most beautiful garden in a formal Italianate style surrounded by a wild garden. In 1921 a remarkable garden was made at Mount Stewart, Newtownards, in which, with a sense of humour not usually found in gardens, skilfully placed among beautiful formal gardens of clipped hedges, topiary and high shrub arches, is a dodo terrace with an ark and other creatures reminiscent, perhaps, of the animals in the fables of the labyrinth at Versailles.

In Europe the story was different. The turmoil and disasters of the First World War, the instability of the inter-war period, followed by the devastations and privation of the Second World War, left little scope for garden activity in the first half of the century. This was not, however, the case in America where, although there were checks, development continued with comparative steadiness.

15
Westward the Land is Bright

Azaleas glowed with fierier red
To mark the spot where warriors bled
And still amid the ancient trees
In flaming brightness take the breeze,
But now in peace for those who seek
Of noble gardens soft they speak.

In the early days of the exploration and settlement of America and Canada, both were surrounded by enemies and so occupied with urgent day-to-day problems of survival that little could be expected in the way of garden development. It is therefore surprising to find that evidence of land set aside for pleasure gardens appears as early as 1604 in a map drawn by Samuel de Champlain of Neutral Island in the St Croix river between Maine and New Brunswick, which has been interpreted as showing two little patterned gardens in the formal sixteenth-century style. Later in the century, in 1682, William Penn's Commissioners laid out Philadelphia in square ornamental plots with spaces sufficient for the town to develop as 'a greene country town, which will never be burnt [because of the space allowed between the houses] and will always be wholesome.' An open square ten acres in extent was provided in the centre of the town and there were five public squares altogether within the town limits. From 1750 onwards trees were planted in the streets.

In the New England villages there were similar central open spaces, like the village greens of the old country, the layout prefiguring the later American park system. Gardens of the early houses of Philadelphia, where the inclinations and the resources of the owner permitted, would have been made in the very formal William and Mary style and this was probably also true of the gardens of the houses in Williamsburg, Virginia, and of Washington's house at Mount Vernon in that state. Further south in Virginia, Maryland and the Carolinas, settlement was on more aristocratic lines. Many houses of distinction were built in the eighteenth century, some of which remain. They had 'stately patterned gardens with boxwood' like those of the old country. Similar gardens were laid out by owners in New England who had visited Europe, but many of the gardens that now claim pre-Revolution status, both in New England and the southern states, were, in fact, made after 1800. Thomas Jefferson's Monticello, three miles west of Charlottesville in Virginia, the most

LEFT *A semi-formal scene in the garden of the Governor's Palace at Williamsburg, Virginia.*

ABOVE *Old-style garden buildings among the box-edged beds of the restored eighteenth-century garden of the Governor's Palace at Williamsburg, Virginia.*

TOP *This house at Old Westbury, Long Island, built in Edwardian times in the Italian style, with terrace steps reminiscent of the Villa Garzoni, stands on the top of rising ground in leafy parkland. Preserved by the John S. Phipps Foundation, it is a fine example of the gardens made for the wealthy in America in the early twentieth century.*

ABOVE *The box-edged beds of the eighteenth-century garden of Gunston Hall in Virginia look out over a wide scene.*

notable of the older gardens, was built in the second half of the eighteenth century on a small hill with craggy sides, the name being Italian for 'little mountain'. The hill is 580 feet high and slopes eastward to the Rivanna river and from it can be seen the Blue Ridge Mountains 47 miles away. The top of the hill was levelled, forming a site 600 by 200 feet, and the house was built about 100 feet from the eastern end and set amid level lawn, from which the landscape slopes on every side. The house is designed in a fastidiously classical style but the surroundings have a Brownian touch.

Some of the best of the estate gardens were laid out between the end of the Revolution and 1830. These continued to be formal and showed in the southern states marks of French and Spanish influence. Not until the decade before the Civil War in the 1860s did the English landscape style make an impact in America, Andrew Jackson Downing being the apostle of the fashion. His writings in the 1840s led America into the Romantic Gothic Revival and soon 'natural' landscaping spread across the United States. The change reached New York, which expanded so rapidly in the first half of the nineteenth century that the city authorities commendably moved to acquire 850 acres in the centre before the whole was overwhelmed with building. Frederick Law Olmstead was commissioned in 1854 to lay out the new Central Park and adopted the picturesque style, carefully and successfully designing the park so that traffic flowed through it as inconspicuously as possible.

After the Civil War town-dwellers began to acquire

The delightful garden at Chestnut Hill, Pennsylvania, where the native trees and shrubs, set amid fine lawns, create an all-the-year-round landscape augmented in the spring and summer, as in this picture, by the colour of flowers.

ABOVE *Boxwood parterres and clipped hedges in the European style in the garden of George Washington's home at Mount Vernon, Virginia. This dates from the second half of the eighteenth century; by then this style had long been discontinued in Europe.*

RIGHT *Central Park in New York City, the far-sighted creation of the New York municipal authorities in the 1850s, designed by Frederick Law Olmsted as an English landscape garden in the 'Capability' Brown style.*

houses in the country for weekends and holidays and many gardens were made around these. Boston, where ornamental gardening had begun in the eighteenth century with porches ornamented with flowers and shrubs, made park-like streets radiating into the interior of the city from a great belt of park outside. Washington D.C., designed like a European town, St Louis and Philadelphia, all made similar streets. In some cases independent local park societies formed by the residents supported the local authorities in this work. Chicago made its 'People's Parks', which were characteristic of America towns, consisting of a football ground with walks around it, a gymnasium, a children's playground with a shallow pool and a swimming pool with baths. It also made a belt of outer parks. Fine gardens were developed on the Pacific coast, often influenced by Spanish ideas. California contributed a number of useful flowers to brighten garden scenes elsewhere, among them being eschscholzias, gaillardias, godetias, lupins and penstemons.

The rapid and continued rise in wealth in the United States in the second half of the nineteenth century increased the number of people who could afford to garden as a leisure activity and also the number of those who could afford to lay out larger estates. The appearance of a horticultural press and of large-scale nurserymen and seedsmen was a sympton of the prosperity, as was the growth of garden clubs to cater for the multiplicity of amateurs. By the early twentieth century all these movements were well under way.

Of the gardens made in the north-eastern part of the United States the Whitney garden at Old Westbury, on Long Island, was a handsome formal creation in the grand tradition with shady lawns under trees and informal woodland. Another garden on Long Island was the Tobin garden at Syosset which was actually a collection of gardens, including one of box and tulips, another of perennials, and a third of azaleas, with the chief feature a long naturalistic pool among trees. One of the most attractive gardens on the island was that of Nelson Doubleday at Mill Neck, which made considerable use of box-edged borders, clipped hemlock hedges and specimen pink dogwoods. The garden, which was primarily a spring garden, was specifically designed to enhance its wonderful view over Long Island Sound, special features being pergolas with hardy vines framing views in the garden and distant vistas.

At the Nicholas garden on Oyster Bay, Long Island, the small house, which was no more than a gardener's cottage, did not permit the use of anything tall or

massive and the garden included open fields with low fences (echoing, perhaps, Charles Bridgeman's design at Richmond Lodge in England, made for Queen Caroline 200 years before) into which the long flower-beds filled with low-growing species were allowed to spill over. This garden was noteworthy for its long succession of bloom, from spring bulbs through summer annuals and perennials flowering on into the fall. The Innocenti garden at Roslyn on Long Island was another of original design. The protection of dense borders around the garden was designed to lengthen its growing season. It was furnished with both deciduous trees and evergreens, particularly dwarf and spreading types, and there were also flowering shrubs and perennials marginally planted around the lawns. The

great feature of the garden was the turf which grew naturally without walks, fences or gates and only a few clipped shrubs here and there so that the visitor might wander without hindrance from scene to scene.

The garden of Oakleigh Thorne at Millbrook, New York, echoed colonial grandeur, being spacious but nevertheless restrained. Colour was derived principally from flowering shrubs and trees. There was a formal French-style *allée* of maples and an elaborate topiary garden; in the less formal parts there were naturalistic pools. The Kouzmanoff garden at Port Chester, New York, which was begun in the late 1940s, was on a different scale, being a small low-terraced garden divided into specialist areas which were very successfully linked by paving, a style which has been

ABOVE *The lake which was part of the original estate at the Du Pont gardens at Longwood, which have been subsequently developed into one of the great gardens of the world.*

LEFT *The Italian garden in the Du Pont gardens at Longwood.*

emulated or separately devised elsewhere. In an experiment in communal gardening, a number of owners on East Sixty-Fifth Street in New York City joined their gardens together to make a much larger area, furnishing it with a marble fountain and sculptured figures which created a most pleasing effect with a distinct European flavour.

In New England, the Adam garden at Dover, Massachusetts, construction of which began in 1917 on a derelict farm, cleverly used an existing pond to form the main water of a stretch of naturalistic woodland of great charm. The Stoddard garden at Worcester, Massachusetts, made about twenty years later, was a garden of great originality of planting. It was densely wooded and on very uneven terrain, making use of natural stands of mountain laurel and fine specimens of juniper, relying not on exotics, but on large groups and sweeping masses of native plants. A fine feature was the Maidenhair Glen containing a long bank completely covered with maidenhair fern. Silver and grey plants were used with fine effect and there was continuous bloom from spring to fall.

There could not be a greater contrast to these two gardens than the Brewster garden at Dublin in New Hampshire, commenced in 1925, which was essentially a summer garden. The gently sloping land enabled a series of different gardens to be made, each on a level with an enclosing hedge, the terraces gradually falling from the house to the lake. There was a walled garden featuring English elm, now so devastated, alas, in Britain, by Dutch elm disease, that it has almost disappeared from the countryside. There was also an English sunken garden, a rock-garden, a French garden, a waterfall, and a white garden and sanctuary. The Dacre Bush garden at Cape Neddick in Maine represented what could be done in the more northerly areas where spring comes late, the garden being sheltered by pines to bring things on as early as possible, with the emphasis on summer bloom.

Further south in Pennsylvania, fine gardens were made for Mrs Lewis H. Parsons at Appleford, Villanova, where there was an old-style Pennsylvania house, around which a garden began to be made in 1920. The garden was designed for the production of early bloom only. In its eighteen acres were fitted almost every landscape feature, meadows, woodland, waterfalls, brooks, a swimming pool and even a duckpond. Around the house there were paved terraces and specialized gardens, potted plants being used there in profusion. The gardens included a small old-type boxwood garden, a rose-garden, a walled garden and a garden of flowering shrubs. There was an extensive wild-flower garden, rock wall plantings and dogwood and lilac walks. The arrangement of all these elements within the confines of this comparatively small garden so that each was impressive and attractive in itself was a *tour de force*.

The Dixon garden at Chestnut Hill, Pennsylvania, was of a different kind, seasonal colour having been subordinated to structure. There were interlocking terraces along the south front of the house, the rest of the estate being given over to lawn, native trees and flowering shrubs, which were skilfully arranged to create, very effectively, an all-the-year-round land-scape, an aim not common in American gardens because of the extremes of climate. Somewhat the same object was achieved, but in a rather different way, in the Phillips garden at Butler, Pennsylvania, laid out in 1930, which was European in style, being architectural and planted for permanent shape, structure and colour, and possessing a courtyard garden. The Mahony garden at Bryn Mawr, Pennsylvania, which was commenced in 1930, opted on the other hand for colour in both spring and autumn, being mainly woodland in type and using azaleas among trees with tulips in spring along the edges.

TOP *A scene in one of the 3½ acres of glasshouses at the Du Pont gardens at Longwood.*

ABOVE *Blossoming shrubs at Winterthur, Delaware, displaying a mass of bloom so thickly carried that nothing of the rest of the bushes may be seen.*

The greatest garden in Pennsylvania, and one of the great gardens of the world, is the Longwood garden of the Du Ponts at Kennett Square, in which an attempt has been made to gather in one garden as many as possible of the world's ornamental plants. This very large garden contains 3½ acres of glasshouses, the flower-beds and borders being rearranged and replanted with the changing seasons. The use of illuminated colour fountains and organ music recalls the Italian gardens of the Renaissance, in particular the Villa d'Este, with its water-driven organ fountain,

ABOVE *Long terrace borders, carpet bedding and treillage set against a background of noble trees in the Vanderbilt garden at Biltmore House, Asheville, North Carolina.*

FAR RIGHT *Used as a setting for sculpture, of which there are 340 examples, from the hands of 178 artists, on the estate, Brookgreen Gardens at Murrell's Inlet in South Carolina is a very beautiful estate, containing dogwoods, crape myrtles, oleanders, camellias, azaleas and Atamasco lilies growing in great drifts.*

BELOW *A beautiful water-garden, the lines of which are reminiscent of the parterres of Jacques Boyceau, at the mansion of Dumbarton Oaks, Georgetown, Washington, D.C.*

although this was a curiosity, the sounds it produced being only doubtfully classed as musical. Another Du Pont garden at Wilmington, Delaware, was mainly a formal French-style garden.

The Dudley Clark garden at Elton, Wilmington, Delaware, was begun in 1929 as a carefully planned all-the-year-round garden, but used only hardy herbaceous plants, not shrubs, being protected against the weather on three sides by a wall and pergola. One of the most interesting of all American gardens, the Crowninshield garden at Eleutherean Mills at Montchanin, is in Delaware. The garden here was begun in 1919 and was an adaptation of the ruins of an old powder works of E. I. Du Pont dating from the early 1800s. The basements of the old mill houses were converted into pools furnished with columns and statuary, set off by columnar cedars, giving a distinctly classical look to the scene, even though modern rock plants were planted in the paving. There were no clipped lawns or beds; the garden was designed to be at its best mainly in spring and autumn.

The Sherwood gardens at Baltimore in Maryland were far enough south for the heat to make summer bloom a little more difficult and this garden, commenced in 1930, was primarily a spring garden. It was in a woodland area; a network of grass paths between the trees were edged with pansies and tulips. More than 100,000 tulips were planted. Azaleas were similarly prominent, and there were about 10,000 of these. Behind the borders were flowering crab apples and pink and white dogwoods. The site and conditions

were very cleverly used, having been treated as allies rather than as opponents. Another garden which made clever use of the site was the Read and Auchincloss garden in Washington, D.C. This garden was within the town and formed from the long narrow garden lots common in older cities, being terraced in sections.

The Vance Norfleet garden in Memphis, Tennessee, was also terraced with gardens and lawns, but in this case although the house opened on to the upper terrace it was screened from the garden by a natural wooded area. The Howe garden at the Wildings, Nashville, Tennessee, was again different in type, being open woodland, eight acres in extent, filled with flowering shrubs, most of which were native, and having half an acre devoted to native wild-flowers. The Hale garden, created about 1930, also at Nashville, was hidden away behind high walls, to give shelter to what, in style, was an attempt to create an old English garden.

The coast of the Gulf of Mexico from Texas to Florida and up the Atlantic coast as far as North Carolina is the zone of cypress swamps, with an acid soil and abundant rainfall. Many evergreen trees grow in this zone, including the swamp cypress itself *Taxodium distichum,* the 'Bull Bay' magnolia *(Magnolia grandiflora),* the 'Sweet Bay' *(Magnolia glauca),* holly, wax myrtle *(Myrica cerifera)* and live oak. Two magnificent flowering trees, the dogwood and redbud *(Circis canadensis),* are native to the area and there are numerous handsome vines, yellow jessamine *(Gelsenium sempervirens)* and smilax being the most important.

BELOW *The Scroll Garden on the Orton estate, a former rice-growing plantation belonging to the Sprunt family near Wilmington, North Carolina. A novel feature is the untrimmed bush in each section of the parterre.*

NEXT PAGE *A deceptive scene in the Middleton Gardens at Charleston, South Carolina, resembling an English landscape garden: the palm in the right foreground, however, destroys the illusion.*

ABOVE *A typical swamp scene in the Cypress Gardens at Charleston, showing swamp cypresses* (Taxodium distichum) *growing in the black water and azaleas visible in the distance throught the veils of Spanish moss.*

RIGHT *Azaleas lining a walk in the Magnolia Gardens near Charleston, a scene which, but for the overhanging grey Spanish moss, might come from a British 'plantsman's' garden.*

The first gardens in the area in Spanish times would have been Renaissance in style, but the early gardens of New Orleans, Mobile, Savannah, or Charleston probably differed little in design from those of Virginia or New England, although the sub-tropical temperatures and high rainfall made familiar plants grow differently. Exotic importations also grew well and were easy to get because all the settlements were ports. Azaleas, camellias and gardenias flourished but the special conditions gave the gardens a very different appearance from those further north. The formal *allée* approaching the great house of the plantation became draped with the melancholy grey of the Spanish Moss. There was much natural water; this was incorporated into the gardens, which lost formality and became naturalistic.

The oldest garden in this area which survives is that founded by Henry Middleton at Charleston in 1741, known as the Middleton Gardens. It was his avowed intention to make a garden that rivalled those of the Old World but displayed a profusion of blossom impossible

to attain there. Two·great old live oaks from the original garden are still alive as are also three of the first camellias to be seen in the colony, supplied by the French plant-collector and nurseryman André Michaux in 1787. Middleton gardens are the best-preserved remnant of the most ambitious formal garden of the days before the Revolution and far exceeded estates like that of Mount Vernon of the same period in scale and richness. The gardens were approached by a water-gate which gave on to a vast system of patterned pools and terraced cascades. Most of this has disappeared leaving surviving specimen plants casually placed in a formal

pattern of beds and walks. The area covered by the original garden has been greatly extended by the addition of azalea-lined walks and today contains one of the finest camellia collections in the world.

Also at Charleston are the Magnolia Gardens on the Ashley river which were begun in the 1840s. The first imported *Azalea indica* was planted here and a collection of camellias made, which now includes some giants 25 feet high. This garden shows the classic pattern of all gardens in this region: informal paths following black pools, the black coming from the bark of the cypress, with moss and wistaria-covered cypresses acting as foil to the flaming azaleas. It also has, however, lawns and space with scattered trees resembling English parkland.

About fifty years ago another garden was established at Charleston on the site of Dean Hall, one of the old rice plantations on the Cooper River. Part of the banks were cleared of a freshwater lake which was formerly used for the irrigation of the paddies. Bulbs and azaleas were planted with such success that clearance was continued, islands landscaped, bridges built and azaleas multiplied until a magnificent water garden was formed which has become known as the Cypress Gardens. The natural growth of the area has been preserved, the garden being primarily a spring garden. Conditions are so favourable in this garden that azaleas will grow outdoors in it that normally elsewhere must be kept under glass.

In the Sharples garden at Palm Beach, Florida, a very clever effect was achieved by using palm trees and tree

ABOVE *A fine re-creation of an Italian garden of the Renaissance at the Villa Viscaya, Miami, made for James R. Deering in 1912.*

BELOW *A bridge seen through a frame of ancient trees draped in Spanish moss in the Middleton Gardens.*

ferns to create what appeared to be a tropical island. West along the coast on the shore of an arm of Mobile Bay in that corridor of Alabama that comes down to the sea was the Bellingrath garden which was begun in 1928. This was a plantsman's sub-tropical garden designed to give all-the-year-round colour; a great range of plants was grown in it. There were a quarter of a million azaleas, both exotic and native, the latter being naturalized in the woodlands, and also 2,000 camellias. Also grown was a wide selection of summer-flowering shrubs, crêpe myrtle, *Hibiscus* and *Althea* being among them. Innumerable herbaceous annuals and perennials were grown and, for the cooler period of the year, many thousands of pot plants, including *Amaryllis,* poinsettia, chrysanthemums, cinerarias, calceolarias and fuchsias, with *Dracaena* and crotons

for foliage effects. The rock-garden carried African violets.

Another semi-tropical garden in a different environment was the de Golyer garden in Dallas, Texas, which was made at about the end of the Second World War. Spanish influence was very marked in this garden. There were walls, arches, paved terraces with massive pottery and plants in pots, one of the features of the garden being the surprise vistas. The house was approached by a long, curving, heavily wooded drive leading to an octagonal court and loggia. The great terrace at the back of the house looked across the lake. An expanse of lawn led to a magnolia avenue which was terminated by a fountain. Paths branched off from the avenue to the flower-garden and the rose-garden and it was also connected to the great terrace by a

LEFT *Trees festooned with Spanish moss in the garden of Bellingrath in Alabama on the shores of Mobile Bay.*

FAR LEFT *A Japanese garden at Bellingrath in Alabama with an island, waterside stones, lanterns and clipped shrubs and, in the background, a pavilion and bridge.*

BELOW LEFT *Impressive Spanish-style pool and fountains in a formal setting at Longue Vue, New Orleans, Louisiana.*

In the Davis house at Minneapolis this winter difficulty was overcome by constructing a glass-roofed garden in the heart of the house like a Roman atrium. The Mather garden at Cleveland, Ohio, on the shores of Lake Erie, which was commenced in the 1920s, was far more imposing than most; it was made on a grand scale in the traditional Italian style. The Peabody garden at Lake Forest, Illinois, was made in 1928. To reduce the effects of the difficult climate, each part was enclosed in trees and shrubbery, with separate spring, summer and fall gardens. The Reingold garden at Highland Park, also in Illinois, was architectural in concept, being a garden mainly without flowers; it might well have come from the time of William and Mary in England. The whole emphasis was on design, there being strictly formal geometrical patterns of box in panels and scrolls, with larger clipped specimens as accent points. Ivy was used for infilling.

In the far West the Nixon garden at Holden in the Utah valley made about 1930 was a triumph against difficult circumstances but liberal use of water made it possible to grow in the semi-desert a good proportion of standard species. The Girard garden at Sante Fe in New Mexico was made in even more difficult desert conditions, hot sun, freezing nights, drying winds and blowing dust, but suitable plants set out in a checkerboard pattern of plant squares and paving succeeded. West over the Rockies in California the climate is extremely variable, including both killing frosts and extreme heat, there being also much variation with altitude because of the irregular terrain. Much of the area is sub-tropical and because the soil is very fertile almost anything will thrive. To those accustomed to less favourable conditions it is surprising to see apple trees, roses, iris, zinnias, geraniums, cacti and other succulents and palm trees growing together. Early gardens reflected those of the Eastern states but from the 1930s onwards styles have emerged dictated by local conditions.

The Green garden at Sausalito, California, was an example of the influence of Japanese ideas on American gardening. It made use of a very steep hillside, the garden consisting of potted plants set out on a large stilted wooden deck. Dwarfed pines and cut-leaved Japanese maples were used and the Japanese effect further enhanced by the use of bamboo screens and clever borrowing of the view of the trees on adjacent land, one of the main devices of Japanese gardening. The Hein garden at Mill valley in Marin county was built in five levels on a sunny and wind-free slope. It relied mainly on trees and shrubs selected for colour

redbud *allée*. A beautiful garden in which architecture and vegetation were mixed to the great advantage of both.

Gardening in the Mid-west of America is conditioned by the more extreme climate normal to inland continental areas. The Kanzler garden at Detroit was laid out before the First World War in a rather formal French design with considerable use of sculpture. A large *tapis vert* ran east from the house to the lake outlined in flowering borders. The Chapin garden at Grosse Point Farms, Michigan, made fine use of the changing levels of the terraces, being architectural in design and feeling. Each main view from the house terminated in an architectural feature. The fine Pillsbury garden at Lake Minnetonka in Minnesota was a garden for a summer home, snow-covered in winter.

and foliage texture, but there was also a wide range of flowering shrubs and a rock-garden. The Esherick garden at Kentfield was, like many West Coast houses, built with the house and garden integrated as one, but in this case it was not by the use of a patio or court. The gentle knoll on which the house was built possessed a magnificent white oak alongside of which the garden was carried up to the house by a series of paved and grassed terraces, each smooth and level. Shrub and tree borders were made around it to give a sense of seclusion.

Of the gardens in semi-desert country, the Moore garden at Ojai was one of the most interesting. The difficulties of low rainfall and lack of humidity were overcome by trapping water from the hillside in ornamental pools which girdled the house, forming the boundary between the garden and the desert. The house was sheltered on all sides by deep overhangs or treillages and the garden became a man-made oasis in which the supply of water was so lavish that plants made very lush growth. At the Tremaine garden at Santa Barbara there were parklike areas of lawn and live oaks which, because of the similarly dry climate, could be maintained all the year round only by constant watering. There was a rock-garden of succulents at this house in which the plants were massed so that,

A colourful garden among the rocks at Santa Barbara, which 'borrows' the scenery of the distant mountains in the Japanese fashion.

whatever the season, there was always something providing a sheet of colour either of flowers or foliage.

The Spanish influence from the state's early years was revived in the Young garden at Pasadena, which was modelled on the old Spanish style, with long *allées* of olive trees, pools with water in constant movement and geometric beds and paths. In contrast the Martin garden at Aptos was very modern in design. It was situated right on the beach; the garden was made of slatted wood tilted a little to allow the sand to be swept off. The U-shaped plan of the house enclosed a small garden the major planting in which was that of hardy plants with grey foliage, such as mesembryanthemums. The curved beds enclosed a small sunbathing beach, the wind being kept off by a redwood fence. The Donnell garden at Sonoma was set in a hillside overlooking the meandering shoreline of San Francisco Bay, the curves of which were cleverly echoed in the lines of the pool which was the central feature of the landscaping, and also in the shape of the terrace lawn and planting beds, giving an almost Japanese sense of unity with the surrounding landscape. The Emery garden at Carmel similarly overlooked Carmel Bay, the garden being linked directly with the beach, wind being kept off by a tall glass windbreak. Colour was maintained throughout the year by the use of plants in large boxes and pots, and evergreens were planted in the grounds.

In the Perlberg estate at Palm Springs the garden was protected by making it in a patio surrounded by the house, somewhat in the ancient Roman fashion.

High in the foothills of the Sierra Madre, the Mueller garden at Pasadena was begun in 1948. This garden was another based on a Japanese conception; it was constructed to form a foreground for the hills and used them as a backcloth into which it merged naturally. This effect was obtained by using as a framework the plants already growing there. The altitude enabled plants of temperate lands to be used which cannot normally be grown in the region. A final garden in the Californian region worth noticing was the Simon garden at San Francisco which differed from all the others in being a roof garden. Plants able to stand the heat were grown in tubs, and in flat pebble areas between, the whole having a desert feeling. Among the plants which tolerated the harsh conditions were *Alyssum, Artemisia,* sedums, Irish moss and *Festuca glauca.*

There were notable gardens further north on the West Coast above California. The Isaacs garden at Bellevue, Washington, was made on a hilltop with a magnificent view over Seattle. The U-shaped house surrounded and protected a patio, but the climate is temperate enough to enable lawns and evergreens to be grown in informal plantings. The terraces at this house give a fine view of the mountains in clear weather. The Nicholson garden in Seattle itself was an example of what could be done with a small garden area, between house and street, within the town. A sense of seclusion was created by heavy borders of cut-leaved maples, bamboos, rhododendrons and conifers, the path to the front door passing through what was virtually a bower of foliage.

The Merrill garden at Seattle was in total contrast; it was much larger, formal in conception and reminiscent of a French parterre. Beautiful turf and flower-beds of massed annuals confined in a frame of clipped box-wood made a summer garden; the annuals were low-growing types of bright colour to create a carpet effect. There was a circular pool in the centre and four small rectangular rose beds. Another large garden in this area was the Worthington garden. Here the house, with many walls of glass, sat in the garden on a platform of interlocking walls, terraces, pools and planting areas, the main emphasis being on spring bloom from hardy evergreen plants.

The gardens of America that have been described are representative only of the burgeoning of the great American love for gardens which began in the early pioneering days but which had to wait until more settled times before it could swell into the great national passion that it is today. There are innumerable other gardens tended with care and love that could equally well have been mentioned. More limited in most areas by its climate than the favoured British Isles, lapped and warmed by the waters of America coming to them as the north Atlantic drift from the Gulf Stream, Americans sensibly soon ceased to strive for European effects, although, nostalgically, some of them still do, and turned their attention to developing styles to suit the varied conditions of their own marvellous country. Their achievement up to the end of the Second World War was considerable but, as the aftermath of that war died away, changes took place not only in America but elsewhere, leading to the situation at the present day.

TOP *A garden coming down to the sea at Laguna Beach, California, in which clever use has been made of the hillside to provide a cascade of colour tumbling down to the very edge of the beach.*

ABOVE *Flat table-like rocks used with good effect round a swimming pool at Woodside, California, to simulate a stream cutting its way down through flat rock strata. The garden was designed by Thomas Church.*

16
Chateaux and Chalets

Who can tell what memories
Of lost beloved Paradise
Saddened Eve with sleepless eyes?

Christina Rossetti

The great gardens of America probably reached their peak in 1930. Although some of those that have been mentioned were founded after that, the Depression years of the 1930s took their toll and one by one the great establishments all across the country began to disappear. The same factors began to operate as had affected the gardens of Britain: rising costs, shortage of skilled labour, expansion of the cities and pressure on available land. As one American writer put it, 'the American house stands on a steadily shrinking plot.'

Gardens made in America since the Second World War have been influenced by many styles, Chinese, Japanese, Arabic, Persian, English, French and Italian, but they have developed characteristics of their own. One American feature which is different from European practice is the lack of fencing between gardens, so that they flow into one another. It is, indeed, expressly forbidden by law in some localities to erect such fences: this has been claimed to demonstrate what is unique in the world, a socially peaceful countryside of well distributed wealth. Another characteristic of American garden owners is a firm belief in the necessity for a stretch of well-manicured front lawn to set off the house; this in spite of the difficulty of maintaining it in many areas because of adverse climatic conditions. Climatic reasons have given rise to another feature of the modern American garden, the shaping of the garden to present the best view from the house because of the large windows required to maintain tolerable living conditions, walls often being made entirely of glass. As this problem is precisely the same as that of the Japanese, who design their houses with a sliding wall to give a view of the whole garden, interest in Japanese gardening has continued in America and many gardens have a Japanese flavour.

One element that has become popular in American gardens is the rock-garden. Such gardens came late to the United States. There was a vogue in the early part of the century for what was derisively called the 'peanut brittle' garden, in which small round boulders were

LEFT *The modern scene at Fredericksborg, Denmark.*

ABOVE *A modern American garden, showing a fountain and pool reminiscent of older styles, leading on to an outdoor living area in the contemporary fashion.*

used in a more or less 'polka dot' arrangement but an exhibition of rock-gardens staged in America by the English landscape gardener Ralph Hurcock in the 1920s introduced true rock gardening and displaced previous efforts of this kind. The new and more natural method of growing rock plants was immediately taken up and spread so effectively that it is found even in sub-tropical high rainfall gardens such as Bellingrath on Mobile Bay. The use of rocks in Japanese gardens has had much to do with their ready acceptance in American gardens.

There is now an almost universal acceptance of the idea that the garden is not merely to be looked at but

part of it at least incorporated into the living area of the house. As amenities spread in America, the garden plot had no longer to contain the woodpile and all the other essentials for living a self-contained life but could be devoted entirely to ornament and pleasure. Gardens are now designed with emphasis on comfort, providing summer shade but not excluding the winter sun. Some provision for privacy is needed, circulation must be easy and maintenance reduced to a minimum. As a help in attaining these ends the patio has been adopted to replace the backyard.

The term 'patio' formerly referred to enclosed areas like the Roman atrium or Moorish courtyard but has now come to mean any paved area. It has affinities with the *giardino segreto* with the terrace of Italian gardens and with the terrace of those gardens derived from the Italian style such as Barry's mid-nineteenth-century Italian gardens on English country estates, which was to some extent used as a living area, tea on the terrace being an English country house social institution. It also has affinities with the New England porch and the verandas or stoeps of houses in warmer climates: affinities, indeed, with all those various modes adopted over the years for the inhabitants of houses to sit outside in privacy or, if they preferred it, in social contact with the passers-by. The modern patio is all these things merged into a living area related to the needs of modern life, the accent being generally on privacy rather than social contact.

The idea of the patio is as well established in the northern countries of western Europe as it is in

America, in both cases probably having spread northward from warmer southern parts. Whatever its origin, a flood of books and magazines on garden design has spread throughout the world a rather standardized notion of what the garden of the average house on a limited site should contain. Many changes are rung in the details and shape of such designs but basically practically all advocate the patio, a sunbathing and play area, a pool and some kind of provision for outdoor living. The plants used and their arrangement vary according to the climate and the area available but the framework is the same everywhere.

The more highly developed countries of the world still contain a high proportion of older style gardens, but where new gardens are made or old ones remade they follow the new pattern, even the smallest plot with no room or money for a pool having its paved area or even being wholly paved, decorated with plants in pots or tubs and provided with garden furniture so that it can be used as an outdoor living space. Many ideas are being circulated for the making of gardens in such confined spaces. Taking another leaf out of the Japanese book, recommendations have been made to paint scenes on the end wall or fence, so that the view from the house seems to look out over a landscape, the living plants in the garden merely being those in the foreground of the larger scene. The Japanese, of course, 'borrow' real scenery for their background but this not being available in most western urban gardens, the painting would be a necessary substitute. It has also been advocated that the picture on the end wall or fence

TOP LEFT *A Chinese garden in San Francisco: an example of one of the many styles that have influenced American gardens since the Second World War.*

TOP RIGHT *Outdoor living in the modern style.*

ABOVE *A modern pool and fountain in a garden at Baltimore, Maryland, U.S.A.*

RIGHT *A patio leading to a wild garden.*

ABOVE *A well-furnished patio bright with flowers and foliage plants.*

RIGHT *Here at Cedres in the South of France climate allows the giant water-lily of South America* (Victoria amazonica) *to grow and flower out of doors.*

should appear to be seen through a window, harking back to an even older practice, that of the Romans, who, as may been seen at Pompeii, painted such effects upon the walls of the atrium or within the peristyle so that a feeling of space was achieved.

The gardens of America suffered neglect rather than physical injury during the Second World War, but many of the gardens of Continental Europe were both uncultivated and damaged. Recovery from the war brought with it, however, a great revival of interest in gardens in Europe. In France the great parks of Paris were restored to their former beauty. The 62 acres, mainly formal, of the Jardins du Luxembourg, the 60 acres of the Tuileries garden, still much as it was, the Parc Monceau, with its eighteenth-century grotto, tomb, pyramid and colonnade and the two vast areas, more than 2,000 acres each, of the Bois de Boulogne and the Bois de Vincennes, are a great asset to the city. The movement to preserve and repair, where feasible, the ancient châteaux of France and their gardens was revived and strengthened and there are a number within easy reach of Paris so that they attract many visitors. These include the Le Nôtre gardens of Courances, St Cloud, Chantilly, Dampierre, Fontainebleau, Sceaux, Vaux-le-Vicomte and Versailles, as well as Champs and Rambouillet in the same style. Bagatelle and the Hôtel Biron (the Rodin Museum) represent the eighteenth century.

Those who like masses of flowers enjoy Bagatelle's 200,000 tulips and 20,000 roses. They also enjoy the Fleuriste Municipale of Paris, from which more than a million plants each year are produced for the parks of Paris. Fine gardens in the older styles have also been remade in other parts of France, of which the restored sixteenth-century garden of Villandry, near Tours, only one among a number of châteaux in the Loire valley, is perhaps the finest. Beautiful gardens open to the public may be seen from the Jardin Botanique at Caen in the north through many variations to the sub-tropical gardens of Cap Ferrat in the south. There are probably upwards of a hundred gardens of all kinds in France that will stand comparison in their genre with any in the rest of the world. New gardens continue to be made, such as the Japanese garden at the Unesco building in the Place de la Fontenoy in Paris but, as elsewhere, economic conditions make such new creations rare.

French home gardens are usually walled in for privacy and the greater part of them differ from the

gardens of other European countries in being devoted almost wholly to vegetables and fruit, the back garden being used for this purpose, only the front being ornamental. Gardening is also mainly the province of men, few women concerning themselves with it. Homes are not, however, devoid of colour: window-boxes, pots, and balcony gardens add a very attractive brightness to the scene both in town and country. Interest in ornamental gardens has increased greatly lately because of the popularity of second homes for holidays and weekends. As the owners are not there all the time they furnish the garden with trees, ornamental shrubs and roses, which require only occasional attention. In 1959 the French Government Tourist Office initiated a 'Fleurir la France' (Make France Flower) campaign designed to encourage local authorities to use flowers in their localities, annual prizes being awarded for the best efforts. The increase in interest in gardening may be measured by the great success of Les Centres Jardinières, hypermarket and supermarket garden selling centres, and the specialist Garden Centres that have been set up in France in great numbers in recent years.

Belgium has been called a 'land of flowers', for everywhere are flower stalls in the open-air markets as well as window-boxes, parks and railway platforms alive with their colour. Of the parks in Antwerp, Brussels and other towns, the Château de Beloeil is probably the finest, being a French-style garden with English parkland, totalling in all 240 acres. Of private

estates, Annevoie, formal garden with many pools, cascades and fountains, modelled in the eighteenth century on Versailles and the Villa d'Este, is the equal of the best of its kind elsewhere. Another fine French-style garden is that of Leeuwergen at Oombergen which is famed for its Théâtre de Verdure, the stage, auditorium and boxes of which are made from clipped ash trees. The gardens of Attre at Ath, Freyr at Dinant, which is supposed to have been designed by Le Nôtre, the Parc de Bruxelles, and the garden of Gaasbeek near Brussels are all French in style. Interesting historically is the garden of Rubens' house at Antwerp which he himself designed and has been carefully preserved.

About 60 of the larger gardens of Belgium are open to the public. Ghent is the capital of the world for begonias and azaleas and produces vast quantities of other ornamental house plants, the growing areas being a tourist focus in flowering time. Home gardens in Belgium are not as uniformly used for vegetables and fruit as those of France, but as in that country the tradition is for the gardening to be done by men, although this is now changing. Formerly Belgians had little national pride in their gardens but this is now changing also. As in France, the rising enthusiasm is marked by the development of garden sales in supermarkets and garden centres. Although there are less shows of the smaller kind in Belgium than elsewhere, the enormous Ghent Floralies which takes place every five years is one of the great shows of Europe.

Near Zandvliet in Belgium there are vast tulip fields like those of Holland, an overflow, as it were, from that country, which is known world-wide for its bulb industry. Those who buy Dutch bulbs abroad, however, may only guess at the appearance of Holland itself. Not only is there the marvellous Keukenhof estate at Lisse, showpiece of the bulb world, with 65 acres of lawn, small ponds, brooks, cherry trees and bulbs everywhere, six million of them being planted, but the whole country is overflowing with bloom all summer long. Roses, annuals and perennials are found in every park, house and place of business. Outside public buildings, on street corners and on islands are placed large wooden tubs of geraniums and heliotrope and many houses have window-boxes. Where they do

ABOVE LEFT *The garden of the seventeenth-century château of Courances, a few miles South of Paris, one of a number of older French château gardens that have been restored in modern times, as part of the movement, common to all countries, to save something of the garden heritage of the past.*

LEFT *Such is the desire of men to have gardens near them that in urban surroundings they will make them on the rooftops, as in this example at Monaco.*

ABOVE *The French-style château at Beloeil, with its adjacent water, set in English-style parkland, one of the fine gardens of Belgium.*

not the windows are lined with indoor plants. Even the shopping streets are brightened by baskets of plants suspended overhead. Not content with this, the Dutch, with their irrepressible love for flowers, seize every opportunity to hold elaborate flower shows and to parade floats decorated with realistic scenes made entirely from flowers. The Dutch are also expert producers of trees, supplying nearly half the world's needs.

There are superb collections of trees in the Netherlands, but the country has few large-scale gardens, Kasteel Twickel at Delden being the finest. It is a garden in the French style with flower-beds, topiary and orange trees, but there is also a rock-garden, a large rose-garden and a grand rhododendron walk with ancient trees. Poort Zuylenstein at Leersum, Raaphorst at Wassenaar, De Hartekamp at Bennebroek, Kasteel Middachten at De Steeg and Kasteel Weldam at Goor are other fine gardens. There is a noteworthy Japanese garden in the Clingendael at The Hague.

A feature of Dutch life not found in France or Belgium is the use of what are called 'chalet' gardens. These spring from plots of land lent to the poor for food production about a century ago which began to be used for flowers and on which in the 1930s small chalets used as summer sleeping quarters were erected, the plots being converted to ornamental gardens. This is now a thriving well-regulated garden movement hampered by the lack in Holland of available land, so that there are long waiting lists for the chalet plots. As elsewhere, the increasing interest in gardening in Holland is reflected in the recent rapid establishment of garden centres.

The Scandinavian countries, Denmark, Norway, Sweden and Finland have a climatic range from that of Denmark in the south, where there is a mild climate approximating to that of Britain, to the icy Arctic tundra of the far north. Much of the area is covered with snow during the winter months, the white expanse being broken only by the spruce and silver birch. There are therefore fewer large-scale gardens than in the countries further south, but some beautiful gardens have nevertheless been made in Scandinavia. Denmark possesses a fine French-style garden in Fredericksborg at Hillerød containing all the standard features, parterres, avenues and long vistas. Knuthenborg at Bandholm is an enormous *jardin anglais* of 1,500 acres

ABOVE *Fountains in the pool at Rottneros Park, Sunne, Sweden, play merrily in the sunshine among modern statuary, reminding the visitor of warmer lands and garden styles further south where ornamental water is a prime essential of the garden, unlike the northern countries where there is more often too much rather than too little.*

ABOVE RIGHT *The very modern terraces at Frogner Park, Oslo, Norway, with roses and bedding plants in bold colour blocks in the foreground.*

RIGHT *An arbour at Schwetzingen, Germany, through which can be seen the Temple of Minerva.*

ABOVE FAR RIGHT *Parterres in the garden at Schwetzingen, Germany, filled with coloured chippings in the manner of seventeenth-century gardens. Francis Bacon, Lord Verulam, had a contempt for these coloured patterns, where flowers were absent, and said of them, in his famous essay 'Of Gardens', written in the early years of the seventeenth century, that 'they be but toys; you may see as good sights many times in tarts.'*

FAR RIGHT *A painted scene, called 'The End of the World', viewed through an arch in the old garden of Schwetzingen, Germany, showing how additional distance and space can be effectively suggested by such devices. The idea has been put forward that there is scope for such effects to increase the apparent size of the modern small garden.*

of parkland, lake and woods. Vallø at Køge and Gavøn at Naestved specialize in bulbs. Gisselfeld at Have, made in the nineteenth century, is small, being only eighteen acres in extent, but squeezes in five lakes with roses on the islands and many rhododendrons and rare trees. The castles of Bregentved and Vemmetofte also have fine gardens. For those who love flowers, the magnificent displays in the pleasure garden of the Tivoli at Copenhagen are as big an attraction as the concerts and firework displays. The rugged terrain of Norway can show the beautiful lakeside woodland garden of the home of Edward Grieg at Bergen and also the very modern garden at Frogner Park, Oslo, where bedding plants are set in bold colour blocks in abstract patterns in the lawns, an up-dated version of Victorian carpet bedding used to set off the statuary of Gustav Vigeland.

Sweden has a number of fine gardens of which the chief is Drottningholm Palace at Stockholm, previously mentioned, a full-scale formal French-type garden. Norrviken gardens at Båstad resemble the gardens of Compton Acres at Poole in Dorset in England, being a museum-like collection of modern replicas of ancient garden styles, mediaeval, Renaissance, baroque, Japanese and Scandinavian. The royal palace garden of Sofiero at Skane is famous for its rhododendrons and roses and contains many rarities. One of the noteworthy memories I have of my tenure of the Secretaryship of the Royal Botanic Gardens, Kew, is seeing King Gustav VI of Sweden periodically going out with Sir George Taylor, the then Director of Kew, to

ABOVE *Bulbs in flower at the unique bulb garden at Keukenhof, Lisse, Holland, which is the showpiece for Holland's vast bulb industry and a place of pilgrimage each spring for those who love the masses of vivid colour to be seen everywhere in the bulb-growing areas of Holland at that time.*

BELOW *Terrace and pool at the old garden at Kasteel Twickel, Delden, Holland, as it is today, conveying some of the quiet and repose of the more leisurely age when it was made.*

look at newly-acquired rarities in the Kew rhododendron collection, some of which were propagated for Sofiero. Trädgårdsförenigen at Gothenburg is noted for flowers and also possesses a palm house. The island of Gotland off the east coast of Sweden is a Mecca for flower lovers, containing many wild orchids in the Alvena Lindang Wildflower Reserve. The Milles garden at Lidingo houses statuary by Carl Milles among the trees, shrubs and flowers on the terraces made on the cliffs near Stockholm. Even more striking is the 100-acre garden of Rottneros Park at Värmland created around the end of the Second World War which, as well as beautiful natural areas within its formal gardens, contains a collection of statues by the principal Scandinavian sculptors.

The short outdoor season in Scandinavian countries has led to the placing of houses so that the garden remains part of the natural countryside. Garden trees, shrubs and flowers are fitted into the existing scene so as to harmonize with the surroundings. The more northerly gardens, such as those of Finland, are so restricted by the climate that effort is diverted to indoor gardening rather than work outside. All the Scandinavian countries are, indeed, great cultivators of indoor plants. When the contents of the window-boxes, balconies and plants in tubs and pots have to be moved indoors at the approach of winter, the gardener turns to the house plants, of which he makes much more than do other countries, often having planted troughs running the length of the room and specially adapted windows. The Danes are celebrated for the *vinterhave*, a kind of conservatory in which plants ostensibly grow in the ground in landscaped conditions.

The patio is an important feature of the gardens of Scandinavian countries, usually being made of stone in Sweden and Denmark, but of timber in Norway. Many Scandinavians have second homes for holidays where they also have a small natural garden. Denmark is one of the leading supporters of chalet gardens, having 20,000 in Copenhagen alone, but the other Scandinavian countries are not prominent in this movement.

Germany's garden record in the past has been one of adopting styles first developed in other countries and, while producing many grand gardens, sometimes going over into the absurd. There is a different picture since the war, Western Germany being in the forefront of the European revival of interest in gardening. A number of the grand gardens of the past still exist and are preserved with care, and some new large gardens have been added. Herrenhausen in Hanover, ancestral home of the English Georges, lost its royal palace during the war but the garden remains one of the finest in Germany, containing both French and Dutch styles of the time it was created. Augustsburg garden at Bruehl near Cologne remains a perfect example of the Le Nôtre style. Schwetzingen at Mannheim still contains the original French-style garden merging into another garden in the English landscape style. The old garden at Nymphenburg near Munich shows the same combination.

The eighteenth century is still well represented in Germany by Ludwigsburg near Stuttgart, the garden of which has been nicknamed 'Baroque in Bloom';

ABOVE *Present-day bedding at Fredennsburg Palace, Denmark.*

BELOW *Spring colour in the Tivoli, Denmark.*

Veitschoechhaim near Wurzburg, full of rococo sculpture; and Frederick the Great's garden at Charlottenburg, near Berlin, with its famous Great Parterre. The nineteenth century was the age of public park making and the great public parks then created are its memorial. The most noteworthy of these are the Grosse Tiergarten in Berlin, two miles long and half a mile wide, with a mixed bag of woods, rhododendron plantations and more formal gardens as well as the animals; the Rheinpark at Cologne, which may be seen from a cable car which runs over it; Westfalenpark at Dortmund with famous fountain displays and a Japanese garden; Nordpark, Dusseldorf; Gruga Park, Essen; the Stadtgarten at Karlsruhe; and the Englis-

The eighteenth-century garden at Ludwigsburg, Germany, is famous for its baroque sculpture, but it also possesses this more modern rock wall with 'cushions' of rock plants.

chergarten at Munich, one of the first English-style landscaped gardens to be made in Germany, or, indeed, in Europe generally.

Of more modern gardens the Planten and Blomen at Hamburg is one of the best public parks in Europe. There is also a beautifully landscaped rhododendron garden along the autobahn on the outskirts of Bremen. At the other end of Western Germany the unique garden of Count Lennart Bernadotte of Sweden on the island of Mainau in Lake Constance benefits from the very mild climate, which brings roses into bloom outdoors in May. The most famous part of Mainau garden is, however, the tropical garden, where even date palms and bananas grow outdoors, as well as oranges and lemons and the more exotic bougainvillea and hibiscus. The Germans cleverly combine the improvement of their parks with their desire for shows. Apart from the grand international exhibition held in the Planten and Blomen at Hamburg every ten years, shows are held every two years in selected individual

towns which last from spring until autumn, the proceeds of which are put either to extending an existing park or making a new one. Other countries might well take a leaf out of this book.

It is in their private gardens that the Germans are mainly ahead of the rest of Europe. Fifty per cent of them have patios and are fully adapted for outdoor living on the lines described earlier. The paved area, which in the new designs uses a wide selection of materials, large smooth pebbles, concrete with various finishes, dressed stone and even metal, extends beyond the immediate area of the house to take in most of the front garden and, behind the house, a part in which square or rectangular beds are planted with perennials or dwarf conifers. By an amazing persistence the

ABOVE *Rococo sculpture from the garden of Veitshoechhaim near Wurzburg in Germany: Pegasus rises from the pool in a crowded scene around the fountain base.*

RIGHT *The flourishing Alpine Garden in Vienna: such gardens were unknown before the second half of the nineteenth century.*

ancient tradition of the garden divided into four by the Four Rivers of the Garden of Eden is still perpetuated in this section of the modern German garden. It is still called, even though the divisions are paths and not water, and there are more than four of them, the *paradiesgartenlein,* the 'little garden of paradise'. As well as its home gardens, Germany has more than half a million chalet gardens, lineal descendants of Dr Schreiber's Leipzig gardens of a hundred years before. These gardens are so popular that Germans are going over the border into adjacent French territory and buying up land to make these gardens, even to the extent of creating, in effect, small German-speaking settlements inside the borders of France. Gardening is the most popular hobby in northern Germany, but is still, as in France, mainly the province of the men, although the interest of the women, always concerned with cut flowers and indoor plants, is growing.

The survivors of the grand gardens of Austria described in earlier chapters are now all public parks. Principal among them is the famous Schönbrunn in Vienna, the grandest of all the Hapsburg imperial gardens, made originally in the French style and still principally in that style with enormous parterres

around the palace, but with additions in later styles. Also at Vienna is the Belvedere, a French-style garden showing strong Italian influence, with cascades, terracing and simple parterres. Bishop Sittich's pleasure palace of Hellbrun in Salzburg, with its ancient water devices, still survives, as does the garden of the Mirabelschloss, also at Salzburg. More recent are the Volksgarten, famous for its association with Johann Strauss, and the Englischer Garten of the Türkenschranz. Of the many fine parks in Vienna the largest is the Prater which extends to 5.3 square miles. The Wertheimspark is notable for its garden for the blind, which was created in 1959 and contains handrails to guide the visitor, Braille labels, and plants to smell and touch. Even the fountain is made to sing as it plays. A most popular park is the Donaupark which was made in 1964 on 250 acres of a rubbish dump for an International Horticultural Exhibition. There are so many public parks in Vienna that almost every home has one close at hand, which accounts perhaps for a lack of enthusiasm for home gardening in Austria. Home gardens are in the main like those of Germany, many having a paved area and a pool. Two modern additions are the alpine gardens at Frohnleiten and that on Patscherkofel Mountain at Innsbruck; there is a similar garden at Rannach at St Veit.

Italy still has its grand Renaissance gardens, more or less altered over the years in most cases and to these were added Sir Thomas Hanbury's garden at La Mortola, Ventimiglia, in 1867, which is virtually a botanical garden, and that of Captain Neil McEacharn at the Villa Taranto on Lake Maggiore, a marvellous

269

plantsman's garden begun in 1930. Only a small proportion of Italians own home gardens and enthusiasm for gardening outdoors is low, partly because the four hot dry summer months make maintenance difficult. Homes are, however, decorated with balcony gardens and pot plants.

Spain also has its ancient gardens, Moorish and later. As elsewhere in Europe, these are mostly public parks. A high point of those in or near Madrid is the collection of roses in the Parque de Oeste, in which 30,000 bushes are set out among pools and fountains in a most attractive fashion. There are also fine parks in Seville, from the gardens of the Alcazar, where Moorish, Renaissance and modern gardens exist side by side, to the ultra modern Rosaleda opened in 1973. Until ten years ago, few Spaniards apart from the wealthy had a garden but the scene is now changing with the making of suburban estates of houses with gardens on the outskirts of some of the larger towns. Although they did not individually own gardens the Spaniards were still great lovers of flowers, decorating their courtyards, steps and walls with plants in pots or tubs.

A few of Portugal's gardens of the past remain, including the royal garden at Queluz and that of Fronteira at Benfica, both showing, in basically French-style gardens, the distinctively Portuguese touch of coloured tiles. The Estufa Fria at Lisbon is a modern garden opened in 1930 which houses a large collection of tropical plants growing together in almost jungle-like fashion. Only a small percentage of the people owned their own gardens until recently so that there was no activity around these such as exists in northern European countries.

Information is scanty about gardens in the countries behind the Iron Curtain but some of the grand gardens of the past such as Sans Souci, pride of Frederick the Great, the Grosser Garten and the Moritzburg garden at Dresden in East Germany are still maintained, and so is the tremendous Peterhof at Leningrad. In the main the Russians and those in the occupied countries of eastern Europe probably rely mainly on the public parks, home gardens being unusual, since most of the population in the towns are flat-dwellers. Some favoured Russians, however, have the second home habit, retiring to *dachas* (weekend cottages) in the woods or on the river banks, in their leisure time. *Dachas* are somewhat larger than the chalets of the chalet gardens of the West, having to accommodate families for a period and not just for an overnight stay. The *dacha* garden usually grows a few flowers, fruit and vegetables. Over a great part of Russia, of course, the winter climate, as in Scandinavia and Canada, makes gardening difficult.

There is nothing to add to what has been said in earlier chapters about gardens to the east of Russia, in China, Japan and India, torn as they have been by wars and political upheavals. Interest in gardens has increased greatly in recent years in the countries of the Middle East stimulated by the wealth available from oil and there may be noteworthy developments in countries of that area of the world in the future. Gardens in the tropics and the southern hemisphere, apart from the striking work of Burle Marx in Brazil,

LEFT *A splendid spring scene in the garden of the Villa Taranto, Italy;* Cornus florida *in the full flush of bloom against the background of the Alps sets off the gaudy tulips.*

TOP Dicksonia *palms lend an exotic air to Villa Taranto.*

ABOVE *Gardening in the southern hemisphere: the beautiful modern garden designed by Burle Marx under cover at the Palacio dos Arcos in Brasilia, Brazil.*

have in the main followed the patterns and reflected the ideas of the countries of the northern hemisphere as applicable to their own climate and position. One country only, Britain, has not yet been dealt with in this survey of the modern situation. It remains, therefore, to see what is the present state of affairs in that 'nation of gardeners', as the British have been called.

17
Down the Long Valley

*Look down the long valley and there stands a
mountain
That someone has said is the end of the world.
Then what of this river that having arisen
Must find where to pour itself into and
empty?*

Robert Frost

In Britain the modern gardening picture is a mixed one. As landowners over the years have found it increasingly difficult to maintain the larger houses and their gardens, many have taken advantage of the existence of the National Trust. Founded in the 1890s to preserve places of historic interest or natural beauty likely to be lost, the Trust is independent of government, carrying out its functions by means of endowments, gifts and bequests, and such money as it raises from admitting visitors who are not members of the National Trust to its properties. It has performed a service of great value in preserving much that is unique, but its function is that of a longstop. It has no funds from which it can make new gardens or even extend gardens in its possession, and thus acts in a museum capacity only. The number of properties with fine gardens which it has been asked to preserve is a proportion only of the whole. Since the end of the Second World War several hundred larger houses and their accompanying gardens have been broken up and the gardens lost.

The number of estates on the grand scale still in private hands is comparatively small. Those that remain, like Chatsworth, make a charge to the public for admittance and augment their finances in this way. Others like Longleat, Alton Towers and Woburn Abbey adopt the methods of the showman and add attractions such as the lions at Longleat to keep themselves afloat. This keeping of animals on large estates recalls the days when every such estate had its menagerie. In addition to these there are the historic gardens like Hampton Court and the Royal Parks of London, which are in the very competent and thorough care of experts of the Department of the Environment: this, like the National Trust, exercises a museum function in respect of these gardens. Then there are the public parks that exist in almost every town and are financed by local authorities.

Carpet bedding, invented in the nineteenth century, carried out today in the seafront gardens at Eastbourne.

Of the middle-sized gardens that remain in private hands a good proportion share their beauties with the public by opening at times in the summer for charity. The owners must always have had sources of income other than the estates but have great difficulty now in finding money and labour to maintain them, so that many are run on a shoestring and suffer accordingly, labour-demanding styles such as those involving planting sequences, carpet bedding and the like, being a thing of the past. As much is done as minimum labour permits. Both the larger gardens and those of medium size supplement their income by the marketing of produce where this is feasible.

Some of the smaller houses have remained in existence as multi-family residences after the bulk of the land has been sold off. They join the larger number of comparatively small properties that have an acre or so of garden manageable by one gardener or with part-time help, or are even run entirely by the owner himself. These contain among their number many of the most enthusiastic, knowledgeable and dedicated of gardeners. There remains the great bulk of British gardeners, who have gardens attached to their village, suburban or town houses, varying from a few square yards at the smallest to half an acre or even more in the case of the largest. Although a proportion of these are neglected and others kept no more than tidy, a good many of the occupiers are interested in their gardens and make an effort to cultivate them.

The British have always had a reputation for being garden-makers but, just as in the other countries of northern Europe, there has of recent years been a great surge of enthusiasm for gardens and gardening. The average worker now has more leisure and money than he had in the past and some of it is spent on gardening. Although they are not as influential as in the United States, general and specialist garden clubs, generally in Britain called 'horticultural societies', flourish everywhere, the leading society being the Royal Horticultural Society which maintains its own garden at Wisley in

Surrey and runs the largest horticultural show, the Chelsea Show, in May of each year. Sales of garden material and equipment are thriving and the shelves of the bookshops are filled with 'how-to-do-it' books, outnumbering any others on the 'do-it-yourself' shelves. As on the Continent, many garden centres have sprung up in recent years and crowds may be seen thronging to them at weekends; plants are also bought elsewhere, in supermarkets, chain stores and garden shops in the towns. All this presents a picture of a thriving national hobby; there is, however, another side to the coin.

Predominantly, the gardening world in Britain is now the world of the small garden and the amateur. Above him there are only the remnants of grand gardens kept going on a museum basis, a minority of middle-size gardens precariously hanging on to existence, and the public parks plus a limited number of advisory and specialist jobs, to employ the professional, comprising all together career prospects hardly likely to attract men of the calibre that served great gardens in the past. The aspiring trainee, if he wishes to do well for himself, must go out into the nursery, pest control or similar world to make his way.

Of the great amateur public now so enthusiastic about gardening many are below the level reached by the Royal Horticultural Society's journal *The Garden*. The needs of the average small gardener are, however, met by several other gardening papers, the continued activity of which is a measure of the extent of the interest of the small gardener in getting the most from his garden.

Of the plants that the British small garden owner uses the rose must come first. Modern varieties are vigorous, prolific and colourful, and will grow almost anywhere, requiring a minimum of attention. They will still give a

FAR LEFT *An attractive view through the parterres, in the garden of Hidcote Manor, Hidcote, Gloucestershire, England.*

LEFT *Restored parterres, filled with coloured chippings, and a shady* allée *in the garden of the sixteenth-century Moseley Old Hall, Wolverhampton, England.*

BELOW *A beautiful modern walled town garden with a classical flavour in Chelsea, London.*

borders severely straight, following the lines of the fences, as if the curve had never been invented, a situation a long way removed from the serpentine line and Hogarth's 'Line of Beauty' of the eighteenth century. The average British gardener's inheritance from his illustrious gardening forebears is precisely nil. Let me not, however, paint the picture too black. Of late years, with the spread of what might be called 'patio' gardening, the small gardener has been becoming gradually more knowledgeable and, helped by the new garden centres and the sale of plants in containers, is trying his hand at once-rare plants and shrubs. Is there not a great field lying fallow here for education in beauty and the relationship of man to his environment?

In spite of his numbers, and the fact that more houses in Britain have a garden than in other countries in Western Europe, the British small gardener is in some respects behind his Continental counterpart. Probably because so many houses in Britain have gardens there is little pressure to turn vegetable allotments into the chalet gardens that are so popular on the Continent but which, to establish in Britain, would require a change in planning policy and, doubtless, of law, a step governments would be reluctant to take because Britain is not self-supporting in her food supply. The average small gardener on the Continent who establishes or takes over a garden is very much more interested in garden design, and shows in European mainland countries feature garden designs more prominently than do British shows, which lay great emphasis on flowers.

The last point raises a general question which concerns not only British gardeners but those of the Netherlands and Belgium and, indeed, any other countries where new varieties of ornamental garden plants are bred. Every year the flowers available for planting become showier, the blooms larger and the colours brighter or more bizarre, as the breeders produce ever more varieties, often differing only marginally from something previously grown, to make the money by which they and the nursery trade survive. Each new and more striking variety of flower, shrub or tree is hailed with enthusiasm as an advance and if it is striking enough a fortune may be made from it by the lucky breeder whose rights, if he has registered them, are protected by law.

An observer from another planet, or even a Japanese gardener, whose ideas on his craft are so far removed from those of the West that he might well come from another planet, may question what intrinsic value there is in all this effort, apart from making money for the worthy breeders, as it seems to have very little to do with the beauty of plants or gardens. Why is a blue rose,

good show in comparatively poor soil conditions even if neglected, and the British gardener buys them in millions. He also buys large quantities of spring bulbs every year and every garden has its snowdrops, crocuses, daffodils and tulips. He also buys bedding plants by the million for summer colour in his beds and borders, and many gardeners with a glasshouse and frame raise their own. To the less sophisticated William Robinson might never have lived. They still like their bedding in the local park and even try to make something like it in their own gardens. Every garden, too, of any size, has a herbacous border stocked with perennials and a lawn, both front and back.

Hand-in-hand with this lack of imagination in planting goes a similar lack of imagination in garden design. Look along any suburban road or village street and you will find most of the lawns are rectangular or square, the flower-beds the same, and the herbaceous not yet achieved, but supposed to be the ultimate aim of rose breeders, and likely to make a large fortune for whoever is successful in producing it, so desirable? There are already many beautiful flowers in all shades of blue. What special virtue is there in another? Why is a new and larger flower of any species to be preferred to the original? What virtue is there in size, which, after all, is only relative? A 'large' pansy is measured on a different scale from a 'large' dahlia. Is the ultimate aim to breed a pansy as large as the largest dahlias?

At camellia shows I have seen flowers detached from the plant laid out in rows for comparison. It is hard to think of anything more unrelated to the marvellous beauty of a camellia flower nestling among the glossy dark green foliage of its parent plant than this process, which can spring only from a total lack of appreciation of its true beauty. Gardeners have been brainwashed, and British gardeners are among the worst affected, to expect continual changes and to regard size and striking colour or combination of colours as the main criteria by which to judge a plant. These are crude values, surely. There are, of course, many discerning gardeners not influenced by this state of affairs, but they are in a small minority.

The lagging of the British small gardener behind his Continental counterpart is repeated in the parks. A fine show is put up in British parks on a meagre budget but there is nothing in Britain like the town shows organized in Germany to raise money to extend or make new parks, so that the situation in this sector is static and likely to remain so, or even to deteriorate still further if the pressure to reduce public expenditure continues. In the sphere of larger gardens there is an even more serious situation. Nothing can now be expected of private owners and the remaining gardens of note, apart from those 'cocooned' as museum pieces by the National Trust or public authorities, will disappear year by year, continuing the erosion that has taken place steadily since the Second World War. Only industry and the government could find the money nowadays to make and maintain large gardens of the kind that were made by private owners in the past and here, although Britain continues to be the reference point, the view must broaden beyond Britain to deal with matters that concern mankind as a whole. What is said about Britain from hereon is, translated into local conditions, true in some degree of every country where large populations have been crammed into large cities, since all have shown, in greater or lesser degree, the same symptoms and to all is applicable the same cure.

Fundamental to the situation is the attitude to large building developments. Opportunities occurring here are the only opportunities that now exist to garden on any scale above the miniature, but the approach is almost always entirely the reverse of that calculated to produce great effects. Architects are told what kind of building they must produce and are instructed to set it suitably in the land selected. Irrespective of what their own views may be, in few cases do they have the final say. Financial considerations rule almost entirely the appearance of the building and when these have dictated what is to be built and where, the architect must make whatever garden or landscape he can

around it. The task of producing something satisfactory is often impossible. Here and there, however, there is a success story, such as the town of Tapiola in Finland, where the rule was made that the direct link between man and nature must be maintained and the resulting design married natural forest, stone and gardens into a satisfying whole that has become a showpiece. Generally the reverse is the case as the usual mode of proceeding puts the cart before the horse. To consider why this is so, it is necessary to go back to the ideas put forward in the first few pages of this book and look again at the nature of man, and to see how he behaves in a modern environment.

One of the most marked features of modern life is the revolt of men against the city and all for which it stands. The rich have always retreated into the country when

LEFT ABOVE *A modern counterpart of the* giardino segreto *furnished for outdoor living, at the base of a large tree.*

LEFT *Patio and steps of a modern house.*

TOP *Modern style patio with space for plants so cleverly designed that they appear to grow naturally.*

ABOVE *Paved area for outdoor living with plants in pots in a secluded garden.*

they felt like it, but the poor have had to stay in the city. Now even they, in Britain at least, have opportunities to leave it and the deserted inner city is becoming a problem. The truth is that narrow streets, cliff-like buildings and boring repetitive tasks performed without any immediate possibility of direct personal advantage, the condition that the city has produced for billions of people in the last few thousand years, is the opposite of the natural landscape in which our ancestors lived for millions of years before that and in which man feels instinctively at home. The sight and sound of natural water, the sight, scent, sound, feel and taste of vegetation, the shade of trees in the heat, the grateful warmth of sunshine in the cold, the smell in the nostrils of unpolluted air and, above all, the sense of open sky and freedom, are for the city-dweller rare experiences and far removed from what he can experience for most of his labouring day. It is not surprising that evil effects have followed the cutting off of men from their origins and that the cities are filled with legions of people unhappy and dissatisfied, and afflicted with depression and mental illness.

The things that people do who can escape, if only for a period, show what they really want. The rich avoid the city except to protect their wealth or for short visits to enjoy its entertainments. The better off forced to spend time there return to homes in areas in the suburbs where some of the things of nature surround them and from this base find the rest of what they crave on the golf course, in the country club, in riding, hunting, racing, shooting, salmon-fishing and a host of

similar outdoor activities, varying from country to country but all basically the same pattern. Lesser fry follow these things as well as their resources permit. There are, for example, two million anglers in Britain, most of whom catch very little, but have a great time in the open air. Hundreds of thousands of people every weekend and holiday take their cars to those spots where they find the light and air and natural things; and many of them camp there. Those forced to remain at home do the best they can with their gardens and their football, and use the parks and recreation grounds. Where these are absent, the chance of resentment against society in the form of crime and deliquency increases, particularly where unemployment reduces hope of any change.

The actions of those who work voluntarily for the welfare of others shows that often, with little consciously formulated appreciation of what drives them they, too, strive for the same end for those they seek to help: to give them a chance to experience for a while something nearer to their original natural surroundings. From the Boy Scout and Girl Guide camps, and similar things run by other associations, through holidays by the sea for poor children, 'adventure' holidays, nature trails, and a host of activities of the same kind, to the recent move for 'city farms', the theme is basically the same. Even package holidays abroad satisfy the same need for light and air, and open surroundings. There are many people doing a multitude of things, all part of the same search, the search that I have called, in the title of this book, *The Quest for Paradise*. The most fundamental expression of

TOP *Play area at Tapiola, Finland, showing a touch of artificiality in the angular flower-beds but only, as it were, in a clearing in the forest, which can be seen a few yards away beyond the houses.*

ABOVE *Residences at Tapiola, Finland, where the buildings have been married into the countryside with as little disturbance to the natural surroundings as possible.*

RIGHT *Some enlightened industrialists have incorporated gardens in the design of their office or factory premises. Here is one such garden in the block occupied by Wiggins, Teape at Basingstoke.*

this quest, pursued through many styles over the millennia, from ancient Sumeria in the days of Abraham's forefathers to the *paradiesgartenlein* of the modern German house, still in modern times perpetuating the original design, is the making of gardens: the re-creation of the environment remembered from the early time of man, a description of which was written down in Genesis by the old Hebrew poet and called the Garden of Eden.

In so far as human policy does not take notice of this fundamental urge, so far will it perpetuate and increase the evils that afflict it. In the poorer countries of the world, with teeming populations with a far lower material standard of living than the West, where most of the people live outside the cities, the incidence of mental illness is less than in the West, whereas in the United States, the richest industrial country in the world, it has become a joke that every business man must have his psychiatrist. The pursuit of an ever-rising standard of living judged from the myopic standpoint of quantity and quality of material possessions fosters a delusive dream. Human happiness will not be found that way. There must be a *volte-face* of opinion. To every project must be applied the crucial test. How far does what is mooted accord with the basic human need for natural surroundings?

When we propose a development of any kind, we must look at the landscape first and make our arrangements to suit that, and not as we have hitherto done, propose the venture with little regard to the environment it will create, paying belated service to that after everything else, and then finding to our surprise, as we did with tower block flats, that the people compelled to inhabit or use the creation become unhappy. Garden cities began with the right notion but execution fell short of what was prompted by the imagination. Although the idea may seem at first impracticable and wildly expensive, and contrary to all ideas of business efficiency, there is no reason why, for example, we should not marry our parks and our pedestrian precincts, so that the supermarket looks out from its grove of trees on to a tree-lined brook, or even, in a hypermarket, the brook should not run through the centre of the store. The creation of human environments of this kind might even remove the basic cause of vandalism.

The advance of technology is bringing changes, such as those even now being brought about by the silicon chip, that will release many pairs of hands for other work, whose energy and time could be diverted to bringing into being new and more natural environments for life and work. If there were a will to do this the money would be found, as it always is if anything is wanted enough. Human ingenuity, that has solved so many intractable problems, and brought about so many bloodless revolutions, would find ways through the whole range of human activity to devise changes similar to those suggested above designed to produce acceptable human environments.

It is fashionable now, when any serious conclusion is arrived at, or a line of activity advocated, to dignify it, in reality only half-humorously, with the mock title of a law or principle, such as Parkinson's Law, or the Peter Principle. To create such environments as are envisaged would, indeed, involve the application of a principle: it is not new, but since its adoption is vital for the health of mankind, I suggest that it, too, deserves a title. It might be called *The Paradise Principle* and defined as: 'Nature and man are one: whatever divides them invites failure.' It seems unlikely that such a principle will be generally adopted, so far is it removed from the notions of present society. Until, however, it is followed, the 'Quest for Paradise' will of necessity continue, because man is relentlessly driven along that road by his unconscious, and so far as he continues to stray from it, as he has strayed in the past, he will continue to embroil himself in self-created difficulties.

Select Bibliography

Addison, Joseph, *The Spectator*, No. 414 (June 25th, 1712)

Blomfield, R. and F.I. Thomas, *The Formal Garden in England* (Macmillan, London, 1892)

Cartwright, J., *Italian Gardens of the Renaissance* (Smith, Elder, London, 1914)

Cecil, E., *A History of Gardening in England* (John Murray, London, 1910)

Chambers, Sir W., *A Dissertation on Oriental Gardening* (London, 1772)

————, *Plans, Elevations, Sections and Perspective View of the Gardens at Kew* (1763, reprint. Gregg Press, Farnborough, 1966)

Clifford, D., *A History of Garden Design* (Faber, London, 1962)

Condor, J., *The Flowers of Japan and the Art of Floral Arrangement* (Hakubunsha Ginza, Tokyo, 1892)

————, *Landscape Gardening in Japan* (Kelly and Walsh, Yokohama, 1893)

————, *Supplement to Landscape Gardening in Japan* (Kelly and Walsh, Yokohama, 1893)

Cox, E.H.M., *The Modern English Garden* (Country Life, London, 1927)

Crisp, Sir Frank, *Mediaeval Gardens* (John Lane, London, 1924)

Crowe, S., and S. Haywood, *The Gardens of Mughal India* (Thames and Hudson, London, 1972)

Czullik, A., *Wiener Gärten im Jahre 1890* (A.D. Lehmann, Vienna, 1891)

Dilley, A.D., *Oriental Rugs and Carpets* (Lippincott, New York, 1931)

Duppa, R., *Illustrations of the Lotus of the Ancients and Tamara of India* (Bensley, London, 1816)

Fitch, J.M., and F.F. Rockwell, *Treasury of American Gardens* (Harper, New York, 1956)

Gothein, M.L., *A History of Garden Art* (1928, reprint. Hacker, New York, 1966)

Hadfield, M., *Gardening in Britain* (Hutchinson, London, 1960)

Harris, J., *Sir William Chambers* (Zwemmer, London, 1970)

Hearn, Lafcadio, *Kokoro* (Gay and Bird, London, 1895)

————, *Glimpses of Unfamiliar Japan* (Jonathan Cape, London, 1927)

Hessayon, D.G. and J.P., *The PBI Garden Book of Europe* (Hamish Hamilton, London, 1973)

Hirschfeld, C.C.L., *Théorie de l'Art des Jardins* (Leipzig, 1779)

Hunt, P., ed., *Shell Gardens Book* (Phoenix House, London, 1964)

Hyams, E., *English Cottage Gardens* (Nelson, London, 1970)

Jekyll, G., *Colour Schemes for the Flower Garden* (Country Life, London, 1914)

————, and Sir L. Weaver, *Gardens for Small Country Houses* (Country Life, London, 1912)

Kincaid, P., *Japanese Garden and Floral Art* (Hearthside, New York, 1957)

Knight, R.P., *The Landscape, A Didactic Poem* (Nicol, London, 1794)

Labyrinthe de Versailles (Paris, 1679)

Latham, R., tr., *The Travels of Marco Polo* (Folio Society, London, 1958)

Li, H.L., *The Garden Flowers of China* (Ronald Press, New York, 1957)

Loudon, J.C., *The Suburban Gardener and Villa Companion* (Longmans, London, 1838)

————, *Villa Gardener*, ed. Mrs Loudon (Orr, London, 1850)

Macmillan, H.F., *Tropical Planting and Gardening* (Macmillan, London, 1962)

Malins, E., *The Red Books of Humphry Repton* (Basilisk Press, London, 1976)

————, and the Knight of Glin, *Lost Demesnes* (Barrie & Jenkins, London, 1976)

Mangin, A., *Histoire des Jardins* (Mame, Tours, 1883)

Mariette-Bey, A., *Deir-el-Bahari* (Hinrichs, Leipzig, 1877)

Masson, G., *Italian Gardens* (Thames and Hudson, London, 1961)

Matsunosoke Tatsui, *Japanese Gardens* (Maruzen, Tokyo, 1934)

Maxwell, Sir H., *Scottish Gardens* (Arnold, London, 1908)

McCormick, H.H., *Landscape Art Past and Present* (Scribner's, New York, 1923)

McDougall, D., *Two Royal Domains of France* (Jonathan Cape, London, 1931)

Menpes, M., *Japan* (Black, London, 1901)

Petit, V., *Parcs et Jardins des Environs de Paris* (Monrocq, Paris, N.D.)

Prescott, W.H., *The Conquest of Mexico* (Routledge, London, N.D.)

Price, Uvedale, *An Essay on the Picturesque* (Robson, London, 1794)

Quatre Siècles de Jardins à la Francaise (Hachette, Paris, 1910)

Repton, H., *Landscape Gardening* (Architectural Library, London, 1803)

————, *Changes of Taste in Landscape Gardening* (Taylor, London, 1806)

Robinson, W., *The English Flower Garden and Home Grounds* (John Murray, London, 1905, 9th ed.)

————, *Garden Design and Architects' Gardens* (John Murray, London, 1892)

Rohde, E.S., *The Garden Book of Sir T. Hanmer* (Howe, 1933)

Sedding, J., *Garden Craft Old and New* (John Lane, London, 1903)

Sibthorp, J., *Flora Graeca*, ed. J.E. Smith (Oxford University, 1806-40)

The Simple Way of Lao-Tze (Shrine of Wisdom, Godalming, 1924)

Siren, O., *China and Gardens of Europe of the Eighteenth Century* (Ronald Press, New York, 1950)

Sieveking, A.F., *The Praise of Gardens* (Dent, London, 1899)

Stroud, D., *Capability Brown* (Faber, London, 1975)

————, *Humphry Repton* (Country Life, London, 1962)

Teijo Itoh, *The Japanese Garden* (Yale U.P., 1972)

————, *Space and Illusion in the Japanese Garden* (Weatherhill, Japan, 1973)

Temple, Sir W., *Upon the Gardens of Epicurus* (London, 1685)

Tipping, H.A., *Gardens Old and New* (Country Life, London, N.D.)

Treasures of Tutankhamun (British Museum/Rainbird, London, 1972)

Triggs, H.I., *The Art of Garden Design in Italy* (Longmans, London, 1906)

————, *Formal Gardens in England and Scotland* (Batsford, London, 1902)

————, *Garden Craft in Europe* (Batsford, London, 1913)

Valdes, *Jardines di Espana* (Aguilar, Madrid, 1973)

Verney, P., *The Gardens of Scotland* (Batsford, London, 1976)

Villiers-Stuart, C.M., *Spanish Gardens* (Batsford, London, 1929)

————, *Gardens of the Great Mughals* (Black, London, 1913)

Wellard, J., *By the Waters of Babylon* (Hutchinson, London, 1972)

Wethered, H.N., *A Short History of Gardens* (Methuen, London, 1933)

Woolley, C.L., *The Sumerians* (Clarendon Press, Oxford, 1928)

Wright, R., *The Story of Gardening* (Dodd, Mead, New York, 1934)

Index

285

287